FLYING SAUCERS—
SERIOUS BUSINESS

BY FRANK EDWARDS

My First 10,000,000 Sponsors
Strangest of All
Stranger Than Science
Strange People
Strange World

By FRANK EDWARDS

Flying Saucers— Serious Business

LYLE STUART • NEW YORK

Queries regarding rights and permissions
should be addressed to Lyle Stuart
at 239 Park Avenue South, New York, N. Y. 10003.

Published by Lyle Stuart Inc.
Edited by Eileen Brand
Manufactured in the United States of America

Affectionately dedicated to the
memory of my long-time buddy

RAY ALLEN

May 25, 1911—December 30, 1965

Table of Contents

Illustrations

9

I wish to express my thanks to the Inspector General of the United States Air Force for issuing the special order from which the title of this book is taken.

Frank Edwards
May, 1966.

"Defense Department orders jets to shoot down UFO's which refuse to land when ordered to do so."

—WASHINGTON, D.C. *Daily News*
July 25, 1952

"Flying Saucers exist only in the imaginations of the viewers."

—PRESIDENT DWIGHT D. EISENHOWER.
December 16, 1954

1

What Goes On Here?

Hundreds of persons near a huge frozen reservoir watched a glowing egg-shaped object darting about from place to place, intermittently shooting downward beams of light. Reservoir guards who later ventured out on the frozen surface reportedly found unexpected thawed places in the area where the object had hovered.

It happened on the night of January 12, 1966, within thirty miles of Times Square—but most Americans never heard of it.

Why not?

A glowing red object crossed the United States from New York to Utah, tracked by radar every foot of the way. It landed beside a power station and put the station out of operation. Forty-eight minutes later it exploded in mid-air while pursued by armed jet interceptors.

It happened on April 18, 1962—but most people never heard of it.

Thousands of people stood in the streets of Duluth, Minnesota, and watched jet interceptors vainly chasing seven Unidentified Flying Objects (UFO's). The presence of both the jets and the UFO's was confirmed by the Radar Base on the Keweenaw Peninsula.

It happened in August of 1965—but most Americans never heard of it.

Sixty-eight Unidentified Flying Objects roamed the skies over Washington, D.C., in one night. They were tracked on radar. They were reported by the airline pilots whose planes they approached. A government agency published a special booklet dealing with the events of this one remarkable night . . . August 13, 1952.

But most Americans are still unaware that it ever happened.

Even some of the persons who deal with this phenomenon have difficulty gathering information.

For instance:

One night early in October of 1965, I addressed an audience of radar experts who had hired me, at their own expense, to come and tell them all that I could about the ubiquitous Unidentified Flying Objects. These were the men (Air Traffic Controllers) who see these things on their radar screens. These are the same men who are required by regulation to give out prefabricated answers or "explanations" to all who make inquiry about such things.

Why were they paying me, a civilian newsman, to tell them about things they see more frequently than anyone else in the nation?

The reason was simple: Although they were under the Federal Aviation Agency, that agency refused to answer their queries for information on the UFO's.

From the Air Force they received only a suggestion to contact the FAA.

From the FAA they got nothing.

To those radar men I showed enlargements of government documents of which they had no knowledge. I showed them photographs of the types of things which caused blips on their radar screens. But in one hour I could not

14

telescope an adequate briefing of the events of these past nineteen years, even though I tried hard.

This book will give me the time to do a more extensive job, and a more thorough one as well.

That I am prejudiced in this upcoming discussion with you I freely admit. That I disagree with the published viewpoints of the United States Air Force on the same subject, I also freely admit.

But I wish it understood here and now that I have no dislike for the Air Force, and for very good reason. The Air Force is as helpless in its way as you and I are in ours. It is doing a job that was forced upon it—a job that has meant deceiving the majority of the American people for almost twenty years. Notice that I say the *majority* of the people—for there have always been some who were not deceived—and today the number of those who are still deceived, or at least confused, as to the real nature of the Unidentified Flying Objects, hereafter called UFO's, must be very small and they are certainly in the minority.

Sometimes I get the impression that the Air Force might prefer to be rid of the whole shabby task; that it deliberately issues the most ridiculous statements, with the silent prayer that by so doing it will bring closer the day of its own release from this presumably odious assignment. For examples: In August of 1965, when tens of thousands of persons from the Dakotas to Mexico watched peculiar lighted formations hovering and maneuvering in the skies, the Air Force blandly informed the news services that all these witnesses, on the ground and in the air, had been watching nothing more unusual than four stars in the constellation Orion!

The preposterous character of that "explanation" was quickly brought to light when astronomers Professor Walter Webb of the Hayden Planetarium in Boston and Dr. Robert Risser of the Oklahoma Art and Science Planetarium pointed out that the stars in Orion, at the time of the sightings, WERE ON THE OTHER SIDE OF THE EARTH.

* * * * * * * *

Having thus established roughly the opposing forces and their respective viewpoints, let us proceed to examine the evidence.

* * * * * * * *

As a professional reporter I am well aware of the importance of including in my report the very beginning of the story. In the case of the UFO's I must call attention to the regrettable fact that the real beginnings of the story are probably lost in antiquity, unless we are willing to give some consideration to certain accounts which have come down to us through the oldest possible sources—the religions and the legends.

Let us examine a few of them as a possible background to the modern portion of the story which we shall consider in detail.

A literal interpretation of the Bible indicates that some forms of spacecraft, operated by beings similar to—if not identical to—human beings, visited some of the places and characters in the Old Testament, at least. I do not propose to recount those stories here, but to those who may be interested in the details I recommend Morris Jessup's *The UFO and the Bible*.

In those distant days, when Heaven was held to be somewhere overhead, it was only natural that beings who came from overhead should be regarded as heavenly representatives; in other words, as "angels." Yet the same

16

accounts that purport to tell of their coming also give evidence that the creatures from the strange craft were not necessarily of celestial origin. Genesis (6:4) tells of these men from the sky mating with women of Earth, who bore them children. And again in Genesis 19:3 we are told that Lot met two "angels" in the desert and they went with him and partook of a feast at his house.

Most observers will probably agree that breeding and eating ordinary food are surprising deviations for angels—but not altogether surprising for manlike creatures who may exist elsewhere in space.

Scholars of ancient languages have noted many items which lend themselves readily to interpretation as Unidentified Flying Objects, reported by persons who had to describe them in terms understandable to their contemporaries: Flaming chariots, fiery or glowing shields (which were generally circular, dislike, with a small "boss" or domelike center) and of course the glittering lances and other trappings of that distant period.

The late Harold Wilkins did a monumental job of perusing ancient volumes for such accounts. Some of the items are included in various articles he wrote for FATE magazine. And in that same publication for December, 1964, there is a good collection of "UFO's in Ancient Times." And Jessup's *Case for the UFO,* now long out of print, contains numerous additional examples.

A chronicle of ancient India known as the Book of Dzyan is in a class by itself, not only because of its age but because of a surprising account therein. The Book is a compilation of legends passed down through the ages before men were able to write, and finally gathered into manuscript form by the ancient scholars who preserved them for us.

They tell of a small group of beings who came to Earth many thousands of years ago in metal craft which first went AROUND Earth several times before landing. "These beings," says the Book, "lived to themselves and were revered by the humans among whom they had settled. But eventually differences arose among them and they divided their numbers, several of the men and women and some children settling in another city, where they were promptly installed as rulers by the awe-stricken populace."

The legend continues:

"Separation did not bring peace to these people and finally their anger reached a point where the ruler of the original city took with him a small number of his warriors and they rose into the air in a huge shining metal vessel. While they were many leagues from the city of their enemies they launched a great shining lance that rode on a beam of light. It burst apart in the city of their enemies with a great ball of flame that shot up to the heavens, almost to the stars. All those in the city were horribly burned and even those who were not in the city—but nearby—were burned also. Those who looked upon the lance and the ball of fire were blinded forever afterward. Those who entered the city on foot became ill and died. Even the dust of the city was poisoned, as were the rivers that flowed through it. Men dared not go near it, and it gradually crumbled into dust and was forgotten by men.

"When the leader saw what he had done to his own people he retired to his palace and refused to see anyone. Then he gathered about him those of his warriors who remained, and their wives and their children, and they entered into their vessels and rose one by one into the sky and sailed away. Nor did they return."

This would seem to be an account of an attempt by

18

some extraterrestrial group to establish a colony on Earth in the distant past. Like so many colonizing attempts by man, it appears to have ended in dissension and conflict. Most interesting portion of the story is the description of the great "lance that traveled on a beam of light," which bears a surprising resemblance to a modern rocket and its jet of flame. The effect of this so-called "lance" brings to mind a rather detailed picture of a nuclear blast and its catastrophic sequels. If this is a mental concoction of some primitive writer, it is at least remarkable. If it is a reasonably accurate piece of factual reporting, then it is even more remarkable. Since it is unverifiable, we must at this late date classify it as "interesting, but unproved."

Several of the very old Irish manuscripts which are still extant and still legible contain numerous references to incidents which in our day would be classified with the Unidentified Flying Objects.

From the Speculum Regali in Konungs Skuggsa (and in other accounts of that era, about 956 A.D.) come many accounts of what were called "demon-ships" in the skies of ancient Ireland. This one account is particularly interesting:

"There happened in the borough of Cloera, one Sunday while the people were at Mass, a marvel. In this town there is a church to the memory of St. Kinarus. It befell that a metal anchor was dropped from the sky, with a rope attached to it, and one of the sharp flukes caught in the wooden arch above the church door. The people rushed out of the church and saw in the sky a ship with men on board, floating at the end of the anchor cable, and they saw a man leap overboard and pull himself down the cable to the anchor as if to unhook it. He appeared as if he were swimming in water. The folk rushed up and tried to seize

19

him; but the bishop forbade the people to hold the man for fear it might kill him. The man was freed and hurried up the cable to the ship where the crew cut the rope and the ship rose and sailed away out of sight. But the anchor is in the church as a testimony to this singular occurrence."

Singular, indeed! Yet it is but one of many such accounts of "ships in the air" and of manlike creatures aboard and about them, to be found in ancient manuscripts throughout the world.

That account of the cable from the "demon-ship" brings to mind a much more recent report, an account from a prosperous and prominent farmer, Alexander Hamilton, of Le Roy, Kansas.

In a sworn statement dated April 21, 1897, he says:

> Last Monday night about 10:30 we were awakened by a noise among the cattle. I arose, thinking that perhaps my bulldog was performing his pranks, but upon going to the door saw to my utter astonishment that an airship was slowly descending upon my cow lot, about forty rods [660 feet] from the house.
>
> Calling my tenant, Gid Heslip, and my son Wall, we seized some axes and ran to the corral. Meanwhile the ship had been gently descending until it was not more than thirty feet above the ground, and we came within fifty yards of it.
>
> It consisted of a great cigar-shaped portion, possibly three hundred feet long, with a carriage underneath. The carriage was made of glass or some other transparent substance alternating with a narrow strip of some material. It was brightly lighted within and everything was plainly visible—it was occupied by six of the strangest beings I ever saw. They were jabbering together but we could not understand a word they said.

20

What Goes On Here?

Every part of the vessel which was not transparent was of a dark reddish color. We stood mute with wonder and fright. Then some noise attracted their attention and they turned a light directly upon us. Immediately on catching sight of us they turned on some unknown power, and a great turbine wheel, about thirty feet in diameter, which was revolving slowly below the craft, began to buzz and the vessel rose lightly as a bird. When about three hundred feet above us it seemed to pause and to hover directly above a two-year-old heifer, which was bawling and jumping, apparently fast in the fence. Going to her, we found a cable about half an inch in thickness made of some red material fastened in a slip knot around her neck and going up to the vessel from the heifer tangled in the wire fence. We tried to get it off but could not, so we cut the wire loose to see the ship, heifer and all, rise slowly, disappearing in the northwest.

We went home but I was so frightened I could not sleep. Rising early Tuesday I started out on my horse, hoping to find some trace of my cow. This I failed to do, but coming back in the evening found that Link Thomas, about three or four miles west of LeRoy, had found the hide, legs and head in his field that day. He, thinking that someone had butchered a stolen beast, had brought the hide to town for identification, but was greatly mystified in not being able to find any tracks in the soft ground. After identifying the hide by my brand, I went home. But every time I would drop to sleep I would see the cursed thing, with its big lights and hideous people. I don't know whether they are devils or angels, or what; but we all saw them, and my whole family saw the ship, and I don't want any more to do with them.

AFFIDAVIT

"Hamilton has long been a resident of Kansas and known all over Woodson, Allen, Coffey and Anderson counties.

He was a member of the House of Representatives. He staked his sacred honor upon the truth of his story.

As there are now, always have been and always will be skeptics and unbelievers whenever the truth of anything bordering the improbable is presented, and knowing that some ignorant or suspicious people will doubt the truthfulness of the above statement, now therefore we, the undersigned, do hereby make the following affidavit:

That we have known Alexander Hamilton for one to thirty years, and that for truth and veracity we have never heard his word questioned, and that we do verily believe his statement to be true and correct.

Signed: E. W. Wharton, State Oil Inspector
M. E. Hunt, Sheriff
W. Lauber, Deputy Sheriff
H. H. Winter, Banker
H. S. Johnson, Pharmacist
J. H. Stitcher, Attorney
Alexander Stewart, Justice of the Peace
F. W. Butler, Druggist
James W. Martin, Registrar of Deeds.
and H. C. Rollins, Postmaster

Subscribed and sworn before me this 21st day of April, 1897"

Since affidavits are considered evidential matter before the highest courts in the land, we are justified in giving the above story more than usual weight in the annals of these weird craft—and their "hideous people," as Mr. Hamilton called them.

In that LeRoy, Kansas, report we find material that was to crop up again and again in similar accounts down through the years: The machine was silent. It was a glowing red color. It used some sort of revolving wheel-like thing for part of its propulsion system. It was dirigible-shaped. The interior was brightly lighted. It carried some sort of brilliant spotlight which could be flashed on the area or individuals to be examined. It was plainly under the intelligent control of unusual-appearing living creatures of more-or-less humanoid appearance.

As far back as April of 1897 the stage had been set and the principal characters and props had been viewed by an American audience.

[Dirigible-shaped craft built by the Tissandier brothers in France in 1884—and by Renard and Krebs (same year) —were frail and feeble, certainly incapable of crossing the Atlantic. The slow and cumbersome Zeppelins of World War I were still far in the future when Alexander Hamilton and his hired man reported their strange aerial visitor.
—F.E.]

Many persons in many lands reported strange craft in that same era, craft which ofttimes resembled or performed in a manner similar to that in the case we have just mentioned from LeRoy, Kansas.

From Adrianople, Turkey, in November of 1885, came a report of a glowing red cigar-shaped craft or thing which pulsated with an intensely brilliant light that dimmed to faint red. It was huge, and seemingly floated and stopped in mid-air. The French publication L'ASTRONOMIE reported a case off Cape Race, Nova Scotia, in November, 1887, where a huge glowing red object rose from the ocean to a height of sixty to ninety feet, moved against the wind for two minutes . . . paused beside the ship from which it was observed and reported . . . then turned about until its *elongated shape* was discernible . . . and, rising swiftly, vanished in the southeast. Total time of observation, five minutes.

A check of the records indicates that the month of April, 1897, was studded with strange aerial performers in the United States.

On April 1, the NEW YORK SUN reports, a great many people in and around Kansas City, Missouri, reported watching some sort of controlled object roaming the night sky in that part of the country, pausing from time to time to send downward a brilliant white searchlight beam, something no manmade aerial craft could do at that time. Additional reports along the same lines from various parts of Texas: Dallas, Fort Worth, Marshall, and Beaumont among them. Watchers in Benton, Texas, on the night of April 16 reportedly observed a cigar-shaped craft crossing between them and the moon.

The object, whatever it was, was conceivably the same one seen and reported by watchers in Omaha on the night of March 29, and on March 30 over Denver—a brightly lighted thing at great altitude, apparently cruising about among the stars on a course toward the northwest.

The NEW YORK HERALD for April 11 says that on the night of April 9-10, in and around the city of Chicago from about 8 p.m. until two o'clock in the morning "thousands of amazed persons declared that the lights seen in the northwest were those of an airship, or some floating object, miles above the earth. . . . Some declared that they could distinguish two cigar-shaped objects and great wings." The thing, said the witnesses, was illuminated from time to time by the rays of two giant searchlights— a description similar to that given a few nights later by observers in Texas.

It should be noted that this spate of reports from Texas to Chicago covers the time period immediately preceding and following the incident involving Alexander Hamilton's airborne heifer. All these reported craft (or things) are said to have been cigar-shaped, glowing red, carrying bright searchlights and intelligently controlled.

That there was *something* maneuvering around in the night skies at that time, something beyond existing terrestrial technology, was further evidenced by the event of April 19, 1897, at Sistersville, West Virginia, a quiet little town on the Ohio river.

A few minutes past 9 P.M. a luminous red object shaped like an immense cigar approached Sistersville from the northwest [over the state of Ohio—F.E.]. It hovered in the darkness over the little town and began flashing at least two extremely brilliant searchlights on the community. The frantic blowing of the sawmill whistle brought the citizens into the streets to witness this fantastic aerial visitor. Those who were forced to look up into those searchlight beams saw little else, but those who lived on the nearby hills could clearly distinguish the cigarlike shape of the craft. By the reflected light of its searchlights they said they could also see large fins on either side of it. When it sped up and away a few minutes later, all the witnesses said they could distinguish the flashing red, white, and green lights along the sides and at the ends of the object, estimated by those who observed it from the hills to be about 180 feet in length and about 50 feet in diameter [NEW YORK HERALD, April 20, 1897].

In pursuing our discussion of reported flights of dirigible (cigar-shaped) craft of unknown origin through the skies of the United States near the turn of the twentieth century, we find numerous reports around the end of December, 1909, and the first month of 1910.

During much of the autumn of 1908, there had been frequent reports, particularly from the New England states, of bright lights moving swiftly through the skies— but moving too erratically for meteors. So far as I can determine, there were no low-level sightings during that period.

But by December of 1909, credible witnesses were reporting some disconcerting sights. Two fishing boats beating their way up the coast between Boston and Presque Isle reported that they were circled by some huge brightly lighted object in the air on the night of December 18. On the night of December 20, according to the NEW YORK TRIBUNE, the Immigration Inspector at Boston had reported a bright light which passed over the harbor, a light which he felt was carried by some kind of aircraft. The same paper says that on December 23, 1909, citizens of Worcester, Massachusetts, were visited twice in one night by an aerial craft which swept the heavens and the town and countryside with a searchlight of fantastic brilliance. Boston and Willimantic were visited on the following night and were treated to the same display from overhead. Thousands of persons stood in the streets to watch the spectacle, which was beyond the capabilities of contemporary manmade craft. The NEW YORK SUN is source for the report that Marlboro, Massachusetts, had been visited nine times by this sort of object between December 14 and December 23.

[On the night of December 24, 1909, amateur astronomer James Fergusen, of Limerick, Ireland, reported watching a brightly lighted object rise over the northeastern horizon, maneuvering generally southward for twenty minutes, then retracing its course and vanishing below the horizon at two minutes past nine.—F.E.]

26

What Goes On Here?

At Huntington, West Virginia, the newspapers tell of strangely brilliant lights seen moving about in the sky on the night of January 1, 1910. No object could be seen, nor any sounds detected; just the brilliant beams of light which finally glided downward behind the mountain ridges and vanished.

There was no question as to the appearance of the object which appeared over Chattanooga, Tennessee, on the morning of January 12, 1910, shortly after 9 o'clock. Thousands of persons rushed out to marvel at this great white cigar-shaped thing which was in plain view, chugging around above the city at an estimated speed of not more than thirty miles per hour. Most witnesses were certain that they could detect a faint chugging sound, which they regarded as indicative of some sort of motor. Also present in most of the descriptions was the line of flickering blue flames which played along the undersides of the craft for almost its full length. Today we would suspect such flames of representing either a stabilizing system or exhaust; what they *did* represent was unknown and remains so, of course.

But the Chattanooga Chugger sailed around above the city for a while and then moved back over the mountains and vanished, unmolested and unhurried. Fifteen minutes later, the same or a similar object was reported over Huntsville, Alabama, about seventy-five miles distant.

Whatever it was, the thing appeared over Chattanooga on three consecutive days—the 12th, 13th, and 14th of January, 1910. It made headlines in the local papers as a matter of course, and it was duly reported in countless other papers across the nation. On the occasion of its last appearance at Chattanooga it sailed in from the south (toward which it had gone the day before) maneuvered

27

over the city for about twenty minutes while thousands marveled—then vanished into the thick mists over Missionary Ridge.

A careful examination of the descriptions of these dirigible-shaped craft leads to the conclusion that they were at best rather cumbersome and, according to the witnesses, none of them exhibited any spectacular bursts of speed. But at the time of which we have written, they were able to outperform anything that man was able to put into the air, so they had a substantial margin of safety.

But when World War I brought about the development of heavier-than-air craft capable of speeds around a hundred miles an hour, the dirigible-shaped craft of possible extraterrestrial origin virtually vanished from the air. In order to be safe, if they wished to avoid contact with men, they had to have something faster and more maneuverable.

The first disc-shaped UFO of which I can find record is that described in 1926 by the Roerich Expedition of the American Museum of Natural History—a shiny, disc-shaped thing which the members of the expedition spotted high in the skies over Altai-Himalaya.

For twenty years, 1926-1946, there is an almost complete absence of sightings reports of UFO's. Those which I have been able to find were all in the most desolate spots on Earth—and they all involved disc-shaped objects: the desert of New South Wales, the Kalahari Desert, a handful of reports from ships in remote seas, and two fragmentary mentions from Chile and Bolivia—so lacking in detail that they cannot be categorized positively as anything except something unusual darting about the heavens.

But in the spring of 1946 all hell broke loose in the

night skies of the Scandinavian countries and of north-western Russia.

Night after night, thousands of persons watched the show: faintly luminous objects zipping about the skies, ofttimes hovering, changing course abruptly and changing speeds in a manner far beyond the capability of man-made devices. At first they were reported as "rockets"—but as the evidence accumulated it indicated that rockets they were not. No exhaust trail, for one thing. Sometimes moving too slowly for a rocket to have remained aloft. Moving about in formations, breaking formations, changing formation positions, and—above all—moving silently.

Just when it must have dawned on the various governments involved that they were dealing with something new and challenging is not a matter of public record. By putting together bits and pieces of statements, however, it is easy to recognize the deep concern which was surely being felt in places of authority and responsibility.

We will examine the evidence in this new aspect of the UFO a little later and in detail. Let it suffice to say at this point in our study that after twenty years of little activity of this sort, 1926-1946, during which man had developed jet planes capable of 700-mile-per-hour flight, several nations suddenly found themselves confronted with some new type of craft, equal to, if not superior to, the best that man could present to counter them.

After the "flap" of new-type UFO's over northwestern Europe in the spring and summer of 1946, the reports of the dirigible-shaped craft became very rare, as though they were being phased out in favor of a superior device, which they may have been. But there continued to be a few reports from credible sources concerning this old-style craft . . . and they are still reported from time to time even in the spring of 1966.

On the night of June 30, 1947, the coastal steamer *Llandovery Castle* was churning along southward off the coast of Kenya in East Africa. The night was studded with stars but was moonless at the time of this incident, according to the ship's log.

A passenger, strolling toward the rear of the ship, noticed an unusual blackness which was blotting out part of the stars. He thought it seemed to be descending and approaching the *Llandovery Castle*. A ship's officer agreed with him and called his superior. By this time a total of twelve persons, nine of them passengers, were watching the approaching object. Whatever it was, it was huge and it carried no lights.

The ship's log says that the thing leveled off about a hundred feet above the sea and about half a mile from the ship, between the vessel and the shore. At that point it turned on a dazzling white light, which shone from the bottom of the object to the surface of the water, and by the reflected searchlight illumination the witnesses said they could clearly determine that their vessel was being paced by a gigantic dirigible-shaped craft which was under intelligent control. It was about twice the length of the *Llandovery Castle,* which would mean that it was about 1,000 feet long. It was silent and it appeared to be made of some shiny substance which reflected the light that bounced back from the sea, and even the starlight, which might indicate that it was some highly polished metal.

Whatever it was, the craft kept pace with the vessel for several minutes before it switched off the brilliant searchlight and rose swiftly and silently into the night skies from whence it had come.

What Goes On Here?

And again on the night of November 2, 1957—this time near Levelland, Texas—Sheriff Weir Clem and his Deputy, Pat McCulloch, who made the official report to the Air Force, were two of the four police officers who saw the huge glowing object which caused the excitement.

Just before midnight, Pedro Saucedo was driving along Highway 116 toward Levelland, with a passenger, Joe Salav. An immense object, glowing blue-green, swept down over the truck and settled on the highway. The car's lights dimmed, the engine died . . . and Saucedo dived out the door and crawled under the truck, terrified. Salav, admittedly so terrified that he was unable to move, told officers later that the object slowly settled down to the highway surface . . . or just above it. He was unable to be more specific because by this time the glare from the object (which had changed to red) was so intense that Salav could not stand to look directly at it.

Both Salav and Saucedo reported that they could hear faint clanking or hammering . . . and other noises which they interpreted as voices . . . but if they were voices they were as unintelligible to these two men as they had been to Alexander Hamilton and his two companions at Le Roy, Kansas, sixty years before.

After about three minutes the object, estimated to be two hundred feet long and dirigible-shaped, rose swiftly and noiselessly, still glowing brilliantly red—and swept away into the night sky. Significantly, as we shall see, it was going in the general direction of the White Sands Proving Ground, where another interesting chapter in the annals of the UFO was to be written that same memorable night.

The Sheriff and the other police officers saw the same or a similar object a short time later as they went to investigate another report—the fourth that night—a short time after Saucedo and Salav, badly shaken, had reached the Sheriff's office.

As we examine this incident (which made world headlines next day) for its possible similarities to that of the Le Roy, Kansas, case six decades before, three aspects of it quickly attract attention: a seeming design improvement in which the external "turbine wheel" of the 1897 model has either been replaced or revised and moved inside—the absence of a cabin in which the occupants (if any) were visible, as they were in 1897—and the interference with the lights, radios, and ignition systems reported by at least eight witnesses in the Levelland case.

Of this last-mentioned "interference" it must be kept in mind that it may actually have been present at the 1897 case but was not noted then because Hamilton had no electrical equipment with which it might have interfered.

Neither was this the first time—nor was it the last— that this interference with modern electrical gear would be a factor in the sightings—as we shall see.

There remains a singular incident involving a UFO— a strangely persistent craft—which reportedly began appearing rather frequently, in May of 1964, to the residents of the little town of Rio Vista, California. A community of about 2,000 persons, it is located approximately sixty airline miles northeast of San Francisco, which evidently explains the interest of the SAN FRANCISCO CHRONICLE in these strange doings.

The reports which kept coming in to the Sheriff of Solano County described the thing as torpedo- or dirigible-shaped, about three to five feet in diameter and twelve to fifteen feet long. It glowed a warm red and it moved silently, witnesses told the Sheriff. One housewife brought in some color transparencies of just such a thing, which she said she had taken in 1964 as the object hovered near her home.

Deputy Sheriff John Cruz of Fairfield told the CHRONI-CLE that he finally became interested in the case on September 22, 1965, and went to have a look for himself. Residents told him that the thing generally appeared near a watertower about five miles from town. That night, an estimated three to four hundred persons standing patiently in the dark on the hilltop around the tower were rewarded by the appearance of the strange object: Glowing softly red, cigar-shaped, hovering or moving slowly about only a couple of hundred feet above the treetops or the top of the watertower.

What makes this incident noteworthy is not the repeated appearances of the same object in the same area . . . but the fact that some of the witnesses told the Deputy that boys with .22 rifles had shot at the object one night —and the bullets made a metallic "twang"—and caused the object to flare up bright red for a second.

But even this barrage did not deter the object from returning occasionally. Nor did it deter the inevitable Air Force "expert" from Travis Air Force Base from "identifying" the object as the planet Venus!

When the planet Venus gets so close that boys can hit it with .22 rifles, it is time for all of us to head for the hills.

* * * * * * * *

We have seen, in these cases which we have examined, that the strange craft with which we are concerned have undergone design changes, possibly intended to enable them to match or exceed those improvements which our

33

own aircraft have undergone in the past sixty years. If these objects are controlled and directed by extraterrestrial beings, it would be imperative that they be able to out-maneuver us in the atmosphere, or that they send in their less maneuverable craft only in areas where our best equipment was absent, as in the case of the *Llandovery Castle*. While the dirigible-shaped things have undergone considerable revision in shape, size, and speed, still another type of craft has appeared in increasing numbers— the so-called flying disc. But even that was not the ultimate in design, for it seems to be in a process of being replaced by an egg-shaped craft.

It is interesting to note that, while the mysterious objects known as UFO's have undergone drastic changes since 1897, man's reaction to them has been very consistent. The farmer in Kansas rushed toward the UFO in 1897 swinging an axe; in 1965 the witnesses at Rio Vista greeted the new model UFO with bullets from a .22 rifle.

Considering the evidence, perhaps we should not be surprised that the operators of the UFO's have been slow about contacting us.

How would you like to meet a race of people who said "hello" with an axe?

One Sunday night in mid-November, 1957, one of my nephews received the shock of his life.

Donald Dodge, who later became a noted artist at Georgetown College, was then teaching art in the Valparaiso, Indiana, High School. He was a confirmed skeptic on the subject of UFO's and delighted in ribbing me about them.

On the particular night of which I speak, he was driving toward Valparaiso. A program ended at 8 p.m. and he switched off the radio. Just then he noticed some revolving lights settling over a snow-covered field along-side the road. Thinking it might be a plane in trouble he stopped and got out of the car.

The thing stopped about ten feet above the snow and switched on an extremely bright white light. Donald realized that he had never seen anything like this before. He scrambled back into his car and took off down the highway—the object pacing along with him. It banked across the road in front of him. He slammed on the brakes and stopped. The UFO hovered a moment, then streaked upward into the overcast and was gone.

So was Donald. He drove as fast as he could to the nearest phone to tell me what had happened. I suggested that, since he was an artist, and a good one, he should draw a picture of what he had seen while it was fresh in his mind. Next day, I told him, report it to the local paper and then relax—by and by the investigators would come to see him.

He drew the picture. In fact he drew three of them; one for me, one for the paper, and one for the two Intelligence Officers who came down from Chicago and spent the day grilling him at great length.

When it was all over and the officers were getting ready to leave, Donald asked them if they would tell him what he had seen.

One of the officers looked him straight in the eye and said: "Mr. Dodge, you were undoubtedly having some sort of hallucination!"

With that they took his drawing of the "hallucination" and left.

The experience destroyed two things . . . his confidence in official explanations of the UFO's—and his skepticism as to their existence.

The picture he drew is reproduced elsewhere in this book.

A frequently repeated claim is that "no professional astronomer has ever seen a flying saucer."

It is one of the most publicized frauds of our time.

It shows the willingness of some otherwise intelligent persons to repeat, without checking, a remark which supports their own conclusions.

I once watched a network television program on which a learned stargazer was being interviewed by a velvet-voiced announcer. Surely, I thought, they won't let this program end without mentioning the UFOs?

With only a few seconds remaining, the announcer got to the payoff:

"Have you ever [snicker] seen a flying saucer?"

The pompous little astronomer inhaled deeply, leered into the lens and snarled:

"No *professional* astronomer has ever seen a flying saucer!"

[I was encouraged to note that this fascinating declaration was promptly followed by a suggested treatment for hemorrhoids. It was, I thought, in proper sequence.—F. E.]

"No professional astronomer has ever seen a flying saucer!"

Really?

Hogwash!

Professor Jose A. Y. Bonilla already enjoyed international recognition by August of 1883. On the 12th of that month he and his colleagues at the Observatory at Zacatecas, Mexico, made history of a sort by photographing some opaque bodies which were passing between their Observatory and the face of the sun. Even with the slow plates available to them, it was not difficult to make pic-

36

tures against such a light source. Professor Bonilla, unquestionably a professional astronomer, since he headed
the Observatory, says in his report of that memorable day:

"I had not recovered my surprise when the same phenomenon was repeated! And that with such frequency that,
in the space of *two hours,* I counted up to 283 *bodies*
crossing the solar disc. Little by little, however, clouds
hindered the observation. I could not resume the observation until the sun had crossed the meridian, and then only
for 40 minutes."

The record of the Observatory for that day shows that
the objects were streaming across the face of the sun in a
straight path. Singly and in pairs they came, round and
apparently dirigible-shaped things. In about one minute
of time they traversed the solar disc, but sometimes so
many crossed at the same time that Bonilla was unable to
count them accurately, as he admitted.

They were presumably smooth surfaced, perhaps even
polished, for at certain angles they reflected the light of
the sun with dazzling effect.

Altogether, Professor Bonilla and his colleagues photographed several hundred of these things, including 116
of them on the following day, when the strange procession
came to an end. Bonilla had notified other Mexican
Observatories (at Mexico City and Puebla) of this incredible spectacle, but they were unable to locate the
objects from their viewpoints. This probably indicates, as
Professor Bonilla commented, that the objects were somewhere in space relatively close to Earth, where the optical
law known as parallax prevented the other Observatories
finding them by following Bonilla's information.

The pictures he took are still in existence. Some of
them were published in contemporary astronomical jour-

nals and, to those of us who are familiar with the shapes of the present day UFO's, the spindles Bonilla observed crossing the sun seem strangely familiar.

[You will notice that I refer to the topic of our discussion as UFO's—but that the television program called them "flying saucers." We are talking about essentially the same things, of course. The military men who deal with them refer to them as "U-FOBs" (unidentified flying objects); informed civilian researchers call them UFO's. Most others, to whom the subject is of less interest or importance, commonly call them "flying saucers." The "saucer" appellation first came to notice in the newspapers of January, 1878, when a farmer used it to describe the shape of an object which he reported over his farm near Denison, Texas. It cropped up again in June of 1947 when Kenneth Arnold, a flier from Boise, Idaho, so described them to reporters.

The term "flying saucers" was both inadequate and outmoded by 1960. Most of the objects are not disc- or saucer-shaped at all—and to use the expression in 1965 indicates that you are evidently thinking in terms of the phenomena of years gone by—it sort of dates you.]

No astronomer ever saw a UFO?

Bonilla was the exception that proves the rule?

Hardly. Bonilla was just one of the first of a long line.

In fact, we would not need to include that famous sighting by E. W. Maunder, which he described in the Observatory Reports for November 17, 1882. This eminent member of the Royal Observatory staff at Greenwich describes the thing as "a strange celestial visitor." Others, including other staff members, who saw it that night describe it as "torpedo-shaped," "spindle-shaped" and Maunder himself wrote many years later that it was precisely like what was then known as the Zeppelin . . . which was nonexistent in 1882.

It is indeed true that 1882 is a long way behind us in time. Maunder's experience was only a year before Professor Bonilla's, of course, but both of them are admittedly old in terms of our subject. Shall we, therefore, look for something in the more recent past?

We have not far to look.

For many years, Darling Observatory at Duluth, Minnesota, was directed by its founder, Professor Darling, whose apprentice was Frank Halstead. After ten years of study under Darling, Frank Halstead became Curator at the Observatory, serving in that capacity for fifteen years as a representative of the University of Minnesota. His quarter-century of experience had earned for him a place of honor and respect in the field of astronomy at the time of his retirement.

One day in 1959, during the course of a long interview with Frank Halstead (an interview which I recorded with his consent) I suggested that I would like to question him about the moon, since I knew that he had specialized in that subject. Halstead agreed and I inquired whether he had ever seen anything unusual on the moon.

HALSTEAD: "Yes, I have. It happened on the night of July 6, 1954. My assistant at Darling Observatory, Mr. Raymond Matsuhara, and myself and sixteen visitors all observed a straight black line on the floor of the crater Piccolomini. We did not see it move, of course. It was just a straight black line in that crater where no line had been before. We watched it for several hours. Bad weather pre-

39

vented our viewing the thing for several nights and when we did get another good look at it the line was no longer visible.

EDWARDS: Did anyone else see the same thing?

HALSTEAD: Yes, Frank Manning, well known amateur astronomer in New Orleans [using a fifteen-inch reflector telescope] reported the same phenomenon in the same crater that night. Nearby Tulane Observatory was alerted and confirmed Manning's experience. I know that we saw it also from our Observatory. I believe that Mr. Manning also saw it.

EDWARDS: Have you ever seen the phenomenon known as the moon bridge?

HALSTEAD: No. I have searched for it many times but I have never seen it.

EDWARDS: A little while ago you stated that you believe that intelligent beings exist elsewhere in the universe, possibly, or probably, developed far beyond our intelligence levels in some instances?

HALSTEAD: That is correct.

EDWARDS: In that case they would already have solved the problems of crossing space, would they not?

HALSTEAD: I believe that is a reasonable assumption.

EDWARDS: Such space travelers would conceivably have visited Earth, then?

HALSTEAD: This is pure speculation, or *almost* pure speculation, but I think that we should assume that we have had space visitors. The folk tales of many ancient races refer to strange visitors from the skies, and there is ofttimes a lot of truth in these legends—as we have come to realize. I feel that we have had visitors from space— just as I feel that in the universe we are not alone. Through the years I have discussed this prospect with many of my fellow astronomers and almost without exception their convictions were similar to my own.

EDWARDS: In your opinion, Mr. Halstead, could the Unidentified Flying Objects of our time be space ships?

HALSTEAD: Frankly, sir, they could hardly be anything else!

EDWARDS: Why do you say that?

HALSTEAD: For a number of reasons. The technology of mankind at its present stage of development is not now capable of producing anything comparable to the performance of the UFO. Again, I have found that many of my fellow astronomers share this opinion of the controversial UFO. Some of these gentlemen have expressed the belief that the UFO are spacecraft based on some distant solar system.

Mr. Edwards, I have watched the skies all my life. I have excellent eyesight, thank heaven! and I am quite familiar with such things as flights of wild geese, balloons, temperature inversions, and clouds. I do not suffer from hallucinations. I cannot imagine how the public can be misled by the ridiculous "explanations" offered to them from official sources relative to the real nature of these objects reported by credible and competent witnesses!

EDWARDS: Mr. Halstead, do you personally know any professional astronomers who have seen UFO?

HALSTEAD: In addition to myself?

EDWARDS: Oh—then you have seen one?

HALSTEAD: My wife and I saw two—to be precise. We saw them clearly in full daylight. Ann and I were on a Union Pacific passenger train, crossing the desert—the Mojave. It was the Challenger, a fast train.

EDWARDS: Do you recall when this happened, sir?

HALSTEAD: Oh, yes! It was the first day of November,

41

1955. We were on our way to California—we were about a hundred miles west of Las Vegas when it happened. My wife, Ann, was sitting next to the window and she called my attention to an object which she saw—something moving just above the mountain range. Our train was running parallel to this range of mountains and this thing was moving in the same direction as the train, just above the mountains.

At first I thought the thing was a blimp—you know, one of those cigar-shaped dirigibles. That was what I thought it was at first. But as I watched it I realized that it could not be a blimp—they are only about two hundred feet long—and this thing was gigantic. It was about eight hundred feet long. I could estimate that because it was so close to the mountain ridges where trees and clumps of trees were visible for comparison.

While Ann and I were watching this cigar-shaped thing —for four or five minutes as it paced the train—we noticed that another object had joined it. This second object appeared very suddenly, in back of the first one . . . behind it, that is.

EDWARDS: Did you get a good look at this second thing?

HALSTEAD: Yes, we did. It was a disc-shaped thing. In fact, both objects were very shiny, we noticed. But this second one was definitely disc-shaped. If my estimate of size on the first object was approximately correct, then this disc would have been about one hundred feet in diameter—flat on the bottom with a low dome on the top side.

EDWARDS: What happened after the second object appeared?

HALSTEAD: My wife and I watched the pair of them for two—possibly three—minutes. They were moving at about the speed of the train and they seemed very close to the top of the ridge—not more than five hundred feet above it I should say. Then they began to rise, slowly at first, and a few seconds later, much faster. In a matter of seconds, fifteen or twenty, they had risen so high that we could no longer see them from our train window.

EDWARDS: Have you ever known other astronomers, sir, who have had similar experiences?

HALSTEAD: Yes.

EDWARDS: How did they describe their experiences?

HALSTEAD: I prefer not to try to tell their stories. But I distinctly recall what I saw and I prefer to limit myself to describing my own personal experiences."

To settle once and for all the falsehood that "No professional astronomer ever saw a flying saucer [UFO]!" let us pursue this matter a bit further . . . to August 3, 1951, and to a boy's camp of the Toledo, Ohio, Boys Club on the shore of Silver Lake in southern Michigan, three miles south of Pinckney. Our witness is the nature counselor at the camp, Professor Walter N. Webb, Chief Lecturer on Astronomy, of the Charles Hayden Planetarium in Boston. He had been letting the boys observe various celestial objects through a small telescope. Shortly after 11 p.m. he noticed a glowing yellow or yellow-red light moving in an undulating path over the hills at the south end of the lake. He noticed that the object was so low that its wavelike flight caused it to dip behind the treetops. Since neither planes nor planets fly in wavy paths at treetop level (or below) Webb realized that he had seen something most unusual. He quickly ruled out the possibility of its having been an inversion effect of some ground-based lights, because the conditions for such a phenomenon were nonexistent. That it *was* what it appeared to be, a UFO, was the only explanation that fit the observed facts.

Dr. Seymour Hess, head of the Meteorology Department of The Florida State University, was associated with Lowell Observatory in Flagstaff, Arizona, on May 20, 1950.

Of his experience that day, Dr. Hess says in a signed letter to the National Investigations Committee on Aerial Phenomena (NICAP):

"This is a copy of the account which I set down within an hour of the sighting.

"I saw the object between 12:15 and 12:20 p.m., May 20, 1950, from the grounds of the Lowell Observatory. It was moving from the southeast to the northwest. It was extremely prominent and showed some size to the naked eye; that is, it was not merely a pinpoint. During the last half of its visibility I observed it with four-power binoculars. At first it looked like a parachute tipped at an angle to the vertical, but this same effect could have been produced by a sphere partly illuminated by the sun and partly shadowed, or by a disc-shaped object as well."

Dr. Hess noted that the thing was bright against the open sky but darker than the clouds under which it passed —which would be true of a polished metal object. Promptly calling the Weather Bureau station only three miles south of the Observatory, Hess was informed that the cloud base was roughly 12,000 feet at that time. He continues:

"I calculated from the known factors that it was from three to five feet in diameter, for a height of 6,000 to 12,000 feet, and a zenith angle of about 45 degrees. This size could easily be in error by a factor or two, but I am sure that it was a small object.

"The clouds were drifting from southwest to northeast

at right angles to the motion of the object. Therefore it must have been powered in some way. I did not time it but for that elevation I would estimate its speed to be about 100 miles per hour, possibly 200 miles per hour. This, too, means a powered craft. However I could hear no engine noise."

Dr. Clyde Tombaugh is the only living astronomer to discover a planet (Pluto), and is very definitely a professional astronomer, often used in an advisory capacity by the United States government in connection with various space problems.

Dr. Tombaugh was relaxing on the patio of his home at Las Cruces, New Mexico, about 10:45 p.m. on the night of August 10, 1949. His wife and mother-in-law were present. Their attention was attracted by a dark object, apparently cigar-shaped, faintly silhouetted against the sky.

Dr. Tombaugh and his family afterward indicated that the object had at least one row of yellow-lighted openings running from front to back about midway down the object, giving the impression of portholes . . . or possibly small square windows.

Writing to Richard Hall, now Assistant Director of NICAP, in a letter dated September 10, 1957, Dr. Tombaugh said: "The illuminated rectangles I saw did maintain an exact fixed position with respect to each other, which would tend to support the impression of solidity. I doubt that the phenomenon was any terrestial reflection, because some similarity to it would have appeared many times. I do a great deal of observing (both telescopic and unaided eye) in the backyard and nothing of the kind has ever appeared before or since.

"As I have said before, I was so unprepared for such

a strange sight that I was really petrified with astonishment. Consequently some of the details I might have noted were missed."

In LIFE magazine, for which Tombaugh described his experience, the astronomer made it plain that he and his family watched a cigar-shaped thing with lighted rectangular windows along the side. In all of his long years of sky watching, said Dr. Tombaugh, he had never seen the equal of this remarkable craft.

The late H. Percy Wilkins was not only a professional astronomer but was, at the time of his death, probably the world's top authority on selenography.

But more than that, Dr. Wilkins was a man who had the courage of his convictions; as we say in America, he had guts. For example: When John O'Neill reported seeing what looked like an artificial bridge on the moon, he was immediately inundated with hoots from the stargazers who had NOT seen any such structure. They knew there was no bridge on the moon because they had always been told to believe that. Somehow, it seems not to have occurred to them to do what O'Neill had done—to look where he told them he had looked. Or perhaps they could not use their telescopes because their mouths were working overtime.

Dr. H. Percy Wilkins did the obvious thing. He stepped up to the telescope and aimed it at the spot indicated by O'Neill. Dr. Wilkins took a good look. Then he issued a statement: He, too, had seen what appeared to be a gigantic artificial bridge or roadway of some sort right where O'Neill had reported.

One month later, when the viewing conditions were again comparable to those of Wilkins' and O'Neill's observations, that area of the moon was devoid of marvels. Whether such a bridge had been there is not the point which concerns us at this moment. The point is that Dr. Wilkins had the guts to report what he had seen—and that he was of such stature that O'Neill's detractors lost their taste for the game.

So it was on June 11, 1954, Dr. H. Percy Wilkins was in this country on a speaking tour and he was flying from Charleston, West Virginia, to Atlanta, Georgia. About 10:45 a.m. Dr. Wilkins glanced out the window of his seat near the rear of the two-engined Convair and was surprised to see two objects darting in and out of the clouds about two miles away. The things were oval-shaped, burnished brass in color and they had thin edges, the scientist reported.

"They looked exactly like polished metal dinner plates reflecting the sunlight as they flipped and banked around beside the clouds. Presently a third object came slowly out of a huge cloud, remaining motionless in the shadow of the cloud and therefore darker than the others. Presently it zipped away and plunged into another cloud mass. After about two minutes, the first two did the same maneuver and I did not see them again."

When he landed in Atlanta, Dr. Wilkins told newsmen that he had seen three flying saucers and he estimated that they were about fifty feet in diameter.

So the next time some pompous little fellow tells his audience that no professional astronomer ever saw a flying saucer, you are entitled to laugh in his little red face; for the record, with the signed documents to confirm it, shows that Bonilla, Maunder, Halstead, Hess, Tombaugh, and Wilkins have not only seen the things . . . but were

47

quite willing to tell what they had seen . . . and to tell it in writing.

One of the most interesting of such cases involving a professional astronomer was that of Professor Bart Bok, of Mt. Stromlo Observatory, Canberra, Australia.

The headline in the Melbourne paper for May 30, 1963:

THREE ASTRONOMERS SEE SAUCER

It told how Dr. Bart Bok, world-famous authority on the Milky Way, and one of Mt. Stromlo's senior astronomers, along with Dr. H. Gollnow and Miss M. Mowat, another astronomer, watched a strange glowing object that passed over the astronomical Observatory the evening before. The three astronomers described it as circular, lumious, orange-colored, too slow for a meteor . . . and a check with the Department of Civil Aviation showed that there were positively no planes in the area at the time.

At the conclusion of their report to the government and to the press, these three professional astronomers offered an interesting summation. They said:

"Whatever it was, it was definitely manmade!"

Questions crop up at this point in the narrative:

If the astronomers did not know what it was or whose it was or where it came from or where it was going, how did they know who made it?

They did not know, of course. After the story got out and the newsmen called to check it, the astronomers added that last line as an afterthought designed to save themselves from ridicule—for which I think they may be pardoned.

But on the following day, May 31, 1963, the HOBART (Tasmania) MERCURY revealed the official "solution" to the mystery:

48

What Goes On Here?

Phantom of the Night Was a Vampire

The paper said that the Royal Australian Air Force had rechecked their flights and had found that the astronomers had actually seen two Vampire jets and one jet trainer on a "routine training flight at 20,000 feet."

This official revelation prompts two more questions:

If it takes the Australian Air Force twenty-four hours to locate its own planes, how would they know if they were being invaded?

If a professional astronomer really were incapable of telling *one* circular object from *three* jet planes at 20,000 feet, how reliable would his work be regarding an object 40 million miles away?

* * * * * * * *

There is not a single reliable report of a flying saucer sighting which cannot be attributed to an ordinary cosmic (Skyhook) balloon.

—Dr. URNER LIDDEL, Office of Naval Research in *Look Magazine,* February, 1951

For early warning in defense of North American continent—MERINT—radio telegraph procedure. Post in radio room and on bridge. Report aircraft, contrails, submarines and Unidentified Flying Objects. Use International Urgency Signal to clear circuit.

—OPERATIONS BULLETIN issued by Secretary of the Navy under JANAP 146; illustrated with two views of disc and bat-like UFO's; Issued to all U.S. Naval craft since 1954

2

The Heat Waves

Innumerable witnesses from all over the Earth have reported that animals showed signs of having noticed the presence of Unidentified Flying Objects before the humans were aware of the same objects. By and large, such reports were dismissed as exaggerations or mere afterthoughts used to embellish a bizarre story. But the recognition that there was an unmistakable electromagnetic disturbance associated with the presence of the UFO eventually led to scientific research in this field, as it had in so many others. And we now know that animals unquestionably do "hear" electromagnetic waves—and that their detection of the waves is discernibly more acute than that of humans—who also "hear" them in varying degrees.

In the 1897 case at Le Roy, Kansas, the farmer was aroused by the commotion among his cattle. On January 29, 1953, at Conway, South Carolina, an ex-Intelligence Officer for the Air Force, Lloyd C. Booth, was returning to his parents' home at 1 A.M., when he heard the pigs squealing behind his father's barn, and the horses were kicking their stalls. He reported to authorities that upon investigating he found a disc-shaped UFO hovering at an altitude over a clump of trees behind the barn. He said that he got under the object and fired several shots from a .22 calibre rifle, some of which scored audible hits before the object could get underway. Following this report, the military conducted an intensive search of the area, using electronic metal-detecting gear in an attempt to locate the spent bullets which might have fallen after failing to pierce the UFO. What they found, if anything, was not divulged.

In the very unusual case at Kelly, Kentucky, often called the Hopkinsville case, the attention of the men who eventually shot it out with the alleged humanoids was first attracted by the excited barking of the dogs.

More recently, in the Exeter, New Hampshire, case of September 3, 1965, police officers noted the rumpus among the horses in a nearby barn, neighing and kicking excitedly, before the UFO was in sight.

Many persons have reported "sensing" the presence or approach of UFO's—a sort of detection-by-hunch, you might say, but the recent research by Professor Clyde E. Ingals of Cornell University shows that there is scientific support for such "hunches."

Of the ability to "hear" electromagnetic waves, Professor Ingalls reports:

"It appears that this takes place by direct stimulation of the nervous system, perhaps in the brain, thus bypassing the ear and much of the associated hearing problem."

In his experiments with humans, the Professor used a closely controlled radar beam, to avoid possible damage to eyes, brain, or other parts of the body. By carefully screening the radar waves so that they could not possibly be affecting the auditory mechanism of the ear, Professor Ingalls was able to prove that detection of the "sound" actually took place in the brain itself. Interestingly, the subjects all reported that the "buzzing" seemed to be several feet overhead, an effect which varied slightly with the individual. Continued testing disclosed that the ability to sense the presence of these radar waves existed *above* the forehead and was clearly not involved with the normal hearing processes, but was, said Professor Ingalls, "a broad band effect."

Some personal friends of mine were seated in their convertible with their two small children at a drive-in theatre in August of 1965. The children, almost simultaneously, exclaimed that they heard "bees." The parents heard nothing and assumed that the youngsters were being imaginative. But the children persisted in hearing the "bees." Then the father heard it, too. As he turned around to speak to the children he saw a UFO approaching the drive-in at very low altitude; double-convex disc-shaped, with a line of tiny blinking lights around the rim. Along with many other persons at the same place at the same time, my friends watched this object glide overhead at an estimated altitude of about one hundred feet, perfectly silent except for a distinct buzzing sound which diminished as the object moved away. The mother of the two children in this case did not hear it at all, but the father and the two youngsters heard it distinctly—as did some of the other witnesses who reported the same incident to me. In each case where I inquired whether there had been any sound in connection with the phenomenon, those who replied in the affirmative all described it as sounding like bees or hornets. There was one exception: One witness told me that he heard a sound which reminded him of "a paperclip caught in the fan belt of a vacuum cleaner."

It was widely reported at the time (1948) that Captain Thomas Mantell, who died during a UFO chase over Kentucky, had radioed that he was experiencing unusual heat effects as he neared the object. Whether that is correct I do not know. One of the radar operators who was present during Mantell's fatal chase told me that Mantell did say it. Another radar operator denied the quotation. There is no mention of it in the account released to the public by the then-fledgling Air Force. For lack of firm corroboration I think we should dismiss it from the present subject matter as "interesting if true; possible but unproven," although it will no doubt continue to crop up in the accounts of Captain Mantell's untimely death, as the years roll by.

Many of the witnesses whom I have personally interviewed about their sightings reports of UFO's have mentioned both the buzzing and the apparent heat wave effect.

Among them was a group of four boys who in 1956 reported to police in Bloomington, Indiana, that they had been fishing in an abandoned stone quarry on the northwest side of that city, and that about 3 o'clock in the morning they had been awakened by a great buzzing sound accompanied by a blinding white light. They had jumped up in time to see a circular object of dazzling whiteness moving overhead very slowly. It was so bright that they could detect no shape to it through the glare. It crossed the quarry pit in which they were fishing and slowly descended among some sycamore trees near a stone mill. The boys ran around the quarry and kept the mill between themselves and the blinding light. When they got up courage enough to venture out onto the railroad tracks beside the mill, they could see that the object was only about fifteen feet above the ground and that it was directly above the convergence of two railroad switch tracks, about one hundred feet from the mill itself. The boys could feel heat when the light struck them, but there was no sound while the thing hovered. After a couple of minutes of this, the thing emitted a tremendous whine and hum—or "buzzing"—as two of the boys said, and then rose straight up until it was out of sight. The four boys then ran all the way to the police station, about two miles away, to report what they had seen.

I questioned them on the day following the report and they took me to the scene. There I found that the night watchman at the mill had seen both the object and the boys, but had not reported it for fear of ridicule. I also found that, at the point where the boys said the object had hovered over the rails, the trees were seared on the sides facing the clearing, but not on any other side. The leaves which would have been exposed to heat had there been an object there such as described were, indeed, withered and dying.

Could this have been due to heat from a locomotive moving freight cars to and from the mill? The watchman said that such could not have been the case, since the mill had been closed several months, and he pointed out that the rust on the rails clearly supported his statement.

[Bloomington police had the boys involved in this case examined by a psychiatrist from Indiana University two days after the reported incident. The psychiatrist reported to police that he could not explain what the boys had seen, but he firmly believed that they were telling the truth about their experience.—F.E.]

At noon on July 1, 1954, the radar at Griffith Air Force Base in upper New York State picked up a strange blip—a return from some craft that was approaching the Base or the general area of the Base. The customary check for aircraft was quickly made, but none was in the area. An F-94 Starfire jet was quickly scrambled and vectored in on the unknown by Ground Control, while the radar operator in the rear seat of the F-94 watched the blip on his own scope. Within two minutes after takeoff, the pilot of the fighter plane had spotted the unknown visually—a gleaming disc-shaped thing several thousand feet above the jet. The pilot pulled up the nose of his jet, opened the throttle and zoomed toward the unknown.

Nothing happened until the radar operator switched on his radio set and began to call the unknown for identification.

The gap was closing swiftly.

The unknown was easily visible. It was not moving.

The engine of the jet abruptly cut off without warning. And at that instant the cockpit of the plane became a veritable hell-hole. The pilot noted that the instruments showed no fire—but he told fellow airmen later that it was like a blast from a blowtorch right in his face. He started to report to Base but realized that he did not have time . . . instead, he yelled at the radarman to bail out.

A few seconds later he felt the thump as the other man left the stricken jet. Half-blinded and gasping, the pilot blew himself out of the jet and got a fleeting glimpse of the UFO as he went out on his back. The thing was huge and circular—and then he went tumbling toward Earth.

Both fliers parachuted safely, landing near the town of Walesville, New York. Their fighter plane came thundering down and crashed into an automobile and two homes, killing two adults and two children.

Before the military could muzzle them, the fliers had talked with civilians who rushed to help them. After Air Force officers arrived, the fliers made no more public statements. Fortunately for me, one of the parties who was in a position to know the details is a close personal friend of mine, now beyond reach of the Pentagon censorship group.

[Major Donald Keyhoe, Director of NICAP, says that a large silvery UFO was reported later that day from several communities in that part of New York State—but that no planes were sent up to intercept it—probably as a result of the tragic Walesville incident.—F.E.]

Close-up approaches to UFO's have produced numerous reports of the heatwave effect noted in the Walesville case.

Captain Jean V. de Beyssac was the Chief Pilot of a Varig Airlines C-46 cargo plane which took off from Porto Alegre for Sao Paulo on the night of November 3, 1957. [Note sequence with the Nov. 2-3 Levelland landing in the U.S. which marked the beginning of the great 1957 spate of sightings.—F.E.] He took the twin-engined freighter up to 7,700 feet and flew at that altitude above a layer of broken clouds.

At about 1:30 on the morning of November 4, the pilot spotted a strange red light below the plane and to the left, on his side. He told his co-pilot to lean over and get a good look at a real flying saucer. The co-pilot took a look, and they both laughed at this little joke . . . but not for very long. A few moments later when De Beyssac glanced down to his left there was the same red object, but closing rapidly. He started to bank toward it but the object beat him to the move—*it zoomed toward the plane.* Before De Beysssac could make any substantial change in his maneuver the red object was very near at hand. There was a strong smell of something burning—but the fire indicators registered clear. The red glow from the object suddenly began to recede. A quick check disclosed that the radio transmitter, the generator for the right engine, and the aerial direction finder system were all burned out. Captain De Beyssac swung the plane around and went limping back to Porto Alegre. There he made a full written report of the strange encounter, had the co-pilot sign it with him. . . . and, in his own words—"I went home and got drunk."

This was the second time in less than three months that a Varig plane crew had reported an encounter with a UFO. At 9 p.m. on August 14, 1957, one of Varig's C-47 cargo planes left Porto Alegre bound for Rio de Janeiro. At the controls was Captain Jorge Araujo and his co-pilot Edgar Soares, both veterans of their profession. They were milling along at 160 miles an hour above a cloud layer at 5,700 feet, with perfect visibility. They spotted some sort of brilliant object to the left and slightly behind and below them. Seconds later it had streaked out ahead of them and off to their right—a maneuver that required fantastic speed—as both fliers remarked.

The object then swept in toward the plane.

In their written report on the incident, both pilots and

the three other crew members described it as a disc-shaped thing with a low shiny dome on top.

As the UFO drew close to the plane the lights on the aircraft dimmed almost to extinction, the engines sputtered and missed badly, and the radio reception became nil. A few seconds later—anxious seconds for that crew, as they admitted—the UFO plunged downward into the clouds and the electrical systems on the plane returned to normal.

That report made headlines not only in Brazil but throughout South America. And when a similar incident happened to Captain De Beyssac in another Varig plane in November, Varig issued strict orders that pilots were positively forbidden to report such encounters to anyone other than officials of the airline.

The heat projection effect noted in the Walesville, New York, case is not present in either of the Varig Airlines cases we have just examined, but it has been mentioned many times, and not always involving planes.

One of those well-documented "heat cases" took place in Brazil on the same night as Captain De Beyssac's harrowing experience. At the Brazilian Army fort of Itaipu, a glowing yellow-orange orb moved in and hovered over the base. A guard made the mistake of moving out into the open where he could get a better view of this strange sight, which by then was quite brilliant. After a minute or two of this observation, he called another guard to witness the spectacle. The object kept coming in lower and lower "setting gently through the air" until both guards became frightened. They sounded the alarm—just as the electric power system failed and the entire base was plunged into total darkness.

By the time order was restored and emergency power supplies were put into action, the UFO was gone—and so was the emergency. But the two guards were painfully burned by their exposure to it—and both had to be hospitalized. The government promptly clamped censorship restrictions on the incident; but it was a rather futile gesture, since hundreds of the base personnel, including the hospital attendants, knew what had happened—and knowing—they eventually talked.

I investigated one of these "burning" cases myself, on November 6, during that fantastic week of 1957.

Rene Gilham, a young ironworker employed in Terre Haute, lived with his wife and children on the outskirts of the little community of Merom, Indiana, about twenty-five miles south of Terre Haute.

While Gilham was eating his evening meal, a neighbor's child came in and urged Gilham's youngsters to hurry out and see the funny star in the sky. The children rushed out, were properly excited by what they saw, and in turn urged the parents to come see for themselves.

Could this really be one of those strange objects which were being discussed so widely on the air and in the press for the past few days? Gilham and his wife followed the childern out into the street in front of their home. The family which lived across the street was already there. They were watching a circular thing which hung motionless in the sky an estimated 200 to 300 feet overhead. Both Gilham and his neighbor guessed that it was not less than thirty nor more than forty feet in diameter. None of the little group of witnesses heard any sound from it—not even the buzzing ofttimes reported.

When brilliant beams of bright blue light began projecting downward from the center of the object, the family

across the road decided it was time to retire. Mrs. Gilham
suggested that they, too, should get back inside the house.
Gilham laughed and told her to "take the kids and go on
inside. I want to see this thing!"

He stood there under the object for a total of about ten
minutes, in the recurrent blue beams of light, each of
which lasted about half a second. Then, he said, "The
thing made a sizzing—like a high speed electric motor—
and away it went!"

That was on a Wednesday night. He felt no discomfort
on Thursday but by Friday his face was beginning to
swell and to itch; by Saturday the top of his head and his
face were showing such unmistakable swelling and redden-
ing that he went to a doctor: and Dr. Joseph Dukes sent
him to a hospital in Sullivan, Indiana, for treatment. He
was treated there and released a few days later, after being
interrogated by Air Force officers who advised him not to
discuss the matter with civilians. Fortunately, they were
too late, once again.

Dr. Joseph Dukes of Dugger, Indiana, told me that the
burns Gilham suffered were similar to the burns caused
by overexposure to the rays from an electric welding torch.
Gilham contended that he had not been near a welding
torch for three weeks nor, for that matter, anything else
that could have caused burns—except that blinking light
on the UFO. Just by way of leaving nothing undone, I
checked with his place of employment and they confirmed
what he had said, as did two of the men who worked with
him there.

Mr. Gilham fully recovered from the effects of his unique
experience. He was more fortunate than the two ITAIPU
guards; they underwent prolonged hospitalization and one
of them suffered considerable scarring. At last report (1959)

both were back on duty and neither was interested in watching any more UFO's.

In NICAP's monumental reference work on the UFO phenomena, *The UFO Evidence,* on page 97 are listed numerous cases of heat effects. Two of them are from France in 1954; both cases involved foliage damaged by the heat. From San Carlos, Uruguay, in May of 1958, "intense heat and electromagnetic effect." This case occurred on the afternoon of May 5, about 3:40 p.m. and the veteran pilot Carlos Rodriguez was flying a single-engined aircraft near the Curbelo Naval Base when he noticed a brightly glowing disc-shaped object approaching his plane. It came within about 700 yards of him and then seemed to stop, with a perceptible rocking motion. Suddenly the heat in the plane became unbearable. Rodriguez slid back the windows, then took off his jacket and finally had to open the door of the plane in order to endure the heat. A moment later the UFO streaked away toward the sea, leaving a thin vapor trail behind it.

Other cases cited by the NICAP publication include eye damage, burns, radioactivity, partial or temporary paralysis, and various types of physiological disturbances. In many of the incidents where persons have come upon the UFO's on the ground, the objects have sped away as though anxious to avoid contact, or near-contact, with humans. This has been reported so frequently that one is tempted to speculate that the operators of the devices know the menace they present to humans, and seem to endeavor to avoid displaying it unncessarily.

The heat wave effect of the UFO's has been well established by credible witnesses and documented cases from many parts of the world and under varying conditions. The electromagnetic disturbance so frequently associated with this phenomenon is also well known and, as in July of 1965, has been documented by scientific bases which were subjected to it.

The performance characteristics of the UFO's are, by our standards, simply fantastic—in speed, in maneuverability, and in reliability. But they are not perfect—they do have their troubles—and they have, upon occasion, provided some samples.

Air Force press conference in Washington, D.C., at which General Samford explains UFO's as nothing more than "weather phenomena."

—July 29, 1952

UFO investigators sent out from Air Bases "should be equipped with binoculars, camera, Geiger counter, magnifying glass and a source for containers in which to store samples."

—BRIEF from Inspector General of the Air Force to Base Commanders, December 24, 1959

3

Hits and Misses

It would be unrealistic for us to expect any official admission that a plane had struck—or had been struck by—a UFO. Such an official admission would negate all the years of censorship, of course. So in examining the records for evidence of reports in the above categories, we must, as usual, base our conclusions on the testimony of the witnesses and on their relative credibility.

One stormy night in 1953, a big British-built Comet jetliner thundered up and out from the Dum-Dum Airport at Calcutta. There were the customary radio reports for a few minutes as the big plane approached a squall line—then only silence.

The first investigator to reach the scene of the tragedy was a veteran of that type of work. He examined the wreckage and told newsmen: "The Comet struck some

65

sort of heavy solid object while in flight." Since this occurred in May, 1953, when UFO's were reportedly swarming all over the globe, his cryptic statement received widespread publicity. My own copy of it was taken from the United Press newswires.

That startling and disturbing statement was promptly denied by the British authorities—*even before any other investigators had examined the evidence at the scene.* We were informed that the airliner had "probably" been struck by lightning or had been torn from the pilot's control by exceptional turbulence. The subsequent official explanation was that the plane had crashed because of fire in the electrical wiring in the tail.

Still unsolved was the circumstance that had led to the first investigator's conclusion: Much of the wreckage was separated from the main wreckage by a considerable distance, including parts of the upper front portion of the main cabin. How a fire in the tail sheared off the top of the pilot's compartment in the air remains one of the most mysterious facets of this case—unless the first investigator was right.

(Probably not germane to this UFO discussion but interesting for other reasons, was the case of the British Comet which exploded over the Mediterranean near Marseilles. Fortunately for the investigators, portions of the plane could be recovered from the relatively shallow waters. The official treatment of this disaster was reminiscent of the previous Comet crash. After a prolonged study of the physical evidence it was announced that the plane had *exploded* because of a structural weakness along the tops of windows, which broke open at high altitude from the pressurization within the passenger cabin. The long delay in arriving at this conclusion may have been necessitated by waiting for the public to forget that the examination of the bodies of the victims, as announced by French investigators, disclosed the puzzling fact that they had been victims of an explosion which drove the metal *into their bodies from underneath*—in other words, from an explosion either outside the plane or inside it and beneath the passengers. Although the findings of the French post mortems were directly contradictory to the official British statement [an *implosion* as opposed to an *explosion*], the British statement went unchallenged—and the French findings went unchanged.)

Ten minutes past midnight, October 19, 1953.

An American Airlines DC-6 had left the airport in Philadelphia fifteen minutes before, bound for National Airport at Washington, D.C. Pilot: Captain J. L. Kidd.

The big four-engined plane droned along on this milk-run at 8,000 feet. Scattered clouds, bright moonlight, no worries. It neared the Conowingo Dam on the Susquehanna River. Off to the right and some thirty miles away, the glow from Baltimore shone like a huge, misty jewel.

The co-pilot saw it first—a shining thing gleaming with reflected moonlight as it slipped in and out of thin wisps of cloud. It did not look like a plane. It did not act like a plane. And it carried no running lights as required by regulations.

Something strange here!

Captain Kidd cut back his airspeed. The thing was not moving out there—just hanging motionless in the moonlight. The DC-6 was closing rapidly.

"Give him the landing lights!"

67

The co-pilot already had his hand on the switch and both brilliant-white landing lights stabbed out toward the object.

A blinding white beam of light reached out from the object toward the passenger plane. Kidd realized that the thing was streaking toward him. There was no time to warn the passengers—no time for anything but the thing that Captain Kidd actually did—he jammed the wheel forward and the big airliner arced downward steeply. The passengers who had unfastened their seat belts were thrown upward, for the dive was a portion of an outside loop.

At five thousand feet Kidd brought the plane out of it and the free-floating passengers banged down into the aisles or the seats. The pilot got on the horn and reported to National Airport—no planes in the area, he was informed—and the Airport added that it would have medical facilities waiting when the plane arrived.

The story of this chilling near-miss appeared in the WASHINGTON POST next morning for one edition. The paper said that ambulances were on hand to take the injured persons to hospitals—but that first aid was all that was required. The Civil Aeronautics Board (CAB) confirmed the incident to me on the morning of the case but declined to amplify what I already knew. This was the sort of thing the commercial airlines did not like to publicize —and the sort of thing the Pentagon would not publicize.

It was one of many.

Flight 193, United Airlines, was making a routine trip along the California coast and was over Long Beach shortly before midnight, April 14, 1954. Suddenly out of the night came an object that narrowly missed the plane. Captain J. M. Schidel was flying the ship. He later said in his report that the thing—whatever it was—had no running lights on until it was right in front of him. Then a bright red light flashed on the side of the object to Schidel's right . . . he thought they were going to crash. He yanked back on the wheel and the airliner swung up into a steep climbing turn. A stewardess was flung into a galley and her ankle broken. A passenger, C. Barber, of North Hollywood, was thrown down the aisle of the airliner so violently that his left leg was broken. Other passengers, taken unaware by the maneuver, were tossed about and skinned and bruised but they avoided serious injury.

The official C.A.B. report says only that the plane underwent a near-miss with an "unidentified craft" at 5,000 feet in a clear sky over Long Beach. But the description of the thing by the pilot and copilot gives ample evidence that it was no conventional plane that had flung itself toward them.

In the files of the National Investigations Committee on Aerial Phenomena in Washington is an official copy of a bizarre incident which made headlines in early 1957.

Pan-American Flight 257 was a Douglas DC6A, enroute from New York City to San Juan, Puerto Rico. At 3:30 a.m., flying west of the customary course to avoid a storm, Captain Matt van Winkle was about 150 miles east of Jacksonville, Florida.

Van Winkle was startled by an intensely brilliant beam of white light from his right *and below his plane.* The object carrying the light had a defined edge which Van Winkle saw in that split second when he did what comes naturally—he yanked the big plane up into a zooming climb to avoid a collision. Passengers, diaper bags, suitcases, the inevitable stale magazines, lunch boxes, stewardesses, and the co-pilot (who was in the cabin at the time) —all mingled in mid-air as Van Winkle fought to bring the plane under control. Several passengers were injured and the plane was met by ambulances at the San Juan airport.

Four other plane crews in the same general area had seen the same or a similar object within a few minutes of the Pan-Am case just mentioned. They all described it as a glowing thing with a brilliant light on the front and a reddish glow or exhaust on the rear.

The eventual official "explanation" assured the press that Van Winkle had seen only a shooting star, or meteorite. This can be ruled out by the simple fact that he saw the thing *below* the horizon, as did at least one of the other plane crews which reported UFO's that morning.

Thanks to a prompt and thorough investigation by Aerial Phenomena Research Organization (APRO), which carried the report in its May, 1959, BULLETIN, the pertinent details concerning a military incident of this same type are available.

At 7:44 p.m., April 1, 1959, came the first hint of tragedy—a radio emergency call from a C-118 plane with four men aboard, which had taken off from McChord Field Air Force Base, Tacoma, Washington, at 6:30 that morning. "We've hit something—or something has hit us"— A few seconds of chilling silence then the pilot yelled— "Mayday! Mayday"—distress in any language. And then the final and fatal sequel: "This is it!— This is it!"

The big transport tore itself to bits on the side of a mountain between Sumner and Orting. There were no survivors and the military quickly cordoned off the area to keep civilians away from the scene.

APRO representatives were able to locate numerous

witnesses who had seen the stricken plane in its final moments. The witnesses all described two orange or yellowish objects following close behind the C-118. Other similar objects had been reported earlier in the evening from many points in that same general area. The McChord Air Force Base told the press that the glowing objects were only parachute flares, part of a project by nearby Fort Lewis. *The Fort Lewis news chief said that no such activity was in progress that night.*

Perhaps the most damning developments in this particular case are these:

1. Troops were quickly brought in from Fort Lewis to cordon off the area. Other military men interviewed residents near the crash scene and warned them not to talk about anything related to the crash.

2. The pilot had radioed that the plane had been hit by something . . . or had hit something. Part of the tail assembly had been torn off the plane and was later found in the hills on the north side of Mount Ranier, miles from the scene of the crash.

The original "flying saucers," as they were called, were evidently disc-shaped craft which carried no running lights, but by 1950 there were many reports of blinking blue or green lights atop the domes of these devices, and in some cases there were reports of blinking lights both above and below the craft; that is, both top and bottom lights. Why this change took place we can only speculate, but a desire to avoid collision seems to be the only logical conclusion, at least in accordance with our brand of logic.

Before we leave this disturbing facet of the UFO problem there is one more case which is well worth our scrutiny.

In the military the familiar Convair two-engined plane

is known as the C-131-D, and it was a ship of this type which Air Force Major Mervin Stenvers was flying on the night of July 22, 1956. Stenvers, a veteran of many thousand hours in the air, was cruising at 16,000 feet near Pixley, California.

He later told newsmen (before being silenced) that the plane was suddenly staggered and knocked to his right by a terrific blow of some sort. Before Major Stenvers could take action, the Convair had nosed over into a steep dive. Stenvers fought the plunging craft for 9,000 feet before he could get it under control again and, from the way it responded, he knew that it had been badly damaged.

Major Stenvers radioed that the plane had been "struck by a flying saucer," and asked permission to make an emergency landing at the Bakersfield Airport.

When he got the crippled craft safely to earth, newsmen were on hand, alerted by the airport authorities. They got pictures of the badly smashed tail section. Fliers, including Major Stenvers, marveled that they had got down alive. The newspapers carried the pictures and quoted an otherwise unidentified Air Force spokesman as saying:

"Evidently something hit this plane from above. We don't know yet what it was."

One enlisted man aboard the plane had been cut when he had been flung about by the vicious plunge of the Convair. Otherwise the crew escaped, miraculously, alive and uninjured.

Faced with the problem of explaining away Major Stenvers' first radio report that he had struck or been struck in the air—and with the badly damaged tail surfaces which had clearly been bent downward by a terrific impact—the Air Force blandly announced that some rivets had worked loose on the metal skin of the tail surfaces, the airstream had forced the metal backward and downward so violently that Major Stenvers had been misled into thinking that something had collided with his plane.

This "explanation" shows considerable ingenuity and imagination. Convairs have flown hundreds of millions of miles on the commercial airways of this and other countries and *I could not find a single case on record of such a thing ever happening to any Convair—at any time—including July 22, 1956, over Pixley, California.*

Cynics may regard this suggested "explanation" as emanating—not from the Air Force itself—but from that branch of the military under orders to hoodwink the public—a group sometimes referred to as the Hot-Air Force.

Perhaps they are doing the best they can, but it is hardly the sort of thing they could brag about.

*   *   *   *   *

".. . and finally, no physical or material evidence, not even a minute fragment of a so-called 'flying saucer' or space ship has ever been found."

—USAF "NEWS RELEASE," January 19, 1961

"I showed to Admiral Knowles the small piece of a flying saucer which the U.S. Air Force kindly loaned to me for examination. That was in July of 1952."

—WILBERT B. SMITH, head of the official Canadian UFO investigation program

—November, 1961

4

Pick Up the Pieces

The statement has been repeatedly made by the censorship group in the Pentagon that the United States military has "no physical evidence that the UFO's exist."

Like so many statements from the same source, it is written in conformity with the regulations which preclude admitting any indication that the UFO's are real. By simply identifying any physical evidence as something else, for public relations purposes, the denial of physical evidence connected with UFO's is easily arrived at.

The heat waves and the electromagnetic effects are transient phases which are easily brushed off. The holes and burning bushes and fused glass found at some of the landing sites (Socorro, New Mexico, for instance) can easily be construed to be something else—or nothing at all—for public consumption.

If by physical evidence we restrict ourselves to "hard-ware"—fragments or debris seen or known to come from UFO's—then that is a different story. And it does not parallel the official denials.

There are such difficult cases as the rancher near Roswell, New Mexico, who phoned the Sheriff that a blazing disc-shaped object had passed over his house at low altitude and had crashed and burned on a hillside within view of the house. The Sheriff called the military; the military came on the double quick. Newsmen were not permitted in the area. A week later, however, the government released a photograph of a service man holding up a box kite with an aluminum disc about the size of a large pie pan dangling from the bottom of the kite. This, the official report explained, was a device borne aloft on the kite and used to test radar gear by bouncing the signals off the pie pan. And this, we were told, was the sort of thing that had so excited the rancher. We were NOT told, however, how the alleged kite caught fire—nor why the military cordoned off the area while they inspected the wreckage of a burned-out box kite with a non-inflammable pie pan tied to it.

Those were the halcyon days of the "flying saucers" and nobody—or almost nobody—questioned such preposterous statements as the one just quoted. What was actually found in that field I do not know. And those who *do* know are not permitted to discuss it—publicly.

Let us examine a case where the results ARE known; where the UFO fragments were collected and analyzed and the analyses were publicized. It happened in Campinas, Brazil, on the afternoon of December 14, 1954—the year of the great UFO excitement in Brazil.

Campinas, with a population of about 250,000, is an

inland city in southeastern Brazil. On the date just mentioned, the attention of many persons was drawn to the antics of three disc-shaped objects, one of which appeared to be in difficulties. This disc was oscillating violently and seemed unable to maintain altitude. The other two discs circled it slowly, as though trying to help and unable to do so.

When the oscillating disc had sunk to an altitude of about three hundred feet, heavy thumping sounds were reportedly heard by many witnesses, presumably emanating from this particular disc, since the sounds seemed to coincide with the occasional oscillations.

The other two discs came in very close to the ailing member of the trio. The third disc tilted up sharply and began moving forward in short lunges. As it did so, a thin stream of silvery liquid dribbled from somewhere on the underside of the disc. A moment later the disc leveled off with a deep humming sound . . . and all three of the strange objects began to rise and were soon lost in the clouds.

Authorities promptly instituted a search of the area where the silvery stuff had reportedly come to earth from the UFO. They found spatters of metal on rooftops, on sidewalks, and streets and in one instance on some clothing that had been hung out to dry. There were several ounces of this substance (no exact figure was ever disclosed) and the Brazilian government took charge of it.

At a press conference some weeks later, a government spokesman admitted that the material was tin but revealed little more than that, possibly because the material had been seized by the Brazilian Air Force, which vehemently denies the existence of UFO's. However, not all the metal fell into the hands of the officials. A few fragments which had been picked up before the area was cordoned off were analyzed by Dr. Risvaldo Maffei, a chemist, who informed newsmen that the material was indeed tin, containing about ten percent of other metals which he did not identify except to say that they were not antimony, iron, or other common impurities. Dr. Maffei also said that he was unable to determine how or for what purpose the tin had been used. It was not radioactive.

The absence of unusual radioactivity would seem to rule out the possibility that the tin was being used as a lubricant in some source of atomic power, where the very high temperatures might require such a fluid.

But it was tin, and it did come from a UFO, and after the UFO discharged it the UFO was able to function again with no apparent continuation of the difficulties which had preceded the release of the molten metal.

It was physical evidence gathered in the presence of numerous witnesses and confiscated almost in its entirety by the Brazilian Air Force, acting through local military authorities. If our Air Force did not acquire any of this physical evidence, it would indicate a strange indifference on their part—or that they already had more than they needed, but not for publication.

On September 14, 1957, Ibrahim Sued, a columnist for the Rio de Janeiro newspaper O GLOBO reported that he had received several fragments recovered when a disc-shaped object had exploded near the beach at Ubatuba, Sao Paulo. The witnesses reported that the disc was diving toward the ocean at fantastic speed when it suddenly reversed itself, climbed a few hundred feet, faltered, and then exploded in a shower of brilliant fragments. Some of the bits had fallen in such shallow water that the witnesses had been able to recover them. These, said Sued, were the pieces he had received.

Dr. Olavo Fontes, acting on behalf of APRO, was able to secure three of these fragments from the paper and found them to be small (about the size of a U.S. half dollar, or slightly smaller). They were very rough on the surface (scoriated) and remarkably light.

Subsequent metallurgical analysis by Dr. Luisa Barbosa of the Spectographic Section of the Mineral Production Laboratory of Brazil showed the fragments to be pure magnesium.

Ordinarily, burning magnesium could not have been extinguished by water immersion, but where the quantity of water was so great and the pieces of metal so small, as in this instance, the water would absorb the heat of the flaming metal so rapidly that it would soon quench the flame. This probably explains the scoriated surface of the samples—and the magnesium itself, burning in the air, would explain the brilliant bits reported by the witnesses to the original explosion.

Dr. Fontes provided the remaining fragments to APRO, and that organization offered to permit the United States Air Force to examine or analyze the pieces, or both, *provided APRO could have a qualified scientist present to evaluate and interpret the findings for APRO.*

There was a lengthy exchange of letters between APRO and the Air Force regarding this matter, but the upshot was that the Air Force was receptive to the idea of making the analysis, but absolutely unwilling to permit any outsiders to be present while it was done.

Since pure magnesium was a laboratory rarity in 1957, the Air Force interest may have been merely academic.

But their decision to forego the analysis in preference to sharing their ultimate findings with APRO indicates that their interest was based on something more substantial than the privilege of examining an unusual piece of metal. If UFO's do not exist, what did the Air Force have to lose?

[For a detailed account of the above incident, including the search for the witnesses at the beach, read the APRO treatise listed in the Appendix at the end of this book.
—F.E.]

Just what would happen if authorities were to find a crashed UFO—or the pieces of such a craft?

Would it be officially identified as a box kite with a pie pan on the tail?

Would it be identified as a common metal, such as tin, and nothing more?

Would it be admittedly rare, as rare perhaps as pure magnesium in 1957, but so interesting that no one outside the Pentagon could be present when it was studied?

Or, if the full story got out before the censors got in, what would happen?

Perhaps the incident of Spitzbergen Island will serve as an example (I take this report from the STUTTGARTER TAGEBLATT, September 5, 1955, as reported by its own correspondent in Oslo, Norway).

The background to this case goes back to 1952, when the newswires carried an account that Norwegian military pilots had reported what appeared to be a plane's wreckage on the island of Spitzbergen. Rescue crews were flown to the scene, and the Norwegian government was quoted as saying that they had found, not a plane, but an object commonly called a flying saucer, badly damaged, but sufficiently intact to be recognized. United States and British experts had been notified and invited to take part in the investigation, said the Norwegian spokesman.

The story vanished from the newswires as though it had been launched into space . . . until at last the silence was broken in 1955 by a spokesman for the government of Norway. The STUTTGARTER TAGEBLATT account from which I quote is typical of the innumerable papers which carried the story:

Oslo, Norway, September 4, 1955: —Only now a board of inquiry of the Norwegian General Staff is preparing publication of a report on the examination of remains of a U.F.O. crashed near Spitzbergen, presumably early in 1952. Chairman of the Board, Colonel Gernod Darnbyl, during an instruction for Air Force officers stated: "The crashing of the Spitzbergen disc was highly important. Although our present scientific knowledge does not permit us to solve all the riddles, I am confident that these remains from Spitzbergen will be of utmost importance in this respect. Some time ago a misunderstanding was caused by saying that this disc probably was of Soviet origin. *It has—this we wish to state emphatically—not been built by any country on earth.* The materials used in its construction are completely unknown to all experts who participated in the investigation."

According to Colonel Darnbyl, the Board of Inquiry is not going to publish an extensive report "until some sensational facts have been discussed with U.S. and British experts. We should reveal what we found out, as misplaced secrecy might lead to panic."

Contrary to information from American and other sources, Second Lieutenants Brobs and Tyllensen, who have been assigned as special observers of the Arctic regions since the event at Spitzbergen, report that flying discs have landed in the polar regions several times. Said Lieutenant Tyllensen: "I think that the Arctic is serving as a kind of air base for the unknowns, especially during snow storms when we are forced back to our bases. I have seen them land and take off on three separate occasions. I notice that, after having landed, they execute a speedy rotation around their discs. A brilliant glow of light, the intensity of which is variable with regard to speed at landing and at take-off, prevents any view of the things happening behind this curtain of light and on or inside the disc itself."

Colonel Darnbyl's quotation asserting that the experts were unable to identify the materials of the crashed UFO is surprising to me, since this is the only time in nineteen years of research and reporting on this matter that I ever encountered that statement from a credible source. Moreover, as the Chairman of the group conducting the investigation, he was certainly in a position to know whereof he spoke.

The statement Darnbyl makes about the disc having been falsely identified as of Soviet origin was actually a slap at someone in the Pentagon. News services quoted an unidentified "Pentagon spokesman" as saying that the disc which had been found bore markings which said that it had been made in the Soviet Union. If this were true, why did the "spokesman" decline to be identified with his story? If it were true, he could not have been successfully refuted. But if his story was false, as the Norwegian Board Chairman says, it is easy to understand that the story was simply another in a long series of phoney "explanations" which have emanated from the Pentagon evidently to deceive and mislead the American public about the reality and nature and extent of the UFO phenomena.

On the basis of the evidence in this case I think we may

safely assume that the Norwegians found something very unusual on the island of Spitzbergen. They examined it, evidently without fully understanding it. They prepared a statement on their findings in which they had concluded that the object was of extraterrestrial origin. They withheld public release of their findings until they had conferred with the United States and Britain. The U.S. had adopted a strict policy of secrecy on this subject, implemented by the censorship regulations of 1951; Britain had instituted a policy of UFO secrecy during the great European "flap" of 1954. Therefore Norway, in 1955, was discussing with two of the leading exponents of UFO deception the proposed release of this information which would have exposed the falsity of both the U.S. and British official positions!

It is not difficult to conclude that the Norwegians never released the full report because of the advice they received from two of Norway's best customers.

In 1964 when I wrote to a member of the Norwegian Board of Inquiry which had investigated the Spitzbergen case, I received, after four months, a cryptic reply: "I regret that it is impossible for me to respond to your questions at this time."

Could he, then, answer my questions at some other time?

To that inquiry I received no reply.

I am recovering from the shock.

Upon several occasions in this chronicle I have mentioned the name of the scientist who headed the Canadian investigation program to study the UFO's—Wilbert B. Smith, of Ottawa, B.A.Sc.,M.A.Sc., P. Engineering, Superintendent Radio Regulations Engineering for the Canadian government. The original Canadian program was established to duplicate, if possible, the UFO flight characteristics by development of a discoid propelled by some form of electrical field. In 1953 this was abandoned as unworkable at the present stage of our technology in this field, and the program was devoted entirely to intensive study of the UFO's. It was hardly mere accident that this action was taken only a few months after scores of Unidentified Flying Objects had swarmed over Washington, D.C. The pressure was on, both in Canada and the United States.

It was during one of those hectic nights over Washington that a military jet got a radar lock on one of the UFO's and poured a burst from his machine guns into the disc. A glowing fragment was seen to fly from the disc and to fall to earth. The pilot marked it down as best he could and notified Headquarters. Ground crews scoured the area shoulder to shoulder and found the fragment in a farmer's field.

Fortunately for the public, the lid of censorship which was clamped on after the Washington UFO events of 1952 was not airtight at the time of this incident, and Lieutenant Commander Frank Thompson of the Navy Department confirmed the recovery of the UFO fragment. [See page 272, *The Flying Saucer Conspiracy*, by Major D. E. Keyhoe.] The fragment had definitely been milled but the original Navy analysis, so Keyhoe was told, had failed to determine whether the thing was artificial or part of some unknown type of meteorite. It had later been sent, so the Navy admitted, to W. B. Smith of Ottawa, for study.

The Defense Department has frequently denied that it has any fragments or parts of UFO's, and similar denials are regularly issued by the Air Force. In fact, I have one dated January 19, 1961, which says: "—not even a minute fragment of a so-called 'flying saucer' has ever been found."

There again, note the tricky wording to trip up the unwary. No mention of Unidentified Flying Objects—but merely a claim that they have never found any portions of a thing that officially does not exist. Sly, but safe, from the standpoint of the censors.

It was in 1952 that the UFO which had reportedly crashed on Spitzbergen was recovered by the Norwegian Air Force, according to their statements given to the press. This does not entirely negate the Defense Department claim, however, since they could contend that they were referring only to the lack of such evidence in their own possession.

Was such a fragment torn off a UFO during the 1952 July-August UFO activity over Washington, D.C.—and if so, what was it, and what became of it?

Speaking on the subject of Unidentified Flying Objects before the Illuminating Engineering Society, Canadian Regional Conference, at Ottawa on January 11, 1959, Wilbert Smith said: "Various items of 'hardware' are known to exist, but are usually clapped into security and are not available to the general public."

Mr. Smith may well have qualified as an authority on that statement, for he had been said to have been the recipient of the fragment collected by gunfire from that Navy jet. But was that report factual—and if so, how to confirm it—if it could be confirmed?

This riddle absorbed the time and attention of countless interested parties, but apparently none of them made any real attempt to solve it. That job finally was taken on by two patient, thorough, and indefatigable researchers who had already made several major contributions in this field; C. W. Fitch of Cleveland, Ohio, and George Popovitch of Akron, Ohio.

They arranged an interview with Mr. Smith, and they had the foresight to record what was said. Thanks to them, I have a copy of that tape and it is from that source that the following material is taken.

The interview took place in November, 1961.

FITCH: Have you ever handled any of this hardware yourself, sir?

SMITH: Yes. Quite a bit of it. Our Canadian Research Group has recovered one mass of very strange metal . . . it was found within a few days of July 1, 1960. There is about three thousand pounds of it. We have done a tremendous amount of detective work on this metal. We have found out the things that aren't so. We have something that was not brought to this Earth by plane nor by boat nor by any helicopter. We are speculating that what we have is a portion of a very large device which came into this solar system . . . we don't know when . . . but it had been in space a long time before it came to Earth; we can tell that by the micrometeorites embedded in the surface. But we don't know whether it was a few years ago—or a few hundred years ago.

FITCH: You mean then that you have about a ton and a half of something metallic, of unknown origin.

SMITH: That is correct. We can only speculate about it at this time—and we have done a great deal of that. We have it but we don't know what it is!

FITCH: You are a friend of Admiral Knowles, Mr. Smith?

[Rear Admiral H. B. Knowles, U.S. Navy, Retired.]

SMITH: Oh, yes. Admiral Knowles and I have been very good friends for many years.

FITCH: I have been told by a mutual friend that in

1952 you showed Admiral Knowles a piece of a flying saucer. Is that statement correct, sir?

SMITH: Yes. It is correct. I visited with Admiral Knowles and I had with me a piece which had been shot from a small flying saucer near Washington in July of that year —1952. I showed it to the Admiral. It was a piece of metal about twice the size of your thumb which had been loaned to me for a very short time by your Air Force.

FITCH: Is this the only piece you have handled which definitely had been part of a UFO, Mr. Smith?

SMITH: No. I've handled several of these pieces of hardware.

FITCH: In what way, if any, do they differ from materials with which we are familiar?

SMITH: As a general thing they differ only in that they are much harder than our materials.

FITCH: What about this particular piece from that UFO near Washington . . . did it differ from conventional materials? Was there anything unusual about it, sir?

SMITH: Well, the story behind it is this: The pilot was chasing a glowing disc about two feet in diameter—

FITCH: Pardon me, sir. But did you say *two feet* . . . ?

SMITH: That is correct. I was informed that the disc was glowing and was about two feet in diameter. A glowing chunk flew off and the pilot saw it glowing all the way to the ground. He radioed his report and a ground party hurried to the scene. The thing was still glowing when they found it an hour later. The entire piece weighed about a pound. The segment that was loaned to me was about one third of that. It had been sawed off.

FITCH: What did the analysis show?

SMITH: There was iron rust—the thing was in reality

87

a matrix of magnesium orthosilicate. The matrix had great numbers—thousands—of 15-micron spheres scattered through it.

FITCH: You say that you had to return it—did you return it to the Air Force, Mr. Smith?

SMITH: Not the Air Force. Much higher than that.

FITCH: The Central Intelligence Agency?

SMITH: [Chuckles] I'm sorry, gentlemen, but I don't care to go beyond that point. I can say to you that it went to the hands of a highly classified group. You will have to solve that problem—their identity—for yourselves."

In view of this statement by the man who headed the Canadian research project in the field of UFO's—a conscientious, courageous, and respected scientist—it may be that the Defense Department and the Air Force claims of having no UFO pieces are true. It may be that the fragments are taken out of their hands on specific instructions from the same high-level body which laid down the censorship restrictions in the first place. Taking possession of the evidence would justify the issuance of the public statements that *those who issued the statements had no evidence.*

It would be weasel wording, of course, but when the final showdown came, it could then be shown that such statements were literally true . . . even though they twisted the meaning to arrive at the effect.

Smith said that the thing from which the fragment had been shot was a two-foot disc. It must have been a practicable device, for that size UFO had been reported before —and would be reported again and again.

In January of 1966, to be precise.

"We are interested in the truth concerning reported sightings and are fully aware of our obligation to keep the public informed on such matters."

—LETTER from Richard Horner, Assistant Secretary of the Air Force for Research and Development, July 3, 1958.

". . . The public dissemination of data on Unidentified Flying Objects . . . is contrary to Air Force policy and regulations."

—LETTER from Captain G. H. Oldenburgh, Information Services Officer, Langley (Va.) Air Force Base, January 23, 1958.

5

Some Classic Cases

Nineteen years of reports from all over Earth have produced an accumulation of tens of thousands of cases in which the witnesses describe a variety of unusual objects moving about in weird ways. It is not difficult, as the Air Force emphasizes, to conclude from the descriptions that a high percentage of these reports actually represent conventional objects or conditions, seen under circumstances which confused the viewers.

But this still leaves a substantial number of cases where competent witnesses report objects which are not readily identifiable as either manmade or conventional in terms of natural space bodies.

These are the classic cases—and these are the cases with which we shall concern ourselves at this point in our study.

It is customary in the treatment of this subject to include the fantastic incident at Fort Knox, Kentucky, on January 7, 1948, in which Captain Thomas Mantell, a veteran fighter pilot, lost his life while in pursuit of a huge spherical object which was crossing the State of Kentucky. We have dealt with that incident, certainly a classic case since it was the first of its kind, elsewhere in this book. Another case which we shall omit here, even though it qualifies, is that of Eastern Airlines pilots Chiles and Whitted (July 23, 1948) whose plane loaded with passengers was rocked by the turbulence of a near-collision with a long, cigar-shaped object with brilliantly lighted windows which swept *upward* to avoid collision. (Official explanation: "A meteorite.") [With windows?—F.E.] Both the Mantell case and the Chiles-Whitted case have been adequately reported many times and those who may have missed them will find them in the books of Major Keyhoe, among others.

Let us turn our attention to other reports from credible witnesses which will indicate the worldwide nature of the phenomenon and some of its unusually interesting aspects.

Shortly after midnight, May 24, 1965, three guests of the Retreat Hotel, in the isolated Eton Range about forty-two miles from Mackay, Australia, watched a strange, brilliantly lighted machine of unfamiliar design approaching the hotel. The witnesses were J. W. Tilse, veteran airline pilot with Trans-Australia Airlines; John Burgess, an Australian army veteran of World War II, and Eric Judin, an engineer. The three men admitted to government agents that they had been frightened at the time of the incident.

Burgess wanted to get his rifle and open fire on the object but was restrained by Tilse.

Tilse's account reads:

"This strange craft was about three hundred yards from the hotel veranda when we first saw it, moving just above some treetops. It had a bank of spotlights, twenty or thirty of them, below a circular platform. It was solid—metallic looking—and was about thirty feet or more in diameter."

It was at this point that Burgess wanted to open fire on the object. Tilse warned him that the craft might fire back and Burgess dismissed the idea.

"The object moved across the treetops until it came to a little ridge, where there were some openings or clearings," Tilse continued. "It seemed to be looking for a place to touch down to earth. Its lights were all shining downward—brilliant yellow or orange—and, as we watched, it settled gently to earth on the top of the ridge. As it did, its lights dimmed, but the glare was still so great that we could not tell whether it actually touched the soil or merely hovered a few inches above it. We did not see any movement on or around the object which might have been due to occupants.

"For thirty minutes the thing was motionless. We made no attempt to approach it, for frankly we were afraid of it. Presently it began to rise, and as it came up over the treetops we could see beneath it in the glare of its lights three massive legs—which appeared to be tripod type landing gear. Each leg had a light on it, but by the time the craft had reached an altitude of three hundred feet we could no longer see the landing gear or the landing gear lights. We assumed that this disappearance was due to the legs being folded or retracted but we could not actually tell—they just disappeared—as far as we are concerned.

"At about three hundred feet it began to pick up horizontal speed. The acceleration was rapid and it moved away toward the northwest and vanished in the night.

"I had always scoffed at these reports," Tilse added. "But make no mistake about it—we saw this thing—we all saw it. It was under intelligent control and it was certainly no known aircraft."

The three men were interrogated at length by Australian authorities, whose number and persistence would seem to indicate that the government attached considerable importance to the incident—as well they might.

The Tilse case just reported was preceded by another report dealing with the night of March 14, 1965.

On that night a professional dog trainer, James W. Flynn, of Fort Myers, Florida, had taken a couple of his clients' dogs into the Everglades for training. He pitched camp on a hummock and prepared to spend the night there. At about 1:30 the next morning he was awakened by the dogs. They were watching a brightly lighted object of indeterminate shape which was slowly settling down into the swamp; in fact, it appeared to be on the ground or just above it when Flynn first saw it.

He had a vehicle known as a swamp buggy; a small, light construction with huge tires capable of operating on soft ground or water. Flynn drove over to the spot where the lights of the object were clearly visible. When he reached a point about a hundred yards from it, he stopped his vehicle and made the rest of the way on foot.

Flynn later told authorities that he was about a hundred feet from the object at his nearest approach. He described it as circular, seventy-five to a hundred feet in diameter, with the lower ten feet taken up by four rows of what

92

appeared to be small lighted windows. He did not see any occupants. The thing appeared to be shiny and metallic—and its rounded dome was about twenty-five feet high. The object was resting on the earth.

Flynn said he thought it was probably some experimental craft that had been forced down . . . and he had intended to inquire if they needed transportation, which he could provide. He took a few steps toward the object and suddenly found himself flat on his back. He told authorities that he saw no one . . . no flash . . . no weapon. But something had struck him a stunning blow that left a gash which required medical attention. When Flynn regained his senses the object was gone.

Flynn's character and integrity were vouched for by many prominent citizens of Fort Myers, including the editor and publisher of the newspaper.

By way of proving his report, he led a party of prominent citizens and police officers, including a NICAP representative, to the spot where he said the incident had occurred. They found, on a low swampy hummock, a circle which measured seventy-two feet in diameter, in which the grass was seared. Nearby trees were also seared and scorched on the sides facing the burned circle.

January, 1965, was a period of considerable activity by Unidentified Flying Objects, including several interesting landing reports, two of them on the same night in the same state, not far from Washington, D.C.

The Virginia State Police report that on the night of January 25, 1965, a huge, aluminum-colored machine (closely resembling the one reported by Flynn in the Everglades two months later) dropped down beside the highway near Williamsburg and caused engine failure in the automobile of a Richmond real estate executive. After hovering just above the ground for an estimated twenty-five seconds, the object rose swiftly with a clearly audible whoosh!—and the involuntary witness was again able to start his car.

On the same night, about half an hour after the case cited above, the same or a very similar machine stopped the car of another Richmond businessman, according to Virginia State Police. A few seconds after touching down near the highway, the object jumped upward and sped away . . . as did the motorist.

Two nights later, January 27, two engineers of the National Aeronautics and Space Administration (NASA), one of them a former Air Force jet pilot, reported watching a UFO with flashing lights descend near Hampton, Virginia. In a statement to NICAP, one of the witnesses, Engineer A. C. Grimmins, says that the unconventional craft zigzagged sharply just before it touched down . . . was on the earth a few seconds . . . then rose rapidly and climbed out of sight.

One of the most interesting cases of the first month of 1965 was that which occurred a few minutes past midnight on the morning of January 12. On a farm near Custer, Washington, not far from Blaine Air Force Base, the farm family reported that a circular, glowing device with a rounded domelike superstructure landed in a snow-covered field. Only a few minutes before, the Base's radar had been tracking a thirty-foot disc which had buzzed the automobile of a federal law enforcement officer a few miles from the field, an experience which the officer confirmed in a signed statement for NICAP.

The object was on the ground at the farm for a very short time . . . but long enough to melt the snow in a thirty-foot circle and to scorch the earth in that same manner. Members of the farm family said they had been told by the Air Force not to discuss the incident. The scorched circle was promptly plowed under, also at Air Force suggestion. There was some speculation that the plowing under was done because of possible radiation; however, in view of the reported Air Force desire to end discussion of the incident, the prompt elimination of the visible evidence would be a logical procedure.

One of the most bizarre incidents in the long and strange history of the UFO's occurred on the afternoon of October 31, 1958, at the town of Iguape, Brazil.

Iguape is located in Sao Paulo Province, on the banks of the Peropava River, a broad, sluggish stream about fifteen feet deep at that point.

Around 2:30 in the afternoon, at least a score of persons told authorities that their attention was attracted by a loud roar overhead, interrupted at short intervals by metallic clanking sounds. Coming along spasmodically toward the river was a shiny disc-shaped object about sixteen feet in diameter and perhaps four feet thick at the center. It lurched over the rooftop of the home of Mrs. Elidia Alves de Souza, a house which stands on a slight ridge beside the stream. As the object passed Mrs. Alves de Souza's house, barely missing it, the craft seemed to be trying to bank but was evidently unable to do so; for it struck the trunk of a palm tree, gouging out a deep notch in the tree.

All the witnesses, including some professional fishermen who were directly in front of the object, agreed that the collision with the tree caused it to become more erratic. It tipped upward and seemed to be trying to climb . . . then it shot sideways for perhaps thirty feet. Roaring and clanking, the gleaming object hung above the river for a few seconds, then abruptly turned on edge and plunged into the water.

Police (and later, military) investigators interviewed all those—twelve in number—who had seen the strange object plunge into the river. All accounts agreed that as the thing touched the water there was a hissing sound as though the object had been red hot—but it should be noted that there was no steam. The hissing phenomenon was due to some factor other than heat. As the object sank into the stream, great bubbles surged up. The disturbance was unmistakably on the stream bed, for within seconds the roiling water was extremely muddy. It continued to seethe in this fashion for more than an hour at the point where the object had last been seen. Meanwhile, professional fishermen who had witnessed this eerie spectacle had driven stakes into the river bank so that the location of the object could be determined by triangulation.

By November 7 there was a variety of gear and experts on the scene: mine detectors, sonar gear, skin diving equipment, long probes for "feeling" into the ten-foot deep mud and silt on the bottom, searchlights, and of course conventional diving equipment. Day and night the search continued, with news photographers working around the clock to keep their papers supplied.

The object was not found. Whether it managed to escape by moving upstream or downstream under cover of darkness—or whether it simply sank deep into the soft muddy bottom of the river is unknown. But every effort was made to find it—a two-week search so thorough that it seems unlikely that the thing could have gone undetected had it still been there.

[Many South American papers had representatives on

96

UFO'S SERIOUS BUSINESS

Unidentified flying objects - sometimes treated lightly by the press and referred to as "flying saucers" - must be rapidly and accurately identified as serious USAF business in the ZI. As AFR 200-2 points out, the Air Force concern with these sightings is threefold: First of all.. the object a threat to the defense of the U.S.? Secondly, does it contribute to technical or scientific knowledge? And then there's the inherent USAF responsibility to explain to the American people through public-information media what is going on in their skies.

The phenomena or actual objects comprising UFO's will tend to increase, with the public more aware of goings on in space but still inclined to some apprehension. Technical and defense considerations will continue to exist in this era.

Published about three months ago, AFR 200-2 outlines necessary orderly, qualified reporting as well as public-information procedures. This is where the base should stand today, with practices judged at least satisfactory by commander and inspector:

- Responsibility for handling UFO's should rest with either intelligence, operations, the Provost Marshal or the Information Officer - In that order of preference, dictated by limits of the base organization;

- A specific officer should be designated as responsible;

This order was issued by the Inspector General of the Air Force to every Air Base Commander in the continental United States, on December 24, 1959. The title of this book has been taken from the title of this official AF order.

Each year, from 1954-1959, Air Force released this 'artists conception' of their 'secret', jet propelled flying saucer being built in Canada. Finally, in mid-1959 the finished product was tested. (See photo on right.)

AVRO Disc, 1955 Portrayal
(Official U. S. Air Force Photo)

AVRO Disc, final product
(Official U. S. Air Force Photo)

The most widely advertised "secret" turned out to be nothing more than a huge ducted fan . . . a monumental fizzle. *The boast had become the bust!*

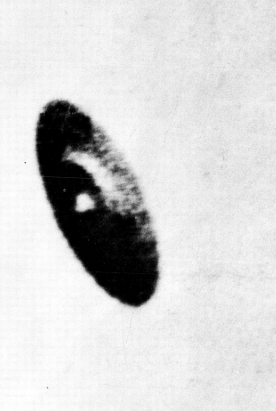

Early type UFO, with top post modified into low rounded knob. Taken by chief photographer for El Cruzeiro magazine, Rio, Aug. 1954, as UFO moved slowly along cliff and above parade on beach several hundred feet below.

McMinnville, Oregon, photograph number 1. Object about 25 feet in diameter over shed in field behind utility pole.

McMinnville photo number 2. Taken about ten or fifteen seconds after picture number 1. Published in LIFE magazine June 26, 1950.

Early type of disc shaped UFO, very similar to McMinnville object. This photographed by French military pilot near Rouen, France on March 5, 1954.

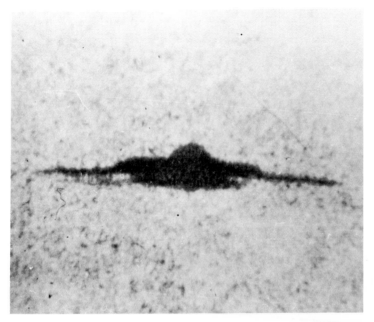

Rare view of old style disc shaped UFO taken edge-on by Argentine pursuit plane, late 1954. Top tower so prominent in original models (McMinnville and Rouen photos) modified in this type. Note also that compartment has been added below rim. Estimated size, twenty five feet.

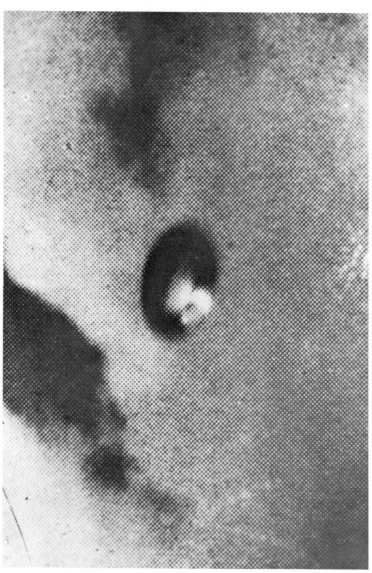

Secondary type of disc shaped UFO. Flat bottom, rounded dome, no protuberance from top. Photographed near Darmstadt, Germany, in August, 1953.

AF INTELLIGENCE MANUAL SHOWS FLYING DISCS

This official flying-disc (or "flying saucer") illustration—NEVER MADE PUBLIC BEFORE—is taken from an Air Force Intelligence Manual, AFM 200-3, Chapter 9, page 3. (See details below photo-copy.)

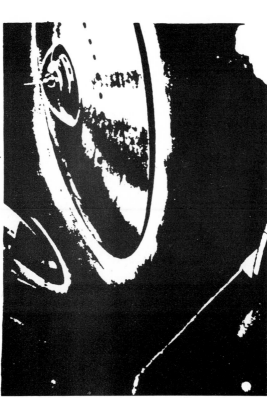

Air Technical Intelligence

Page from an Air Force Intelligence Manual for September, 1953. Drawings were designed to alert AF Intelligence personnel to configuration change then taking place as disc-shaped UFOs were being replaced by double-convex type of craft.

Pilot Chases 50-F "Saucer"

The recent pursuit of a "f by a Utah pilot, fully other pilots and airport being investigated by AF The chase occurred about near Utah Central Airpor City.

Two National Air Guar scrambled after the private a report. But the stra eluded them in a swift ver

The disc-shaped UFO w by Waldo J. Harris, he taxied out for a take-o toward the object, which at 6500-7000 feet, he clos three miles.

"It appeared to be a Harris later reported. "I like a pair of saucers, on side down on the other, was light gray, and it' 50 feet across and four There were no visible opend or exhaust.

"I was about three miles it suddenly moved upward, vator." As the disc b Harris pursued it. Durin he radioed the FAA tower ity's Municipal Airport ed a "flying saucer" gh Utah C

Photograph of UFOs over Taormina, Sicily, in summer of 1954. Objects were about 100 feet in diameter, silent and were filmed by United Press staff photographer. Thousands watched the UFOs until Italian jet arrived and chased them away.

Book deriding UFOs, written by Air Force Public Relations Officer Lt. Col. Lawrence Tacker, called this picture a "meteorite, often mistaken for UFOs."

Tacker's alleged "meteorite" was actually a photograph of a comet. It was another boo boo by this Air Force Public Relations Officer.

U. S. "Listening Station" at Porto Rico

Huge metal-lined bowl is radio telescope station at Arecibo, Puerto Rico, when staff of Green Bank worked while that 'closed' station was being modernized at tremendous cost. Story on page 153.

the scene, among them A NACIO, of Sao Paulo, and DIARIO DA NOITE, Sao Paulo. If you understand Portuguese, their coverage of this bizarre incident makes excellent reading.

—F.E.]

After an intensive search which yielded only frustration, the divers packed their gear and went away. But we should not forget that the government authorities carefully cut out the top of the palm tree beside the river . . . and took with them the notch which the witnesses all testified had been made by the object which had vanished in the muddy Peropava river.

Modern science can deduce a great deal from such a piece of evidence. Lacking the object itself, scientists took the proof of its passing.

For a somewhat different type of case involving credible witnesses, let us shift the scene to a lonely highway near Pretoria, South Africa. It is a few minutes past midnight, September 16, 1965. Two veteran police officers, John Lockem and Koos de Klerk, are driving slowly along the blacktop highway between Pretoria and Bronkhorstspruit, on a routine patrol.

It was routine until they came around a bend in a wooded section of the highway and their lights showed a huge, shiny object blocking the road. Lockem jammed on the brakes. Both men testified later that the thing was copper-colored, disc-shaped, about thirty feet in diameter. The low, rounded dome seemed to be glowing faintly. The whole object was clearly visible and it was unmistakably resting on the highway.

Ten seconds or so after the police car came upon the strange craft it leapt into the air with a roar, rising on two jets of flame which the officers said streamed out of two short tubes on the underside.

113

Heat from the blast was so fierce that the witnesses could see fragments of the asphalt highway flying outward. And long after the UFO had vanished in the darkness, flames were leaping up three feet high from the shattered road surface.

The official investigation took into consideration the possibility that the police had been mistaken—that someone had poured a volatile substance, possibly gasoline, on the road and had ignited it as the police car approached.

That theory had to be abandoned when examination by highway engineers showed that the asphalt at that point had been depressed and broken by a very heavy weight and that the gravel had been separated from the asphalt in a deeply burned area slightly more than six feet in diameter. Experts who examined the physical condition of the road were unanimous in their conclusion that burning gasoline could not have been the cause.

An estimated three hundred persons saw the damage and some of them photographed it. The newspaper DIE VATERLAND published a drawing of the object based on the description given by the two police officers. The South African government belatedly ordered the officers to discontinue their descriptions of the object. Censorship, you see, is an international ailment.

Lieutenant Colonel J. B. Brits, District Commandant of Pretoria North, told newsmen: "This event is considered as one of highly secret and important nature. A full inquiry is underway in top circles."

The crushed condition of the highway in this 1965 case at Pretoria brings to mind one facet of a case which French authorities investigated at the village of Quarouble. There a young metal worker in the Blanc-Misseron mills,

114

34-year-old Marius Dewilde, reported an experience which in fact foreshadowed many others that have followed, in other years and in other parts of the globe.

Briefly stated, Dewilde told authorities that he had gone to bed about fifteen minutes past ten, as was his custom, on the night of September 10, 1954. A few minutes later his dog began to howl and Dewilde got up to investigate. He put on his trousers and slipped outside, taking with him his flashlight. The dog came crawling to him, rather unusual behavior for that particular animal.

Dewilde told authorities that he could make out a large, dark mass faintly silhouetted on the nearby railroad tracks. He heard footsteps and flipped on his flashlight. In its beam, and not more than twenty feet from him, were two very small manlike creatures. He described them as being about three-and-a-half to four feet tall, wearing some sort of shiny helmet which was similar to diving gear that he had seen.

As Dewilde started to run across his garden to intercept the creatures by getting between them and the object on the railroad tracks, a dazzlingly bright beam shot out from the object and he felt stunned. He told police: "I could only stand there as if I were paralyzed. I could not move my arms or legs. I could not yell. I was helpless while that light was on me."

He saw some sort of opening appear in the dark object. A moment later the thing began to rise slowly, straight up, and then it shot upward with a roar.

As soon as he could move, Dewilde ran about a mile into Quarouble, only to have the police refuse to listen. He then went to the home of Commissioner Gouchet, who *did* listen. Gouchet reported to the proper French officials and a probe was promptly instituted by the police, the investigators for the French Air Force, and the Department of Territorial Security.

After lengthy questioning they came to the conclusion that Dewilde was telling the truth. But equally as important, they found physical evidence which concerns us here. At the point on the railroad tracks where Dewilde had reportedly seen some strange object resting, the authorities found five deep indentations in the wood of the crossties. Experts who examined the marks and the wood of the crossties calculated that it would have required a pressure of thirty tons to create such marks. They also found that the gravel used for ballast between the ties was exceptionally frangible, as though it had been subjected to great heat, unlike that to be expected in normal railroad operations.

Other witnesses had also reported watching a strange glowing object in that area on that same night . . . but the report of Marius Dewilde received the most attention from the authorities, for obvious reasons.

In this case, in 1954, we have the physical evidence of extreme weight in connection with a UFO; the report of a beam or ray that could stun without killing and one of the early accounts of the small humanoid (manlike) creatures which were to be reported in association with Unidentified Flying Objects throughout the world.

France had played host to still another strange craft at Marignane Airport, near Marseilles, on the night of October 26, 1952, if Customs Officer Gabriel Gachinard saw what he reported. According to his report to his superiors and to other officials who were interested, Gachinard saw a shiny object glide out from between two of the darkened hangars. It settled on a runway about a hundred yards

116

from where Gachinard stood. He says that it was tapered at both ends, was about fifteen feet long and perhaps three feet thick at the center, with half a dozen small square windows from which soft yellow light glowed. Gachinard hurried toward it for a closer look; when he was about fifty yards from the object it suddenly emitted a shower of sparks and lurched into the air, then streaked away at such low altitude that it barely cleared the fence at the edge of the airport.

The time was 2:30 a.m. Gachinard had been the only one to report the object, which had been well below the ground-clutter limits of the radar.

Customs Officer Gachinard had a long record of excellent service and was highly regarded by his superiors. After he was questioned by some of the government officials who investigated, he changed his story in only one respect. He no longer said that he believed he had seen what was then called a "flying saucer"—Officer Gachinard carefully emphasized that he had no idea *what* he had seen.

[For a lengthy and careful study of this unusual case you would do well to read *The Truth About Flying Saucers,* by the French mathematician, Aimé Michel, F.E.]

On the evening of February 26, 1959, a glowing yellow-orange disc was seen at low altitude over the London Airport. One of the four credible witnesses was the Traffic Control Officer in the Airport tower, who observed the thing closely through binoculars and reported it as "an unidentified flying object." An official Air Ministry statement given to Reuters News Service said the same object was watched at the same time from Royal Air Force Headquarters at Stanmore. The RAF description given to the Air Ministry says:

"Bright yellow light varying in intensity, about 200 feet above the ground. Stayed in one position for about 20 minutes then climbed away at high speed."

By March 6 strange things were happening.

The Air Ministry announced that the glowing disc had been nothing more remarkable than "the nose cone of a civilian plane." How it had hovered in one spot for twenty minutes was not explained, of course.

London Airport, unaware that planes can allegedly hover while their nose cones glow in the dark, issued a statement on that same morning of March 6. The Airport claimed that the hovering object had been "the planet Venus, seen through a layer of clouds." The Airport failed to mention the alleged plane's nose cone . . . nor did they explain how Venus got down to two hundred feet altitude, where the RAF Base reported watching the object.

Some very competent witnesses had certainly seen a very strange sight—almost as strange as the official explanations. It remained for the Air Ministry to explain the explanations: The stationary light was the planet Venus; the light that zipped up and away at high speed was "the wing light of a passing plane."

As jolly old Santa Claus so often says—"Ho! Ho! Ho!"

Leaving the Royal Air Force at Stanmore staring in astonishment at the rare spectacle of "a wing light on a passing plane," we move along to another case and another airport.

The time: 7 p.m. on March 21, 1965.

The place: seventy miles from Osaka Airport, near Himeji, Japan.

Veteran Pilot Yoshiaki Inada had forty passengers on the twin-engine plane he was flying for Toa Airlines. In the report he filed with authorities, Inada said that shortly after passing Himeji, "a brightly glowing mysterious object appeared beside us. It paced the plane for a moment, then dropped out of sight behind us. Then it came up alongside us and paced us, about three hundred feet off our wing tip, for about fifty-five miles."

While the object was near the plane, Inada reported, the automatic direction finder was "violently affected," to use his words. The co-pilot tried to radio Osaka Airport, only a few miles ahead, but the plane's radio did not function. The annoying object vanished as the aircraft neared the city of Matsuyama, in Shikoku.

Inada's co-pilot, Tetsu Umashima, was trying to contact the Matsuyama Communications Tower to report the incident when he heard the frantic calls of a pilot for Tokyo Airlines, reporting that his plane had been buzzed by a greenish, disc-shaped object which had circled him twice and then zipped away. The Tokyo plane was also near Matsuyama and was about twenty miles from Inada's Toa plane at the time . . . so it seems probable that both airliners were approached by the same UFO within minutes of each other.

(As an interesting sidelight to this same case, which was widely reported by both Reuters and UPI, the respected MAINICHI DAILY NEWS reported, on the day following the above incident, that a team of United States investigators was already en route to Osaka to question all the pilots involved in the incident of March 21—experts from the Federal Aviation Agency, the Defense Department, and Palomar Observatory. Purpose of the interrogation, said the Mainichi Daily News, was to try to determine exactly what the fliers noticed when the object was near the plane, in the hope that it might explain "several mysterious aviation accidents" which might involve UFO's.)

Ocean vessels, too, have had their innings with the ubiquitous UFO's. The *Llandovery Castle* incident reported in Chapter One has had many counterparts. Let us consider a relatively recent instance, confirmed by top authorities of the nation involved.

On the night of November 12, 1963, the Argentine Navy transport vessel *Punta Medanos* suffered interference from the presence of a very large unidentified object which was following the vessel at a distance of about one mile. The UFO was round in shape, moved at a steady speed, and made no sound. It did not carry any lights.

As the object reached its nearest approach to the Navy transport, the *Punta Medanos'* magnetic compasses swung wildly and were useless for navigational purposes. This effect was achieved over a distance of about one mile from the mysterious object.

As soon as the UFO had gone, the compasses returned to normal. The Fleet Commander radioed a full report immediately to the Commander-in-Chief, who ordered a full investigation. The subsequent probe disclosed nothing wrong with the compasses and ruled out the possibility that the remarkable disturbance could have been caused by submarines or conventional aircraft. The Argentine officials concluded that the disturbance was the result of the proximity of an Unidentified Flying Object.

The incident was reported in detail to the National Investigations Committee on Aerial Phenomena (NICAP) in Washington, D.C., by Lieutenant Commander O. R. Pagani, who had been named by the Secretary of the Argentine Navy to investigate such cases. Commander Pagani arranged to have the Hydrographic Survey Service of Argentina investigate all future EM (electromagnetic) cases and he also advised NICAP that the Argentine Navy had reported fifteen such incidents by September, 1965.

Then there was the very interesting case of the United States Coast Guard cutter *Sebago,* on the morning of November 5, 1957. Commander Waring said in his report that the radar had picked up an object which was racing around the cutter. Time, 5:10 a.m. Tracking it without interruption, the radarmen had seen it stop in mid-air, then dart ahead at high speed.

Eleven minutes after the radar picked up the UFO blip, four men on the deck of the *Sebago* were able to see it clearly with the naked eye: Lieutenant Donald Schaefer, Quartermaster Kenneth Smith, Radioman Thomas Kirk, and Ensign Wayne Schottley. They described the object as shiny and circular, capable of performance beyond the limits of known aircraft.

Fortunately, the *Sebago* report got on the press wires before the Pentagon was aware of the incident.

[The Pentagon may have been engaged at the moment trying to remove its foot from its mouth. It had just released another of those imposing statistical reports (of the type which Yale mathematicians analyzed and branded phonies), and in this particular report the arithmetic was so badly bungled that they found themselves claiming to be able to explain fractions of single cases: For instance, 54 9/10 percent of bird cases; 74 4/5 percent of balloons, etc.]

But I must admit that the wizards of odds in the Pentagon were equal to this new problem. They promptly "explained" that the officers and men on the *Sebago* had been watching nothing more unusual than a conventional piston engine plane! (You know—the conventional piston engine plane that is silent . . . which can stop in flight

. . . and reverse its direction from time to time. You haven't seen one? Don't worry! The Air Force hasn't seen one either.)

The statement was perhaps more asinine than usual but let us keep in mind that under the regulations the "explainers" had no choice: They can only tell the taxpayers that these strange objects are conventional craft or circumstances. The governments of some other nations, as we have seen, are more candid with the suckers who pay the bills.

One of the most prolonged close-up cases involving UFO's is one which came to my attention in late 1958.

At that time I was a television news commentator on a station in Indianapolis, the terminus for one branch of the Monon railroad. I received a telephone call from a crew member of southbound train Number 91, which, on the night of October 3, 1958, was enroute from Monon, Indiana, to Indianapolis—a trip of about ninety miles.

The five crew members of the train included Harry Eckman, engineer; Cecil Bridge, fireman; Morris Ott, head brakeman. These three were all in the cab of the diesel engine at the head of the train—therefore they were the first to see the objects. Conductor Ed Robinson and flagman Paul Sosby were in the caboose at the rear of the train. The two groups were in communication by means of FM radio, through which they were also in contact with the railroad dispatcher's office in Lafayette.

Bridge reported the case to me and his account, which was subsequently recorded by me on sound film, was corroborated by the other crew members involved in this case. Cecil Bridge is a former Air Force man with 450 hours of heavy bomber time to his credit.

"About twenty minutes past three, on the morning of

122

Friday, October 3rd," said Bridge, "the train had just passed the little town of Wasco—not a town really, just a crossroad settlement. That was where we first noticed four strange lights in the sky ahead of us. They were moving lights. At first they looked like unfamiliar stars but then we realized they weren't stars . . . they were unquestionably moving, we could all see that.

"They were moving in a sort of V formation. By that I mean that there was not actually a light at the front and center of the formation, just the two wings of two lights each, angled off at about forty-five degrees from each other.

"I think I was the first to notice them. After I watched them for about fifteen seconds I called them to the attention of the other two men in the cab with me, Harry Eckman and Morris Ott. They saw them too.

"I am familiar with planes and their performance characteristics, both as a flier and as an observer. All of us on the train are familiar with planes—we see them every night—dozens of them. But these things were NOT PLANES!

"They were moving at about forty or fifty miles an hour when they crossed the tracks about half a mile ahead of us . . . just four big soft white lights.

"We were pulling fifty-six cars—about half a mile of train—at the time, and because the lights were so low just then the boys in the caboose couldn't see them, but I got them on the radio and told them what we were seeing.

"A few seconds after the lights crossed the tracks they suddenly stopped—and came right back. This time they zipped over toward the east and went out of sight, still at very low altitude, barely above the treetops. I'd say they were out of sight about a minute altogether when all of a sudden they came back over the tracks ahead of us . . . approaching the train. I called the caboose and the boys back there could see them now. The dispatcher in Lafayette could hear us talking, of course, but he never interrupted during the whole time of the sighting."

Bridge's account could deal only with what the men in the engine could see. It remained for the crew members in the caboose to witness the objects close up—under most unusual circumstances. On the night of October 3, 1958, about sixteen hours after this incident occurred, I interviewed both Bridge and the conductor, Ed Robinson, on a television program which we recorded. Mr. Robinson said:

"When Cecil [Bridge] called me that second time I was already up in the cupola where I could see over the tops of the freight cars. I saw the four gobs of light, about half a mile ahead of the caboose—the full length of the train. Then I realized that they were coming toward us. Sosby was in the cupola and he saw them too. They were going north and we were going south. They were pretty low, not more than a couple of hundred feet above the cars . . . and they passed over the full length of the train, but going in the opposite direction. I would say they were not going over fifty miles an hour at most, but that is only an estimate . . . I just know that they were not moving very fast—it took too long for them to run the length of the train.

"None of us heard any sound from them but that isn't surprising, for a freight train makes a lot of racket and it would have drowned out anything but a big roar.

"We got a good look at them as they sailed over the train and over the caboose. They were four big disc-shaped things maybe forty feet in diameter. They glowed like white fluorescent things, sort of fuzzy looking around the rims. After they had gone half a mile or so behind the train they seemed to stop for a few seconds and then Sosby and me went out on the rear platform to watch them. They seemed to be bunched up, right over the tracks, by this time about a mile or so away.

"Then they swung off the tracks, one right behind the other, and started moving to the east. The faster they went the brighter they got. The boys in the engine were able to see them again by this time and they yelled at us over the radio."

As the objects swung away, all the crew members noticed the same oddity: The things glowed and dimmed in sequence, first number one, then two, then three, and then number four. As their apparent speed dropped, the objects changed color from a bright fluorescent white to a muddy yellow-orange at their lowest speed. [This sequential dimming and color change are oft-reported characteristics of the UFO's.—F.E.]

The objects were again out of sight of the train crew for a period of about two minutes. Then they reappeared, coming right down the tracks behind the train and overtaking it rapidly. Robinson says:

"They were just a little bit higher than the treetops along the right of way. They approached to within about two hundred feet of the caboose. The two which were over the tracks were flying on edge . . . by that I mean the rims were vertical. The ones on either side of these two were flying at angles of about forty-five degrees, with the upper rims tilted in toward the discs over the tracks. They sort of resembled a huge letter "M" in white lights. If any of them had been flying flat—horizontal—its edges would just about have covered the right of way . . . so they must have been about forty feet in diameter and about eight to ten feet thick. But it was hard to tell, for their light was sort of fuzzy . . . none of us could see any detail of the objects themselves.

"I ran into the caboose and grabbed a powerful five-cell sealed-beam flashlight that throws a good beam a long ways. I switched on the light and put it on them. As soon as the light hit them they jumped sideways out of its beam. When they came back over the tracks, I gave them another shot of that light and this time they scattered. I had the feeling that they didn't like it at all. After we shined the light on them that second time they didn't come in close any more . . . but they hung around beside the train and behind it . . . at considerable distance until we got to Kirklin [about thirty-eight miles northwest of Indianapolis.—F.E.] then they just zipped off to the northeast and we never saw them any more."

Following my interview with the train crew the news wires picked up the story . . . and so did the Air Force. The officials of the Monon Railroad advised the trainmen to keep quiet if they saw any similar objects in the future —and Bunker Hill Air Force Base, about thirty miles east of the scene of this sighting, asked the railroad to contact the base immediately if such objects appeared again. Officials of the Monon Railroad at Lafayette confirmed to me that the Bunker Hill Air Force Base had installed a special telephone line to the dispatcher's office in Lafayette, where the train crew's radio signals are monitored. And the same source informed me that the Air Force had suggested that the train crews be especially watchful "between three and four o'clock in the morning."

[The Monon evidently did not share for long the Air Force feelings that secrecy was advisable in such matters, for the railroad subsequently printed the full story in its employees' magazine.—F.E.]

On the night of December 9, 1965, a brightly glowing yellowish or orange-red object streaked eastward across Illinois, lower Michigan, northern Indiana, Ohio, and finally exploded at tremendous altitude near the Ohio-Pennsylvania border.

Thousands of persons subsequently reported seeing the flash—or the object—or both. Most of them seemed to be trying to report simultaneously to the studios of KDKA in Pittsburgh, were I was being interviewed by Mike Levine on his hour-long, and very popular, radio show. We were planning to discuss unidentified Flying Objects —we had not expected Fate to cooperate with us in such a spectacular fashion.

After hearing many of the descriptions of the object and its performance, I stated on the program that it was almost certainly a meteorite, burning up and finally exploding high in the skies.

I watched developments on this case closely and as late as a month after the event there were many unexplained features. For one thing, the burned patches which had been found, allegedly the result of blazing fragments which had fallen to earth in grassy fields, had left no specimens of the fragments themselves. This could hardly have been true of conventional stone or iron meteorites.

However, the official decision offered to the public was that the object was an exploding meteor, and in that case you may rest assured that fragments *will* be found, at least in the press releases.

One of those who turned a questioning glance at the

127

official "explanation" in this case was noted scientist and writer Ivan Sanderson. His conclusions were developed into an article for North American Newspaper Alliance, subsequently reprinted in FATE magazine for March, 1966.

Sanderson points out that the lowest speed ever recorded for a meteor was 27,000 miles per hour—in sharp contrast to the calculated speed of the object of December 9, 1965, which crossed those states at only 1,050 miles per hour. And when a lady who lived on a farm near Kecksburg, Pennsylvania, reported to State Police that a large object had fallen in a patch of woods nearby and was burning there, Sanderson says that newsmen and State Police officers who converged on the area discovered that sizable contingents of various military units had already reached the scene. One armed services spokesman is quoted by Mr. Sanderson as saying, for the record: "We don't know what we have here, but there is an Unidentified Flying Object in the woods."

I will venture the prediction that the military spokesman who made *that* statement isn't making any more public statements about UFO's!

In January of 1965 the ubiquitous Unidentified Flying Objects returned to one of their favorite stamping grounds—Washington, D.C.

About 4:20 p.m., January 11, a group of Army communications specialists in the Munitions Building at Nineteenth Street and Constitution Ave., N.W., rushed to the windows to watch an interesting spectacle to which they had been alerted by friends in the radar section.

There were twelve of these Army specialists, including Paul M. Dickey, Jr., and Ed Shad, gathered at the windows, where they observed twelve to fifteen white, egg-shaped objects, moving across the sky in erratic fashion at altitudes of 12,000 to 15,000 feet above the Capitol building. And the objects were clearly being pursued by two delta-wing jets, which they easily outmaneuvered in the three or four minutes the spectacle was in sight from the Army center.

One of the first news sources on the scene was the WASHINGTON STAR. In addition to the specialists just mentioned, the STAR interviewed Sam Webb, Jack McBride, and Sam Marrone. Said the STAR (January 13):

"They agree on the shape and approximate number of the discs and the fact that the things were speeding faster than the jet interceptors."

When the STAR inquired of the Defense Department what the objects might have been, the paper was curtly informed that the twelve Army communications specialists had seen NOTHING AT ALL! "There was no such incident. It just did not happen."

Even more intriguing was the experience of a television station which made arrangements to interview the Army group which had seen the strange objects. The interview was to be made on sound film and aired that night.

Word of this development got to the Pentagon and a "spokesman" was rushed to the Army center on the double quick. He found the television crew setting up their gear. The communications specialists who were about to be interviewed were taken into another room and informed that they could not discuss the incident for public consumption. When some of the civilian specialists demanded to know in what manner the Pentagon could force THEM to maintain silence, the flustered officer told

129

them that *since they had observed the objects through a government window they came under the government regulations on the subject!*

There were no television interviews with those witnesses.

One of the best known men in the United States is veteran pilot and television personality Arthur Godfrey. He lives in Virginia, has his own private plane and pilot, and flies back and forth to his broadcasting duties with the Columbia Broadcasting System in New York City.

On his coast-to-coast program on June 25, 1965, Godfrey's guest was comedian Orson Bean, and the subject of Unidentified Flying Objects came up. Mr. Godfrey recounted an experience which had befallen him and his co-pilot, Frank Munciello, on a night flight they were making in Godfrey's plane from New York to Washington.

They were having a routine flight, said Godfrey, and were near Philadelphia when a brightly lighted object suddenly appeared off the right wing of their twin-engined Convair. Godfrey, at the controls, rolled his plane sharply to the left to avoid a possible collision. Then, he told his audience, he contacted the FAA tower at Philadelphia:

"Any traffic near us?"

"None," the tower replied.

"Well, there's darned well something up here!" Godfrey replied.

At that instant the object reversed its course and circled them, coming up seconds later behind their left wing. Godfrey again banked sharply away from the UFO and tried to increase the distance between them. The object

130

banked right with him. Every time Godfrey made an effort to elude the UFO, it duplicated his moves.

"It stayed right there off my left wing," Godfrey told his audience, "no matter what I did!"

He also admitted that he and Munciello, both veteran pilots with thousands of hours of flying time, were scared by what had happened to them. They could not shake the UFO, no matter what they tried. It simply stayed right with them until it got ready to leave, and then it veered upward and away into the night.

Two of the most interesting case reports of 1964 involved three highly credible witnesses: two Nevada ranch owners and a South Carolina businessman. The second case was reported before the first case reached the news-wires.

On June 25, 1964, rancher George W. Rogers, who lives in Spring Valley, near Ely, Nevada, was driving to Ely with his brother Bert. They noticed a peculiar device in the highway ahead of them. When they first saw it, the thing was beside the road and about four feet off the ground . . . they could see only the top of it . . . and their first thought was that it was a jeep off the road. Then it came up and over the road, resting briefly on a sort of slender pedestal which was about two feet long. By this time the men were within a few feet of the thing. They described it as resembling a pyramid-shaped top with the point tapering down to that two-foot-long pedestal. The top was slightly bulging or curved. The object was spinning rapidly.

George Rogers jumped out of the car and ran up to touch the object. As he drew near, the thing made a loud humming sound and shot into the air to a height of about

131

ten feet, coming back down on the highway about forty feet away. George approached it three or four times, and always with the same result. George told authorities later: "It occurred to me that I was fooling around something that I didn't know anything about. Bert was yelling for me to get away from that thing. I decided that was pretty good advice so I went back and got into the car."

A moment later the object rose slowly and began to move rapidly away to the east, finally vanishing in the distance as it passed over a ridge.

Both ranchers agreed that the thing they had seen was shaped like an inverted top. George, who had tried to touch it, said the sides were shiny, as though they were plastic and that there was a red insignia or emblem on one face which he was unable to make out clearly because of the spinning motion.

The Ely, Nevada, RECORD carried the report of the strange inverted top in its issue of July 1.

In the Anderson, South Carolina, INDEPENDENT, of July 1, 1964, we find an interesting sequel to the experience of the Rogers brothers of Ely, Nevada, a thousand miles to the northwest.

B. E. Parham of Wellford, South Carolina, is District Manager of Family Record Plan, Incorporated. He had been on a business trip to Atlanta and was returning, in his late model Chevrolet hardtop, to his home in a suburb of Spartanburg. He was on Highway 59, driving about seventy miles an hour, and the time was about one o'clock in the morning. There was no other traffic near him at the time.

Parham told federal authorities:

"Suddenly everything lit up around me. I saw this bright object coming straight toward me. I thought I was

132

gone—I thought it was a meteor that was going to hit me!"

At the last second it turned straight up and swerved high above the car, a maneuver that Parham says gave him the impression that it was curious about his headlights.

The engine of his car began to fade and he let the car roll to a stop beside the highway.

Said Parham: "The thing looked like an inverted top with sides about six feet long. There were little holes underneath it—it seemed to be propelled by yellow flames of some sort. When it came down low over my car the heat was stifling, and I thought the odor resembled formaldehyde. I rolled up the windows on my car and locked the doors. A few seconds later the thing made a roaring sound and rose up and up until I couldn't see it any more. I really didn't want to see it. I just wanted to get away from there and I did."

Parham drove to the airport at Spartanburg and made his report to the Federal Aviation Agency employees there. They checked and found several spots on the top and hood of the car where some liquid had destroyed the paint. The Anderson INDEPENDENT reported that, when the FAA checked the spots with a Geiger Counter, they found the spots radioactive.

Interrogators came and questioned Parham and they scraped the sticky spots off his car. Then they went away and left him to figure out the answers for himself.

It's the American way—where UFO's are concerned.

* * * * * * * *

During the ensuing year there will be authenticated sightings of roughly 200 Unidentified Flying Objects, of which the Pentagon will be able to disprove 210.

—LIFE MAGAZINE, January 6, 1958, page 16

6

Life Out Yonder

"The United States can eavesdrop on more than one intelligent civilization elsewhere in the Universe *anytime we are ready to set up the gear!"*

The speaker was Bernard M. Oliver, famed electronics engineer and Vice President of Hewlett-Packard Corporation. He was well-informed on what the radio-telescopes *had done and what they were doing* when he appeared before the American Institute of Aeronautics and Astronautics in San Francisco on July 27, 1965.

Mr. Oliver told his distinguished audience that by building a mass of not fewer than one thousand nor more than ten thousand radio telescopes, each about one hundred feet in diameter, in a ten-mile square of flat terrain such as certain areas in Texas, man could scan the skies as they were never scanned before. By coupling all these instruments together we could, he said, "virtually listen to creation itself."

The cost of such a project?

About the cost of the first atomic bomb—or only about one-tenth the cost of landing a man on the moon.

The array of super-sensitive listening gear, Oliver said,

would enable man "to detect the unintended radiation from another intelligent race; their television programs, their FM radio, the communications they would be using in their own commerce and social life."

"These signals are pouring in on Earth today in all probability. It is maddening to think that this is happening now—and that we can't hear it!

"I predict that by such a listening post on the Universe we would find not one—but several—sources of intelligent life."

Mr. Oliver's address to that convention of scientists would have been regarded as pure crackpot material a generation ago . . . or even less. But in the last twenty years many things have happened—on Earth—and around Earth—and out in space, things which all point to the likelihood of intelligent life other than human beings of terrestial origin.

There was no snickering at Mr. Oliver's remarkable proposal nor for his outspoken conclusions. None at all. Instead, he drew prolonged applause; for his well-informed audience knew that the evidence was with him.

The quest for evidence of life elsewhere in the Universe (of which the UFO's may be one indication) is a long, long story. It is a story of top-level secrecy, of prolonged frustration—and of ruinous expense.

In terms of money and manpower, it has become, by 1966, one of our major scientific endeavors.

In the case of the United States it began officially about 1924. There had been some activity in this field by individuals prior to that time, but it was in 1924 that the United States government took an interest and financed certain endeavors. They had reason to expect results—

and they secured results—but hardly what they had anticipated.

Even this experimenting had been preceded by that of Dr. Otto Hahn, a respected German geologist, who reasoned that if microscopic forms of life were preserved in the ancient rocks of Earth then similar forms might be found embedded in the stony meteorites which were presumably fragments of other planets.

Hahn had neither sufficient funds nor time to conduct continuous and thorough research in this promising field but he made excellent use of what he had. From a meteorite which had been seen to fall near Knyahinya, Hungary, in the year 1866, Hahn managed to saw off several tiny slices which he polished to a transparent thinness. Under the microscope he was pleasantly surprised to make out delicate figures which resembled fossilized lifeforms of very early Earth creatures. Some of these things were unquestionably lacelike striations such as a tiny shell would make. And tiny shells themselves are the product of living creatures.

After two years of patient study of his meteorite fragments, Hahn had managed to photograph what he called sixteen family groups of various sponges, corals, and assorted objects which he lumped together as crinoids, tiny living things having stems and "arms" which existed (and still exist) in the sludge of primordial seas.

As a double check on his findings, Dr. Hahn turned the "evidence" over to a noted zoologist, Dr. D. F. Weinland, and asked him for a determination of the nature of the objects.

Dr. Weinland made a careful and protracted study of the material and his findings confirmed what Dr. Hahn

137

had concluded: The corals and sponges did indeed resemble those of Earth, except that they were much smaller. The objects which Hahn had called "crinoids," however, came out in Dr. Weinland's judgment as some form of sponge. But the over-all conclusion—that all those objects had indeed lived somewhere in space—was the same.

Dr. Hahn was a man of eminence, as was Dr. Weinland, but his scientific stature was not enough to protect him from the poisonous barbs of his fellow scientists when he published his findings in 1880. The accepted posture in those days was that there was no life elsewhere in space— that life as we know it was an exclusive and unique development on this little planet of ours. To hint, as Hahn did (with Weinland's concurrence), that somewhere out there another body had once held primitive life forms, and might still hold them, was heresy, no less.

A meeting of scientists at the University of Basle concluded that Dr. Otto Hahn had made an ass of himself, and that Dr. Weinland was his equal. Most of the scientific papers which dealt with Hahn's findings treated them as though they were ashamed to have to offer such fare to their readers. From the Smithsonian Institution Hahn was denounced as "a hapless man who has permitted his imagination to run wild with him."

After this shower of scientific cabbages, neither Dr. Hahn nor his colleague, Dr. Weinland, devoted any further efforts to following up what they had found. For the most part they were unable to induce their critics to even examine the evidence; then, as now, the bitterest skeptics were the uninformed.

It was eighty years before other scientists would take up the work for which Hahn and Weinland had suffered.

We shall examine their research in its proper place, chronologically speaking; for in the meantime other men, using other approaches, had been busy in this field.

One of these researchers was the noted Yugoslav self-taught scientist, Nikola Tesla. He is probably best known for the Tesla coil, but his greatest impact on the modern world was his victory over Thomas Edison which resulted in alternating current, advocated by Tesla, superseding the direct-current system advocated by Edison. (He refused, in 1921, to share a Nobel Physics prize with Edison, for whom he had a strong personal dislike.)

By 1899 Tesla was a wealthy, though somewhat eccentric, figure in the new era of electric power and wireless. One of his pet theories was that power could be drawn from the magnetic field of Earth in such stupendous quantities that it could be used to signal other planets—in case anybody might be listening there.

After a great deal of conferring with government experts to select a highly charged location for his work, Tesla moved to Colorado Springs, Colorado, where he set up his gear.

It was like nothing that man had ever constructed before; it was a giant-size package of electrical equipment designed to deliver a giant-size blast of manmade lightning which could be loosed in such fashion that it would cross space in a sequence indicating that it was the work of intelligent beings.

In the generation of a mighty wallop, Tesla succeeded beyond his wildest expectations. By alternately changing the flow of the current through that immense coil, seventy-five feet in diameter, and finally shooting it into a copper ball atop a two-hundred-foot tower, Tesla produced bolts of artificial lightning which literally rocked the countryside for many miles around. He also burned out a power generating station, and lighted electric bulbs miles away by the immense flow of current from his experimental installation—a fantastic story which you will find in the book *Prodigal Genius* by John O'Neill. And before public outcry forced him to cease and desist to avoid arrest, Tesla felt that he had evidence to support his original contention . . . that somewhere out there in space his gargantuan dots and dashes had been detected . . . and answered.

The signals picked up by Tesla's gear in 1899 were periodic and "with such clear suggestion of number and order that they could not be traced to any cause then known by me."

And he added: "Although I did not decipher their meaning, it was impossible for me to think of them as accidental . . . there was a purpose behind those signals . . . they were the results of an attempt by some human beings, not of our world, to speak to us by [wireless] signals. I am absolutely certain they are not caused by anything terrestrial."

Tesla's contention that he had been listening to extraterrestial wireless signals was well-founded, for at that time Marconi was barely able to send puny little signals a distance of fifty miles—and it was two years AFTER Tesla's experiences at Colorado Springs that Marconi managed to get the letter "S" across the Atlantic in intelligible form. Tesla said that his instruments picked up a transmission with a regular pulse—which is not a characteristic of natural stellar radiation, as we now know after years of study. The regularity of the signals, and the apparent promptness with which they followed

Tesla's gigantic sparks, are unique in this type of experiment.

At the same time that Tesla was blasting the heavens with his artificial lightning in Colorado, young Marconi was tapping out the letter "V"; and his co-workers fifty miles away (Wimeraux to South Foreland) finally succeeded in intercepting the signals.

In 1921, Marconi reported that he had been receiving strange, unidentifiable radio signals on his yacht in the Mediterranean. As with Tesla twenty-two years before, Marconi noted the unnatural regularity of the pulses. He authorized his London representative to quote him as saying that the signals certainly represented some sort of code which he could not recognize, *other than the letter "V" then being used in the Marconi code.*

In 1962, speaking to the American Rocket Society Convention in Los Angeles, researchers C. D. Jackson and R. E. Hohmann presented a superb paper on the long search for life in space. In it, of course, they dwelt at length on the experiences of Tesla, Marconi, and also of the fantastic results of an experiment conducted with the cooperation of the United States government by the Professor of Astronomy at Amherst College, Dr. David Todd, on the night of August 23, 1924.

The Navy was an active participant in this venture for several reasons, one of them being that the Navy had made arrangements with Charles Francis Jenkins to test a device he had just built—an instrument which could record radio signals on sensitized paper tape or on film. Jenkins was best known as the man who built the first successful machine for projecting motion pictures. In later years he built the first practical device for converting television signals into television pictures—the crude and cumbersome (but workable) Jenkins scanning-disc system.

In 1924 Jenkins had progressed as far as this method of intercepting and recording radio signals on photographic material. The Navy wanted to try to record possible signals from Mars during that planet's near approach during August of 1924, when it would be only 35,000,000 miles from Earth. But the Navy was loath to be tarred with the brush of lunacy if the word got out that it had sought space signals and failed. It preferred to remain in the background, furnishing the money and the gear and the necessary technical manpower—while someone else fronted for the project. The "old Army Game" of "Heads We Win, Tails You Lose" was also the old Navy game in this instance.

In Dr. David Todd they found their man. He was a respectable astronomer who was fully justified in being curious about Mars. Instead of the old-fashioned telescope he would try to use the new-fangled radio recording device.

It was a great night in the annals of eavesdropping on space.

For one thing, the government ordered all American radio transmitters to remain silent during the period of the test. Inside the "Jenkins Radio-Camera" a roll of sensitized paper tape crept past a fluctuating point of light—the radio signal being converted into a beam of light that would record on the photographic material. The recording material was about thirty feet long and slightly more than six inches wide.

With the antenna directed toward Mars, and the tiny light flickering the incoming signals onto the paper film,

142

the hours dragged by. Around the world, other nations participated by instructing their wireless stations to listen for strange signals.

Some reported results; some made no reports.

A British Columbia station reported that it had received a baffling series of signals which consisted of four dashes in code, repeated for many minutes.

Amateurs in France and England also reported picking up short bursts of what seemed to be meaningless code. What our own Naval vessels received, if anything, was not revealed.

One thing is certain—none of them got the same results as the Jenkins Radio-Camera being used by Dr. Todd for the Naval Observatory.

It had functioned perfectly—if remarkably.

Along one side of that tape were recorded the dots (and dashes) which other receiving stations had reported. Along the other side of the tape, at intervals indicating a time lapse of about thirty minutes between the markings, were strange clusters of signals.

The NEW YORK TIMES reported on August 28:

"Development of a photographic film record of the radio signals in a period of 29 hours when Mars was closest to the earth, has deepened the mystery of the dots and dashes reported heard at the same time by widely separated operators of powerful stations.

"The film . . . discloses in black on white a fairly regular arrangement of dots and dashes along one side, but on the other side at almost evenly spaced intervals are curiously jumbled groups, each taking the form of a crudely drawn human face."

The scientists who examined that amazing strip of recorded radio signals . . . "of curiously jumbled clusters

each taking the shape of a crudely drawn human face"
. . . were understandably bewildered by this strange turn
of events. Especially so, since the inventor himself had
no idea how the signals could be transmitted to produce
such a bizarre result. The apparent caricatures were a
sort of seven-day wonder until they were finally filed and
largely forgotten.

But the scientists had already noted another aspect of
this experiment which may in the final analysis be of
greater import than the "faces." They had noted that
there was an interesting chronological relationship between this flood of signals recorded in 1924 and the
earlier experiments conducted by both Tesla and Marconi.

For instance, Tesla transmitted repeated regular pulses
of radiation in the high frequency bands at a power of
many millions of volts, in 1899. Marconi transmitted the
letter "V" in the Morse code used by telegraphers, also
in 1899.

In 1921, after a time lapse of twenty-two years, the
Morse code "V" was received on Earth under conditions
which indicated transmission from an extra-terrestial
source.

In the closing days of 1901, Marconi flashed his first
wireless message across the Atlantic. It was the code
letter "S" and it was a much stronger signal than his
earlier efforts.

From December of 1901 to August of 1924, when the
letter "S" came streaming in from space is a few months
more than the twenty-two-year period, but it is still within
the apparent cycle noted before.

It may be pure coincidence, of course, but the seemingly intelligent nature of the signals, duplicating those

we had sent out so many years before, makes coincidence alone rather unlikely.

Which brings us to still another facet of our discussion: Twenty-two years from our space signal experiments of 1924 brings us to 1946, the year the Unidentified Flying Objects swarmed over Earth, in this case over the Scandinavian countries and parts of Soviet Russia.

Here again it may have been pure coincidence, but such an interesting "coincidence" that it deserves inclusion, for we shall see that as this phenomenon develops, coincidence alone becomes inadequate to explain what has happened.

Still another broadcasting experiment which lies precisely on that twenty-two-year line was that conducted by the noted Kentucky eccentric, Nathan Stubblefield, in the summer of 1902. The WASHINGTON EVENING STAR told the story in bold headlines in its issue of May 21, 1902:

BY LAND AND WATER
FIRST PRACTICAL TEST OF WIRELESS TELEGRAPHY
HEARD FOR HALF MILE

The STAR reported that Stubblefield had broadcast voice messages from the Potomac River steamer *Bartholdi* and had interchanged voice messages with prominent members of Congress on the banks of the river, by sending the radiations out through two wires dangling in the water behind the steamer.

To make the record inclusive, we should note that this headline event took place almost exactly twenty-two years before Dr. Todd and the Naval Observatory technicians intercepted those strange signals. And Stubble-

145

field's transmissions of the human voice were, of course, followed forty-four years later by the dramatic appearance of the ubiquitous flying discs.

Did these unexplainable signals mean that somewhere out there in space, at least eleven light years away, somebody was trying to let us know they were listening? Were they recording our signals and sending them back to us —a twenty-two-year round trip? If so, where were they— if they were there at all?

It did not take a great deal of calculation to narrow the field to a pair of probabilities: the stars Tau Ceti and Epsilon-Eridani. If they have inhabited planets which are interested in us, they are just far enough away to fit the time-lag we have noted.

Somebody in high place thought the subject worth exploring after the incredible Jenkins Radio-Camera experiment of 1924; for in 1926 both the Navy and the Signal Corps, this time using Johns Hopkins University as a front, built a huge wireless receiving installation in Nebraska. It cost the government an admitted one hundred thousand dollars; not much now but enough to construct a very powerful receiving station in 1926.

Precisely what happened there that summer has never been a matter of public knowledge. The backers of the project admittedly were hoping to intercept radio signals from space and they admittedly tried. After several weeks of activity, the official statement said only that the results had not been satisfactory, which was probably correct. At any rate the station was closed down, the records were absorbed in the vast government files, and the attempt was virtually forgotten. But it *was* made and it *was* devoted to recording space signals, if any.

Hunting for space signals, in the 1920's, was tantamount

146

to applying for admission to the looney bin. Hunting for traces of fossilized life in meteorites was on the same level, and for the same reason. Orthodox science took the position that there was no life in space; therefore, those who looked for it were daft—and should be dismissed from the society of solid thinkers.

Not until 1950 did space listening become acceptable. That was the year that the public was told that radio telescopes, generally vast and expensive constructions, were necessary for scientists to analyze the hissing of the stars. Millions of dollars were spent in many lands on these gigantic dish-shaped devices for receiving and recording fantastically weak radiation signals from the vastness of space. In the world of science the old fashioned astronomer who examined the evidence of space with the eye was quietly supplanted by a new breed who examined the same evidence by ear. The old order changeth——.

Like begets like, you know, and when space radio listening became respectable, a few courageous scientists dared to examine the innards of meteorites again, and to talk about the results.

A meteorite of the type known as carbonaceous chondrite (granular, containing carbon) had been found near Murray, Kentucky, in 1950. It was turned over to the Smithsonian Institution for study, where scientists subjected it to lengthy observation and chemical analysis. Their report, over the signature of Dr. Melvin Calvin, may easily be construed as evidence that they were aware of the criticism they were inviting. The report was published in the book *Chemical Evolution* in 1961, and it identified their findings as "organic compounds" of the type common to primitive evolutionary processes. Few laymen were likely to see that statement; fewer still were

147

likely to interpret it for what it was—a guarded admission that *the Smithsonian group had found the basic stuff of life in that meteorite.*

So it was in 1953, when a researcher at the University College in London, Dr. George Mueller, set about dissecting a meteorite from South Africa, a carbonaceous chondrite which had blazed to Earth in 1838. The doctor patiently secured from the stony mass a tiny amount of a resin which proved to contain organic acids in complex forms. He also reported finding water which was unlike the water common to Earth. Mueller added his name to the list of those who had found evidence of primitive life forms from space.

For different reasons, neither of those two reports (Mueller's and the Smithsonian's) drew any critical fire.

Not so with the work of their successors in this field in the 1960's.

Dr. Warren Meinschein, an analytical chemist for ESSO (Standard Oil Co.), used a mass spectrometer which brought the revelation that the hydrocarbons of crude oil were evidently the hydrocarbons of living things. Meinschein's discovery came to the attention of two scientists at Fordham University, Bartholomew Nagy, a geochemist, and Douglas J. Hennessy, an organic chemist. Having similar interests, they quickly formed a group to examine the hydrocarbons which a French scientist had isolated from the well-known Orgeuil meteorite, back in 1868.

Their findings stirred up a scientific storm when they were published in NATURE, the British equivalent of the SCIENTIFIC AMERICAN. NATURE said that the study of the Orgeuil meteorite had brought to light evidence of primitive life forms which resembled, but which were not

148

identical to, ancient forms of algae which live in water on Earth.

Actually Nagy, Meinschein, and Hennessy listed and pictured five different fossil forms which clearly indicated elementary life forms in the structure of the meteorite, all of which, they said, had developed in an environment where water had been available to them for a very long time.

Critics showered challenges from all sides. Their principal argument against the findings of the researchers was that the meteorite had been contaminated by striking the earth. Therefore, they said, any earthlike fossils had merely been acquired by contact.

It was not an unreasonable assumption, but it was badly weakened when the scientists pointed out that they had actually studied two different meteors . . . and the one from France (Orgeuil) was identical in content to the one from Africa (Ivuna).

[To further confound the critics, and to startle the researchers themselves, as it turned out, fragments of the Murray, Kentucky, meteorite of 1950, were turned over to the U.S. Biological Survey for study. There, in a carefully sterilized environment, tiny samples of the meteoritic substance were placed in nutrients and carefully attended. By 1961 "some growth" had been noted. In the spring of 1965 they were still growing! F.E.]

Summed up to this point in our discussion, it means that reputable scientists have discovered considerable evidence which indicates that somewhere in space there is, or has been, life. If it developed under conditions which seem indicated by the nature of it and by the content of the material in which it was found, then we have no reason to doubt that it continued to develop—at least until the cataclysm which rent the body on which the life existed.

This in itself is not proof of intelligent beings—not even of little green men—but it is evidence that somewhere out there *life* did exist—and that *is* important.

Is it still there in some recognizable form on some celestial body which is capable of being interested in us . . . and of reaching us, physically, perhaps?

That question has not been neglected, as we shall see.

So far as the records show, there was no *consistent* search for radio signals from outer space prior to about 1952, by which time the equipment used for this work had become sufficiently sophisticated to justify the expense of creating and operating it.

At that time there were no manmade satellites orbiting Earth, of course. Sputnik No. 1 was still waiting to make its bow in the autumn of 1957. But there were thousands of patriotic American citizens watching the skies regularly every night—members of the Ground Observers Corps—and they were reporting some very strange spectacles. And the few existing radio telescopes were flooded with strange radiation signals from space. The problem was to determine whether in this plethora of visual and audible evidence there was any evidence of intelligence.

The experiences of the early experimenters, Marconi, Tesla, and Dr. Todd, were inconclusive, but encouraging. With new techniques, new approaches and ample time and money, the enigma might be resolved.

A well trained amateur, 25-year-old John G. Bolton of Australia, reported in 1947 (June) that he had picked up some interesting signals from a point in space which he was not able to locate precisely with his gear. But

150

four years later Bolton's radio signal source was identified as Cygnus A.

It may safely be said that radio astronomy grew rapidly following Bolton's discovery, although not necessarily because of it. He later became head of the Radio Astronomy Department at Caltech, where he helped install the first two large radio dishes in this country.

In August of 1956, Dr. John Kraus of Ohio State University made headlines around the world with his announcement that he had picked up some very interesting radio signals from Venus.

"The signals come in pulses often lasting one second or more and sometimes there is a string of them, with more or less uniform intervals between," said Dr. Kraus in a paper prepared for the American Astronomical Society. "The impulses appear to be modulated to an audio frequency of about 117 cycles per second," the scientist reported.

This was not the first time Dr. Kraus had reported such an anomaly. In June of that same year he had announced that the signals from Venus were very much like those which might be generated by a tremendous and prolonged electrical storm.

But the signals which prompted Dr. Kraus's second announcement, in August, were vastly different.

"These signals must come from a source of a rather complex type," said the scientist, "and they have many of the characteristics of terrestrial broadcasting stations."

By today's standards the 1956 radio astronomy gear at Ohio State was little short of primitive. It had been designed to collect the signals on a sort of wire fence, the design which gave the most for the money.

151

But for the greatest performance, huge and expensive metal "dishes," riding on rails embedded in concrete, were preferable. They were not long in coming. With the UFO's swarming around the world—with Russia orbiting manmade satellites—with strange radio signals coming in from space—the tracking gear was soon building. Radio telescopes can track satellites as well as they can gather signals from space.

In the early winter of 1959 I reported over the Mutual Network that the giant radio telescope being built at Green Bank, West Virginia, by the National Science Foundation was to be used in a search for intelligible signals from outer space. This was promptly denied, of course, for government agencies dislike having anyone beat them on their own news releases.

What happened at Green Bank?

The Green Bank station's work was officially known as Project Ozma . . . with a bow to the mythical Wizard of Oz. Its first Director was the noted astronomer Dr. Otto Struve, who described it to the newsmen as a "long-range program," which can mean many things, of course. At that time Struve's assistant was Dr. Frank Drake, who later succeeded Struve at Green Bank.

Let it be noted that at the inception of Green Bank Dr. Struve devoted considerable time to stressing the importance of the work to be done there, including what he referred to as the great benefits which would result from communicating with a more advanced civilization.

But in 1961, less than two years after it opened with such fanfare and such an expenditure, the public was told that Project Ozma was no more—kaput!—finished! To make the puzzle more puzzling, Dr. Otto Struve ran under his own goalposts. This time he indicated to news-

152

men that the project was of little value, and in response to questions on when they might expect news of Ozma's renewed study of space signals, Struve suggested that they "come back in a hundred years."

Once again, as was the case with the officially reported closings of Air Force UFO programs, this project was not closed at all. It was merely transferred quietly to a new location, in this case to Puerto Rico.

There, in a huge bowl-shaped valley which had been contoured with the aid of giant earthmoving machines, the Office of Scientific Research, a branch of the Air Force, had set up a tremendous space listening station. It was built by experts from Cornell University, with financial and technical aid from the National Science Foundation—a metal-lined bowl about one thousand feet in diameter, many times more sensitive than the movable radio "dish" at Green Bank. Please note that after it was ready to be put into service the Defense Department took control and assigned the Air Force to actual operations.

[The weakness with such devices or installations as this one is that they are *not movable,* therefore they must take what they can get. Their advantage is that being so much larger than any movable "dish" they intercept signals which are so faint that they would be missed by smaller mechanical "dishes."—F.E.]

The metallic bowl in the mountains of Puerto Rico, near Arecibo, began operations in 1964. It was merely the transplanted version of Project Ozma, but this time its findings were classified and concealed from the public.

And on the staff at Arecibo we find Dr. Frank Drake, formerly head of Ozma—the same Dr. Drake who had disclosed, during the latter days of the Green Bank operation, that the radio dish at that installation had picked up some very strange signals which seemed to emanate from the region of the star Tau Ceti. You may recall that Tau Ceti happened to be one of the two stars (along with Epsilon-Eridani) which were suspected of being involved in the apparent twenty-two-year cycle of signals noted by scientists who had analyzed the matter years before Green Bank. At that time terrestrial receivers seemed to be picking up signals which had been sent twenty-two years before—eleven years out and eleven years back. Then, in the "closing" days of Project Ozma at Green Bank, the scientists pointed its giant reflector at Tau Ceti and once again they began recording strange but exciting signals. And they announced their experience to the press.

The result was widespread publicity and tremendous public interest. The public, which had put up every cent of the money for Project Ozma, wanted to hear more about the success of the experiment. But when newsmen called on Dr. Drake for an amplification of his recent disclosures, he was only able to suggest that a news release would be forthcoming from the National Science Foundation.

And so it was. It purported to be an explanation. It referred to the announcement from Green Bank as a "scare" and dismissed the signals received on that widely discussed occasion as nothing more than "apparently experiments of a secret nature." ([There's something new for you—"secret" broadcasts. You might add to your notes on this subject that the origin or nature of the allegedly secret broadcasts was never clarified nor was the origin, nature, location, or agency responsible for them. Perhaps this is just as well, for even the slipperiest explainers can easily get into difficulties when they endeavor to amplify the nonexistent.)—F.E.]

You will find, in the constellations Pegasus and Aries, two points identified by the cryptic designations CTA-21 and CTA-102. What they are we do not know. They are probably not "suns," for to us they are optically invisible. If they are planets, they would certainly be optically invisible. If they are objects which we cannot see, but can only hear by way of their radio transmissions, then we should be interested in them.

We are.

Soviet scientists reported in 1960 that they were picking up scraps of radio signals which hinted at the existence of extremely advanced civilizations on or near both CTA-21 and CTA-102. The disclosures by the outspoken Soviets brought prompt comment from British, French, Australian, and American scientists: They too had heard the signals. Unusual signals, yet, but they stopped right there. They left the Russians alone on the record with their statement suggesting highly intelligent life behind those signals.

The Soviet studies continued, and in 1964 they resulted in a report in the Soviet Academy of Science publication ASTRONOMICAL JOURNAL, by the eminent astronomer Dr. N. S. Kardashev. He pointed out that the signals were received on the 900-megacycle band, which is near perfect for extreme long-range transmission, since it is *between* the two segments of the spectrum which abound in natural radio "noise" which creates serious interference with radio-telescope operation.

After noting that the signals themselves seemed to fall within the technical classification of artificial transmission, as opposed to the helter-skelter pattern of natural radiation, Kardashev called attention to the regular rise-and-fall characteristics of the signals.

In view of the vast distances between Earth and the presumed locations of CTA-21 and CTA-102, the signals would have to originate from a transmitter with the energy output of our sun. How could such a thing be?

Kardashev suggests that an extremely far advanced civilization may have learned to use the stuff of their uninhabitable planets to enclose their portion of their solar system, including their sun, conserving and utilizing its entire output, minus a small percentage lost in reflection. This would explain why the sources themselves are optically invisible to us—and how they originate signals strong enough to reach us in the broadcast spectrum.

The reality of the signals is undeniable. Their origin is widely accepted. What—or who—originates them and how—we do not know. At this point Kardashev's theory is just that. As with Einstein's Unified Field Theory and Newton's Theory of Gravity. Kardashev's theory remains unproved and unprovable, so we let it remain on the books until we can do better.

I have been trying to show in these recent aspects of our discussion that the interest in signals from outer space is widespread, that it is being pursued diligently and thoroughly at great expense, around the clock and around the world. Some very interesting results have been obtained and made public. The expansion of the projects by our own government and the veil of secrecy imposed upon them, also by our own government, lead me to believe that the meager results which have leaked out are but a small portion of the entire story. The simple truth is that governments do not expand, and squander scientific manpower, on projects which are nonproductive.

Stars are suns of varying degrees. Our telescopes are capable of noting the existence of one hundred billion billion suns. Some of these suns have planets. Do some of these planets have life? Harvard's Dr. Harlow Shapley declared in 1964 that one hundred million of those planets DO have life on them.

Harvard physicist Dr. Edward Purcell observes: "It would be rather remarkable if only one planet in a billion (in our own galaxy, the Milky Way) had become the home of intelligent life."

In the *Yearbook of Science and Technology* (1964) scientists are quoted as saying that about 67 percent of the stars in the Milky Way, of which we are a tiny part, are believed to have planets, because of their slow rotation.

Dr. Harrison Brown, California Institute of Technology, is on record as saying that there are at least hundreds, perhaps thousands, of planets capable of supporting life *in our own galaxy.*

Barnard's star, our second nearest neighbor of that type, is now known to have at least one planet which calculation has shown to be about half again as large as Jupiter. But it is so far from its sun—which emits so little light and heat—that it seems an unlikely abode for life. Yet by its mere existence it is important, for it shows that the pattern of creation which brought our own solar system into being also operated elsewhere.

In a lecture in San Francisco on March 17, 1965, one of the men who was very close to the Project Ozma operation made an interesting, and probably important, speech. On that occasion Professor Harold Weaver, Director of

Radio Astronomy at the University of California, ventured the opinion that extraterrestrial races would probably first be attracted by our radio signals and that they would probably receive these signals from space probes which they would have sent into likely spots in the universe, to intercept and re-transmit such signals, which in their original form would have been too feeble to cross interstellar space.

If such a thing has actually happened to us, we would in all probability have been unaware of it, for it is only within the past fifteen years that we have had gear (radio telescopes) capable of locating such space probes. It would be pointless to speculate whether the strange objects seen in the skies of Earth for so many centuries were, in fact, surveillance craft. They were SOMETHING from SOMEWHERE, seen and reported by credible witnesses to the best of their respective abilities. Beyond that prudence counsels caution.

In that same San Francisco speech, Prof. Weaver also said that if one of these space probes from an extragalactic source were to find an inhabited planet emitting artificial radio signals, the next logical step would be to try to contact that planet. How?

"How does it communicate? How does it let us know? It sends some of our own signals back to us. . . . Maybe that is why we got those 'beeps' in Project Ozma!"

Does this mean that the signals which Marconi and Tesla had noted were actually feedback of their own signals, copied and returned from an unidentified craft or body in space? Were the strange facelike markings recorded by the Jenkins Radio-Camera an effort to alert us to the existence of other beings, humanoid in appearance, who also knew what we were doing?

Another startling incident of this same type will be found in the British scientific publication NATURE (Volume 122, pages 681 and 878, 1928) which carried the reports of a team of eminent scientists, Carl Stormer and Balthus Van Der Pol. They had repeatedly received "echo" signals of their own transmissions, sometimes several seconds after the signals had gone out, at other times *minutes* after transmission. The time lag was so great in either case that the only answer was intelligent and purposeful interception—and subsequent re-broadcast.

Whatever it was, it was largely a forgotten matter when similar phenomena reappeared in modern form in the autumn of 1953.

In a three day period, beginning on September 14, 1953, and continuing until September 17, many television viewers in the British Isles were surprised to see on their television screens the identification card and call letters of station KLEE. The signal would come in so strongly that it would override the local stations to which they were tuned. After a few minutes (generally three or four) the image would fade and the local signal would again be visible.

KLEE was a station in Houston, Texas, and under certain freak conditions such long-range reception of commercial television does occur. Several of the viewers in the British Isles had the good sense to photograph this enigma when it appeared on their sets . . . but when they checked with KLEE for verification of their unusual experience they found themselves confronted with another mystery: KLEE had gone off the air and out of existence three years before!

When the British Broadcasting Corporation began its investigation of this remarkable case, it was informed by the successor to KLEE that no KLEE signal or identification card of any kind had been broadcast since that station had gone out of existence in 1950.

A spokesman for the British Broadcasting Corporation told newsmen that for anyone to have perpetrated such an incident as a hoax would have involved the expenditure of at least a hundred thousand dollars, plus knowledge that *transcended contemporary technology* as well as the use of towers and other equipment which could not have been concealed and which were in fact difficult to secure. American and British authorities alike ruled out any possibility of a hoax, and said so publicly.

The case attracted international attention and international concern. In 1959, long after the facts were dimmed in the public mind, an "explanation" was offered, not by the British investigators, but by our Project Ozma, which was up to its own electronic neck in strange signals from space in 1959.

The explanation? Faith and bejabbers it was that old standby of professional explainers, none other than a mysterious inventor perpetrating a hoax!

For reasons which are easy to understand, the alleged inventor was never otherwise identified. Neither was he ever charged or prosecuted for such a flagrant violation of the British broadcasting regulations. Nor was it ever explained how he managed to blanket the British Isles from one station, something no other television station has been able to do to this day.

It is my personal belief that we should take off our hats to the Hokum Department in our government for dreaming up an invention which is more remarkable than the one they purported to explain: They invented the Nonexistent Inventor, literally incredible.

160

At the conclusion of the original investigation by British authorities, a spokesman for the British Broadcasting Corporation told newsmen:

"We are confronted in this instance with a set of circumstances which are at variance with accepted knowledge of television transmission. It is unthinkable that these signals could have been circling the earth for the time since that station [KLEE] last broadcast them. It is physically impossible that they could have been reflected to us by chance from any celestial body at such a vast distance. That leaves us with but one possibility, however bizarre, that these signals were transmitted to us purposefully and intelligently, from a source and for a purpose presently unknown."

*　*　*　*　*　*　*　*

"There is a total lack of evidence that they (the UFOs) are interplanetary vehicles."

—Letter from Major General Joe Kelly (Air Force) to Senator Harry Byrd, May 1, 1956:

"These objects (the UFOs) are conceived and directed by intelligent beings of a very high order. They probably do not originate in our solar system, perhaps not even in our galaxy."

—Dr. Hermann Oberth, famed German rocket authority and space travel authority, press conference, Innsbruck, June, 1954:

7

Who's Driving?

In early 1950 I received a copy of a newspaper from a personal friend in a large western city. It carried an account which purported to describe the finding of a disc-shaped craft containing several small bodies of manlike creatures. It contained "details" of the spongy food tablets which they supposedly soaked in water, the hammocks in which they supposedly slept, and other tidbits which are familiar to all good science fiction fans who would recognize them as standard equipment of such tales.

I checked out the fellow who had told the story and the verdict was that he was a hyperthyroid who did such things for practical jokes.

I filed it and forgot it.

163

A couple of months later I received a call from Frank Scully, a grand guy who wrote a column for VARIETY. Knowing that I was interested in this matter, Frank wanted my advice on a story about a crashed disc which contained some little bodies—etc. It was similar in many respects to the story that I had checked and discarded, but Scully's version had been embellished with mysterious scientists and electronics engineers . . . which merely strengthened my original suspicions.

I was unable to dissuade Frank from publishing the yarn, I am sorry to say. Scully's book created a little ripple of excitement; gave birth to a score of variations which were recounted by various individuals as their own experiences—but worst of all, Scully found the "little men" to be an albatross around his neck. Subsequent investigation by TRUE magazine revealed that Scully's mysterious scientist was a fellow who was later convicted of peddling a device which purportedly told where to drill for oil. The government views such devices with suspicion and the "scientist" turned out to be no scientist at all. And the "electronics expert" of Scully's story was revealed as the operator of a radio repair shop, which did not qualify him for the description in the book.

Frank Scully, a thoroughly likable and well-known writer, had been taken in. The "little men" story plagued him to the end of his days. But it did more than that: It made everyone who had any regard for his reputation very suspicious of such tales, and in that sense it was a healthy influence. If there were any little men in the discs, their existence was not going be accepted without a great deal of reluctance born of caution.

Eventually, from many parts of the world, reports of small manlike creatures associated with the UFO's began to trickle in. They came from tiny isolated islands in the Pacific; from the American midwest and northwest; from the Scandinavian countries; from Germany and Italy; from Africa—in many instances, from intelligent and credible witnesses, as we shall see.

There were also a few scattered reports of stinking monsters associated with grounded UFO's. The Flatwoods, West Virginia, case is a standard item of this type. Something reportedly settled down on a ridgetop near Flatwoods one September evening in 1952. When a small group of local citizens went to investigate, they assertedly came upon a giant humanoid in a dark green coverall-type garment. The thing was almost ten feet tall, said the witnesses, and had its helmeted head caught on a branch of a tree. It hissed. It scooted its feet and it sprayed them with some sort of noxious mist that made them ill. What it was or where it came from or how it got there are unanswered questions to this day.

Fortunately, such reported encounters are very rare. Like the "hideous" creatures reported by that Kansas farmer back in 1897, most of the reported beings are said to be small, more like pygmies or dwarfs than hissing, stinking giants such as that of the Flatwoods case.

The physical limitations of the 1947-type disc led to the belief that they were remotely controlled, or that the operators were indeed small by our standards. This in turn led to such stories as that on which Frank Scully came to grief. That the occupants, if any, were small creatures was a logical deduction and it was arrived at early in the study of this enigma.

According to records, the first account of any credible witness reporting these little creatures to come to my attention was an experience reported by THE STEEP ROCK

ECHO, which is the house organ of the vast Steep Rock Iron Mines (Steep Rock Lake, Ontario, Canada) in their editions of September and October, 1950.

The full account runs many pages in the publication, and for that reason must be abbreviated here. In the prefatory remarks, the editor of the publication identifies the individuals in the report only as a senior executive of the mine and the executive's wife, who preferred to remain anonymous to avoid ridicule.

The executive and his wife had gone, as they often did, to a cove off Sawbill Bay—a narrow and deep arm of the lake which was surrounded by great rock outcrops. The entrance to the cove is only about a hundred yards wide, with a sharp curve which makes most of the cove invisible from the bay itself. It is, therefore, a very secluded spot, well hidden from the main body of water.

On the afternoon of July 2, 1950, the witness and his wife had pulled their small boat well up on a sandy beach under some overhanging tree limbs. At that point the boat could not be seen from the water of the cove because it was behind a cluster of projecting rocks.

After having a couple of sandwiches and a Thermos bottle of tea, they were just sitting there, relaxing, when the air suddenly vibrated. The executive thought it resembled the shock wave of a dynamite blast, but dismissed the idea because there had been no sound and because they were miles away from the nearest mining operation.

When the disquieting feeling persisted, he climbed up a spear of rock that rose above the surrounding undergrowth. The rock was divided at the peak by a sharp cleft through which, fortunately, he could see without being seen.

In his signed statement to the mine he says:

166

Who's Driving?

"Looking through a cleft in the rock I could see a large shiny object resting on the water in the curve of the far shoreline, not a quarter of a mile across the top end of the narrows. [The entrance to the cove from the bay. —F.E.] I scrambled quickly back to where my wife was. She took one look at me and said "What's wrong?" I tried to be calm and told her of what I had seen. Then we both climbed back up and looked through the opening. The thing was still there. It looked like two huge saucers stuck together, one upside down on top of the other. Round, black-edged ports appeared to be about four feet apart around the edge. As the bottom was resting on the water or very close to it, it was impossible for us to see the underside.

"The top had what looked like hatch covers open . . . and moving slowly around over its surface were about ten queer-looking little figures. Rotating slowly from a central position and about eight feet in the air was a hoop-shaped object. As it rotated to a point directly opposite us it stopped—and so did the figures. Everything seemed to be concentrated on the opening we were looking through. We instinctively ducked behind the stone at that moment. Looking down over my right shoulder to see how we could best get down I caught a movement in the bushes. Directly opposite us, on the far side of our cove, a deer had come down to drink. The figures and the hoop were facing the deer. As the circle, or hoop, began to rotate again it did not stop at the deer as before. My wife and I would count twenty and duck. We feel that the rock before us shielded us from the action of the hoop.

"We could both see that the hooplike thing was being operated by a figure on a small stand directly beneath it. This figure had on what appeared to be a bright red skull cap or helmet. All the others wore dark blue headpieces. All were about the same size: We estimated three and a half to four feet in height. All were dressed the same, with a shiny metallic appearing substance over the chest and their legs and arms covered with a darker material. At that distance [about 1200 feet—F.E.] we could not make out any features—if they had any.

"The most noticeable thing was that they moved like automatons, and did not turn around—that is right around as we do—but they had to turn their feet in order to change direction. . . . I watched one of these figures pick up the end of a flexible hose (a very vivid green) and lift it while facing one way, then laboriously turn the feet around in order to walk the opposite direction. During all this my wife and I could hear a steady humming sound. They seemed to be drawing in water through one hose and discharging something into the water through another hose.

"We had to duck again because of that rotating hoop and when we looked again everything was gone from the surface of the object and it was beginning to rise from the water. It was about eight feet in the air. The water where it had rested was reddish blue, tinged with gold. The thing looked to be about fifteen feet thick at the center and about twelve feet thick at the rim. There was a rush of wind as it streaked away at about forty-five degrees and was quickly lost in the distance. By having lined it up with two trees on the opposite shore I estimated that it was about forty-eight feet in diameter."

B. J. Eyeton, Chief Chemist of the Steep Rock Mining Company and Editor of the ECHO, adds that others reported seeing a similar, or the same, object in that isolated cove. They also mentioned what appeared to be very small manlike figures on the craft, which fled at their approach. But the report of the executive and his wife was the most detailed and Mr. Eyeton was fully satisfied as to their credibility as witnesses, since they were well known to him.

Small humanoid creatures, or "figures" in shiny garments, moving awkwardly by our standards—the strange experience at Steep Rock Lake was to recur many times in the ensuing years.

In September, 1951, a band of aborigines of the Unmatjera tribe, in Central Australia, reported to authorities that they had watched, from a low hilltop, the landing of a shiny circular object which settled down a short distance from a similar object already on the ground. They estimated that the objects were the same size, between thirty-five and fifty feet in diameter and "a man and a half man tall." Afraid to approach the things, the aborigines had remained hidden on their stony hilltop and watched this strange scene. After several minutes, they said, a very small manlike thing had come from underneath the second object and had entered the first through the bottom of the craft. This creature, or figure, had a shiny suit and a round shiny head [helmet?] the natives told authorities. Shortly after the creature entered the craft on the ground it began to rise with a buzz like swarms of insects, and the other object quickly followed it into the sky and both were lost to sight.

It is useless to speculate on the many reasons why a creature from one of these craft would transfer to another, of course. The report reached the Australian authorities about seven months after it happened and, other than questioning the aborigines, there was little that could be done. But it is noteworthy that these primitive people, who had never seen or heard of such things as "flying saucers," should have reported both the objects and the humanoids in such detail. Pure fabrication would seem to be most unlikely, in view of the known facts about the witnesses and the reports from other parts of the world.

Eight miles north of Hopkinsville, Kentucky, on Highway 41, is the little settlement of Kelly. On a farm half a mile from Kelly a weird and perhaps historic incident occurred between 7 and 10 p.m. on the evening of Sunday, August 21, 1955. In a front-page story on the following day the EVANSVILLE (Indiana) PRESS reported KENTUCKIANS REPORT GUNBATTLE WITH "LITTLE MEN FROM SPACE."

Here is the story, taken from the witnesses themselves, the police officers involved, and from the PRESS account.

Three children and eight adults were involved in this case. Billy Sutton, then a teenager, had gone out to the well for a drink of water about 7 p.m. when he noticed a brightly glowing circular object, moving silently on an apparently straight course, abruptly stop and settle to earth beyond the barn and out of view from where he stood. He mentioned this odd sight to the folks inside the house but they dismissed it as a probable "shooting star" and made no investigation. [The same object was seen by several other witnesses from nearby farms, according to statements made later to investigators.—F.E.]

Around 8 o'clock the Suttons' dogs began to bark furiously, as they generally did when an intruder was about. Two of the men went to the back door and peered out. They later told authorities that about fifty or sixty feet distant was a creature of some sort: It glowed, they agreed, like the lettering on a radium-painted watch. It came to within fifteen or twenty feet of where they, admittedly dumbfounded, stood. Both men told authorities that the thing looked like a very small man not over three and a

170

half feet tall, wearing a shiny garment or a nickel-plated suit. Its head seemed unusually large to them, all out of proportion to the rest of the body. The arms, they said, were unusually long and the webbed hands outsize and equipped with claws that glistened faintly in what little light there was.

Mrs. J. C. Sutton also told officers that she saw the same creature at the same time. "It was as shiny as aluminum foil," she said, "and it walked like a very old man— or some sort of monkey—mostly with its hands."

Elmer Sutton and John Sutton both fired at the weird thing that was approaching them. The blast from the twelve-gauge shotgun and the bullet from a .22 calibre pistol caused the creature to fall backward, but it leaped up almost immediately and ran away before the astonished men could take any further action.

The two Suttons hurried back inside the house, badly shaken by what had transpired. All the house lights were immediately turned off and the doors locked.

A porch light was turned on. At that moment one of the ladies screamed that something was peering into the dining room window. The men rushed in to the room in time to see a creature with some sort of helmet and wide, slit eyes—clinging to the screen on the window. Both men fired repeatedly through the window and the thing seemed to be knocked backward by the impact.

After a wait of about twenty minutes, during which no more of the weird creatures were seen, the armed men ventured outside. The dogs were barking at a faintly luminous thing in a tree, but before they could get closer they discovered another of their strange visitors moving along the ridgerow of the house. Elmer Sutton blasted the thing with the shotgun. Both men told authorities they

could clearly detect the sound of the shot striking home
. . . but the glowing thing seemed to dive off into the air
and was seen a moment later running into a weed patch.
Another shot caused the glowing thing in the tree to glide
down into the weeds and be lost to sight. By this time the
dogs had taken refuge under the house . . . and with
all that shooting going on it was probably a very good idea.

One of the interesting sidelights of this most unusual
report is the agreement of the men involved that the bullets from John Sutton's .22 pistol could be heard richo-
cheting into space, as though they were glancing off metal.

After their ineffectual foray into the yard, the men
went back into the house and stood guard at the windows,
while the women and children lay on the floor behind
them. By 11 o'clock, after at least two hours of this watchful waiting, the men decided that the weird beings had
left. After being fired at some fifty or more times with both
shotgun and pistol at short range, it is possible that the
creatures got the idea that they were not welcome.

The eleven persons rushed from the house, piled into
two automobiles and made haste to the nearest police station—at Hopkinsville. The EVANSVILLE PRESS story quoted
the Police Chief, Russell Greenwell, as being skeptical of
the story—which Greenwell promptly denied. On the
23rd, the day after the story appeared in the paper, Greenwell told me:

"There is no doubt in my mind that those people—
every one of them—were terrified when they got to Hopkinsville Sunday night. We didn't find any little footprints—that is true—but that ground was so hard and
dry that a tractor wouldn't have left much of a trace on
it. I didn't make any footprints there either—so the ab-

sence of footprints doesn't prove a thing—nobody with a lick of sense would have expected to find any under those conditions! Those people saw something strange. I don't know what it was . . . but they saw it and they shot at it right through the doors and the windows and the sides of the house . . . the holes are there to prove it."

State Police and four members of the Hopkinsville Police Department accompanied the men back to the farm and investigated—but the weird little creatures and their glowing craft were gone. One of the State Troopers noticed that one of the men involved in the incident was virtually in a state of shock, with a pulsebeat visible in the neck veins at 140 per minute, about twice the normal rate.

Official reaction to this incident was one of pretended indifference. Nearby Fort Campbell sent an officer, Major Albert Coren, to question the witnesses, although the Base Public Informations Officer denied that the Base knew anything about it. Several days later, Air Force investigators questioned the witnesses briefly, as though it were merely a routine matter, and went away. But about two weeks after the event, two men in civilian clothing who claimed to be selling aluminum kitchen utensils, visited the neighborhood. They spent a few minutes talking about their alleged merchandise, and devoted hours to asking questions about the creatures and the craft which had reportedly been seen on the night of August 21.

It may be pure coincidence, but a team of "peddlers" of this same type and product visited the Flatwoods, West Virginia, area five days after the alleged "monster" was encountered there, in 1952. In both cases the men were clearly more interested in gathering information than in selling pots and pans.

173

It would be in keeping with the official government policy of deceiving the public to treat this type of incident in this particular manner. To rush investigators to the scene where the humanoids or monsters were reported would be to disclose the importance which officialdom attaches to such cases. By treating the incidents as relatively unimpressive and unimportant until the public interest subsides, and then conducting the real investigation by subterfuge, the government gets the information it seeks with the least possible publicity. Even if the deception is suspected, the story will get nothing more than local attention. It is a clever way of dealing with the subject and I have never seen it mentioned in print prior to this moment. But this pattern has doubtless been followed many times, with the investigators operating in many guises. It would be difficult to prove which visitors were merely curious and which were there on official business. I know of only these two cases of the disinterested "salesmen" of aluminum kitchenware—who just *happened* to appear on the scenes of these two landing reports—making no effort to sell aluminumware—but making unmistakable efforts to gather information about the UFO cases.

For our purpose of comparing and compiling details of landing reports by credible witnesses, the outstanding case of 1952 came out of Berlin, Germany, on July 7, via North American Newspaper Alliance.

Oskar Linke had been for many years the Mayor of a small city in what had become the Russian-occupied portion of Germany. Fearful of persecution, he and his 11-year-old daughter had managed to escape to the zone now known as West Germany, where he related their amazing experience to authorities and gave sworn statements to both the British and American officials who questioned him.

Linke said: "We lived only a few miles from the frontier [with West Germany] and in order to facilitate our escape my daughter and I took frequent rides toward the border on my motorcycle. She rode in the side car. This way the Russian border guards grew accustomed to seeing us and did not grow suspicious of our real intentions.

"One afternoon last week we were returning home from one of these trips when my daughter called my attention to something shimmering white through the trees in a small forest through which we were passing. It is only about three miles from the border.

"It was such an unusual sight that we let the motorcycle roll off the road and come to a halt. I hid it under some bushes and we hurried into the woods. We reached a point about seventy-five or a hundred feet from a very strange sight. It was a disc about twenty-five feet across resting on the ground in a clearing.

"It resembled a huge warming pan without a handle, and it seemed to be phosphorescent. In the center of it there was some sort of apparatus—a square contraption—a sort of upper works which rose out of the top of the craft much like a top hat. It was slightly darker than the rest of the object, which was the color of aluminum, well polished.

"We were lying behind a low embankment and were well concealed. We saw two small figures, like tiny human beings about three-and-a-half feet tall. They were wearing what appeared to be shiny one-piece garments—like aluminum or silver in color. On the chest of one of these creatures was a box or package about the size of three cigarette packs stacked up, and on the front of this pack-

175

age there was a bright, blinking blue light. What this was for we do not know, for they did not seem to be using it. They just approached the craft from the edge of the clearing, one behind the other.

"When they were within about ten or twelve feet, the one in back reached out and touched the other on the shiny, glasslike helmet. Both stopped in their tracks and one of them turned slowly and faced to the left of us. At this my daughter let out a little gasp. The creatures hastily entered the craft through a porthole on the top of the upperworks—the square part—in the center of it.

"Then we saw that the disc had two rows of circular portholes around its edge. They were about the size of portholes on a ship.

"As we watched, the square upperworks began to retract into the dome and simultaneously the object started to rise slowly off the ground.

"We both noticed that a similar square-shaped construction was emerging from the bottom of the craft and was apparently forcing it up off the ground.

"Then the object began to rise slowly into the air. It rose to about a hundred feet, hovering for a moment, then sped away and was quickly lost to our sight."

The signed statement of ex-Mayor Linke was supported by his daughter's story to officials. The girl added: "I was so terrified that I did not know what to do. I hope I never have such an experience again."

During 1954, South America underwent UFO visitations similar to those being experienced in Europe and the United States at the same time. That was the year, you may recall, in which Lieutenant Colonel John O'Mara of Air Technical Intelligence in Dayton stated that the ATIC was receiving UFO reports at the rate of seven hundred per week, the largest number on record up to that time and very likely still a peak. But the South American cases of 1954 included a large number of reports of landings and of humanoids around the craft. How many of these reports are veridical would be difficult to say, but it can safely be said that many of the persons who made the reports were members of groups, and that many others were public officials—and in several cases, were respected members of the medical profession.

One of the finest civilian UFO research groups in the United States is also one of the oldest, the Aerial Phenomena Research Organization (APRO) of Tucson, Arizona. Through its thousands of members in many lands, including many scientists and experts in various fields allied to aeronautics and astronomy, APRO has done a fine job, year after year, of bringing to light important and widespread UFO activities. APRO does for its members in this country the job that the news services fail to do, by giving adequate and carefully investigated information, especially on South American incidents of note.

Venezuela was a hotbed of UFO activity in the closing weeks of 1954. Police records in many cities contain accounts of humanoids around disc-shaped craft seen on the ground. In some instances where men reported personal contact with these creatures, the men did not fare too well.

In the suburbs of San Carlos is a beautiful park named for the Ministry of Agriculture and used to hold its expositions. On the night of December 16, three young men had dined together at a restaurant in San Carlos and were driving home together. Jesus Paz asked his friends to stop the car in order that he might enter an isolated part of the park to relieve himself. Paz had scarcely gone more than a dozen steps before he screamed for help. His friends ran to his rescue and found him lying stunned and bleeding on the ground. A short distance away a small, hairy, manlike creature was running toward a shiny disclike craft which was resting on the grass. One of the companions of Paz was Luis Mejia, a member of the National Guard, who had only time to snatch up a stone and hurl it at the disc, which was beginning to rise with a tremendous buzzing sound.

Paz was rushed back into the city to the hospital, where doctors found that he was in a state of shock. Furthermore, the man had long deep scratches on his right side and downward across his spine "like claw marks" the doctors said.

Paz told officials that he had walked around a bed of tall flowers, his footsteps deadened by the thick grass. Suddenly he almost stumbled over this short, hairy, manlike creature which was examining the flowers. Paz tried to escape but, when he turned, the creature attacked him, first by clawing and tearing his shirt, then with a blow on the back of the neck which stunned Paz.

Six days before the Paz incident at San Carlos, two teen-age boys, Jesus Gomez and Lorenzo Flores, had been hunting rabbits along the Trans-Andean Highway between Chico and Cerro de las Tres Torres. They had only one old shotgun—unloaded as they started home because they had used all their ammunition.

As they trudged along the edge of the highway they noticed some sort of shiny object in the brush alongside the road and only a short distance from the highway proper. They later told police they thought it must have been an automobile which had gone off the road . . . and they went into the brush to investigate.

The boys found themselves only a few feet from an

object which resembled two huge shiny washbowls stuck together at the rims. They estimated that it was possibly ten feet in diameter and could see, they later told police, that it was hovering about three feet off the ground and that it was ejecting fire from the bottom.

Lorenzo Flores said in his statement:

"Then we saw four little men come out of it. They were approximately three feet tall. When they realized that we were there, the four of them grabbed Jesus and tried to drag him toward the thing. I could do nothing but take my shotgun, which was not loaded, and I struck one of them with it. The gun seemed to have struck something as hard as rock—it stung my hands—and it broke the gun into two pieces. . . . It was too dark for us to see features of their faces, but we did notice the abundant hair on their bodies and their great strength."

Gomez had been dazed by something when the little creatures grabbed him. Flores dragged his friend back toward the road and, when Gomez was able to do so, they ran as fast as they could for the nearest police station. They arrived with their clothing badly torn. Gomez's shirt was in shreds. Both boys were deeply scratched. Doctors who were summoned told police that the young men had been badly frightened by something to such an extent that they were nearly hysterical but were otherwise intelligent and credible.

When the boys led police to the scene of the reported encounter on the following morning, the officers found ample evidence that some sort of struggle had taken place . . . and they also recovered the broken shotgun which had been Flores' most prized possession. But other than a few scorched bushes, there was no trace of the little creatures or their craft.

179

Exactly two weeks before this incident, two truck drivers in Caracas had stumbled into a police station, torn, bleeding, and terrified, to gasp out a story which might have been ignored by the police . . . had it not been for an exceptional witness.

Jose Ponce was a helper on a panel truck driven by Gustavo Gonzales and, in the early morning hours of November 28, they were driving to Petare, about fifteen miles away, to pick up a load of food to be delivered in Caracas in time for the markets, which opened about daylight.

The truck was jogging along a street on the outskirts of Caracas, about 2 a.m., when the men found their way blocked by a glowing disc-shaped object about ten feet in diameter, which was hovering about six feet above the street.

Gonzales brought his truck to a stop and both men just sat there for a moment, staring at this strange object in wonderment. Then, by common impulse, they got out of the truck and walked closer to the object. When they were about twenty-five feet from it, they discovered that they were being approached by what appeared to be a very hairy dwarflike man.

Gonzales grabbed the creature and lifted him off the ground. [He later told police that the creature weighed about thirty-five pounds.—F.E.] But the little fellow twisted out of the truck driver's grasp and gave Gonzales a shove that sent him sprawling backward. Ponce had had enough . . . he turned to run for help at a police station only a couple of blocks away.

Before Gonzales could regain his feet, his tiny antagonist leaped several feet into the air and came for Gonzales —who noted that his attacker's eyes glowed in the headlights of the truck—"like yellow cat's eyes!" Gonzales managed to get up on one knee and to get his knife ready for action. As the little creature lunged at him, Gonzales saw that instead of hands it had webbed extremities that had claws about an inch long. Gonzales later told police that he tried to drive the knife into the creature's shoulder . . . but that the blade glanced off as though he had struck steel. Another of the hairy little men jumped out of the glowing craft and pointed a small shiny tube at Gonzales. There was a brilliant beam of light which blinded Gonzales for a moment and he thought he was gone . . . but when he could see again the object was rising above the trees and was quickly lost in the night.

Gonzales ran for the police station, arriving a couple of minutes after his companion. At first police thought the men were drunk or crazy. A doctor was summoned, who determined that both men were in a state of shock and that neither of them had been drinking. Gonzales was treated for a long deep scratch down his left side and was placed under sedation.

Fortunately for the men involved, and for the others who were interested, a well-known Caracas physician had witnessed the entire incident. He had been on a night call and had been driving behind Gonzales when Gonzales came upon the thing blocking the street. The doctor told authorities that he had witnessed the fracas which Gonzales and Ponce had described but that he had been reluctant to confirm their report for fear of ridicule. Later, after being assured that he would not be publicly identified in the reports, the doctor made his statement to police. [The APRO representative in Caracas was informed by press representatives that the doctor was subsequently invited to the United States for consultation with authorities here regarding the "little men" involved in the Petares case.—F.E.]

Within forty-eight hours of the Petare incident just noted, Arnold Dibble of United Press and John Schell of North American Newspaper Alliance showed up in Caracas. No doubt this was just another of those coincidences with which the UFO problem is replete.

In examining these alleged "little men" cases, widely separated in terms of both geography and time, we note certain similarities.

The creatures in the shiny suits and shiny helmets reported by the young miner near Quarouble, France, in September of 1954, parallel the description of the creature reported by the aborigines of Australia. The beam of light which stunned Dewilde at Quarouble is duplicated in the report of Petare, Venezuela. It is to be found also in the case of a Florida scoutmaster "Sonny" Desvergers, who, with three of his scout troop members, spotted a UFO in a thicket beside the highway near West Palm Beach about 9 p.m. on the night of August 9, 1952. Something fiery shot out of the UFO as he neared it—something that burned holes in his hat and flung him to the ground— badly frightened but unharmed.

The farmers at Hopkinsville, Kentucky, who heard their shotgun and pistol pellets glance off the little creatures, got the impression that the creatures were as hard as stone . . . or metal. That feeling was shared by the boy who broke his shotgun on one of the beings [near Chico, Venezuela, in 1954]—and by Gustavo Gonzales when Gonzales tried to stab the little humanoid and his knife merely glanced off, in the Petare case just mentioned.

The little robotlike figures reported in the Steep Rock Lake case were about the same size as the similar ones in other instances. They wore the same shiny coverall type garments, but they were apparently without the shiny helmets generally associated with these visitors.

And the creatures reported by Oskar Linke near the border between the two sections of Germany—there again the familiar humanoids in the shiny coveralls wearing the helmets, and one of them with a blinking blue light on its chest.

From all parts of the globe, the descriptions of the alleged operators are remarkably uniform. There is either a worldwide conspiracy to lie about these things . . . or a great many people, including some who have never heard of "flying saucers," have seen some very strange creatures of unknown origin.

Among those witnesses we must include the name of Reverend William Booth Gill, an ordained minister of the Church of England and a graduate of Brisbane University.

Nor was he alone. The Reverend Gill had as co-witnesses more than a score of students and teachers at Boainai, New Guinea, all of whom signed the report for the government there.

On the night of June 26, 1957, the Reverend had come out on the porch after dinner and glanced up toward Venus. His attention was immediately attracted by another brilliant light in the sky—considerably brighter than Venus and unquestionably sparkling.

After a few minutes he realized that this particular light was coming toward him—rapidly. He called one of the teachers, and several of the students gathered around also. It came close enough—they estimated four hundred feet— that the witnesses could see that it was a huge disc-shaped construction, thirty to forty feet wide at the base, which had four metal legs projecting from it, diagonally. On top of the disc was a dome which the witnesses estimated to be ten feet high and about twenty feet in diameter. There seemed to be a sort of deck on top of this structure . . . and on that deck several small manlike creatures could be seen. There were never more than four of these figures to be seen at any one time. They seemed to be leaning on a low railing, although the light was not good enough for the minister or his companions to actually see the railing. Occasionally, from time to time, one of the figures would bend over as though manipulating something on the deck. And at intervals of about thirty seconds, a narrow shaft of bright blue light would be projected skyward for a duration of approximately five seconds, as though signaling.

The Reverend Gill told authorities that he felt impelled to try to establish contact with the creatures. He said:

"As one of them leaned over the rail or whatever it was and seemed to be looking down on us, I waved one hand overhead and the figure did the same, as though a skipper on one boat waving to someone on a wharf. The teacher waved both arms over his head and two figures on the craft did the same. Then both of us waved both arms aloft . . . and all four of the figures did the same thing in response. We were all delighted. The boys [students] were jubilant. Some of them called out to the figures on the deck of the disc but we heard no response. One of the boys brought a flashlight [torch, as Gill also called it] and we turned the beam on the object. It hovered—and came quite close to the ground. We thought it was going to land, but it did not. We were all very disappointed about that."

The object, or a similar object, appeared over that particular school several times in the ensuing days and nights, but never again did it come close enough for the watchers to see the little humanoid figures they observed that first night.

Reverend Gill's report filled eleven single-spaced typewritten pages which were signed by all the witnesses. It is one of the most detailed and remarkable cases of its kind and one of the few cases where credible witnesses have reported what might have been intelligent responses to their efforts to communicate.

Paradoxically, the interesting response to their signals reported by Reverend Gill and his co-witnesses is the direct opposite to the results reportedly obtained by the U.S. Air Force. Admiral R. N. Hillenkoetter, first Chairman of the Board of NICAP, asked his friend Air Force General Nathan Twining some questions about UFO's, including whether our government had ever been able to communicate with them. General Twining's aide, replying in the General's name, stated that the Air Force had been unable to communicate, presumably for physical reasons. The same source declined to explain what was meant by "physical reasons."

However, if the little guys on deck who waved at Reverend Gill and his crowd were the same ones who had visited Kelly, Kentucky, I think their reluctance to land is understandable.

On October 28, 1962, a high school teacher, Mrs. E. D. Sylvester, who lives in Norwood, a suburb of Adelaide, Australia, and her three children aged 10, 8, and 6 years, had a strange experience.

According to the HOBART MERCURY of Hobart, Tasmania, Mrs. Sylvester was driving on the Salisbury-Elizabeth road. It was about 7:30 p.m. She and the children

185

saw the object at just about the same time as it glided across the road some distance ahead of them, evidently headed for a landing in a field alongside the highway.

When they reached a spot near the point of the presumed landing, the four of them got out of the car and walked along the roadside until they saw the thing. It was oval or egg-shaped, about fifteen feet long and five or six feet high, and it was on the ground.

Beside it, said the witnesses, was a tiny manlike creature in a shiny suit such as divers wear. The creature wore some sort of translucent helmet and it was connected by tubing to some gear on his back, presumably breathing apparatus. The figure carried a shiny box or container in its hands and appeared to be taking samples of something from the soil around the object. Mrs. Sylvester told authorities she watched the thing for about forty minutes before it re-entered the shiny craft and rose silently into the sky.

Mrs. Sylvester, I find, is highly regarded in the school system where she teaches. Although she reported the matter promptly to government authorities, news of the incident did not leak out to the public until February 5, 1963.

Good solid citizens such as Mrs. Sylvester are not easily ridiculed for the simple reason that too many persons who know them are going to come to their defense, if needed. No government can afford to stir up these pockets of public indignation, not even to mislead the public about UFO's, so the technique most frequently applied is that of stalling and pretending that it certainly is strange —but we just don't have any answer—yet.

Mrs. Sylvester apparently got the stalling treatment— at any rate she was not subjected to any official sneering.

Sergeant Lonnie Zamora of Socorro, New Mexico, was

the same calibre witness and he, too, got hands-off treatment and the long stall.

On the afternoon of April 24, 1964, veteran police officer Zamora was milling around the streets of Socorro on a routine mission when he saw a shiny thing apparently drifting down into the gullied area just outside the town. He said later that he also heard a heavy roaring sound which made him suspect that an old dynamite shed in that isolated area might have exploded. He radioed to headquarters and then drove hurriedly out of town and along a winding dirt road that led to the old shed.

Zamora had to stop about 150 yards from a deep gully in which he could see what appeared to be an overturned automobile, so he radioed that there might have been an accident and that he was moving in closer to investigate.

He was on his way to a remarkable experience.

Sergeant Zamora discovered that he could drive up on the mesa near the wide mouth of that particular draw . . . and he did so. As he approached the edge of the ravine, he found himself looking down upon a strange eggshaped object about twelve or fifteen feet long, white in color, standing on short metal legs. And beside it, apparently oblivious of his presence, were two small manlike beings dressed in white or silvery coverall type garments. They seemed to be examining or repairing a place on the underside of the craft. As Zamora stood there, about seventy-five feet from them, they noticed him, took one look, and scurried around the object.

As Zamora turned and started back to his car, he glanced back . . . just in time to see the object jetting a bright blue flame down into the sand on which it rested. Seconds later it rose out of the gully with what the officer described as "an ear-splitting roar." Sergeant Zamora ran in the opposite direction. The thing was out of sight over the nearby mountains in a few seconds . . . and if Sergeant Sam Chavez had not appeared just at that moment, Sergeant Zamora might have soon been out of sight in the other direction.

Chavez had heard Zamora's radio calls and reached the scene about three minutes after Zamora sent out the first report when he saw the thing on the ground.

Together the two officers went down into the ravine where the object had landed. They found four deep marks where Zamora said the metal legs had rested. They found the bushes charred and still smoking where the flames underneath the object had caught them.

The landing-gear marks were three and one-half inches deep, circular in shape—a familiar description to researchers in this field. The sand in the bottom of the ravine was hard-packed and, in spite of diligent search, the officers could find no footprints of the humanoids. Whatever it was that had pressed those metal legs into the sand had been very heavy—several tons, at least.

White Sands Stallion Site Station was notified, and military men came on the double quick to examine the landing site. They piled rocks around the indentations to preserve them for photography, which was done early the following morning.

Sergeant Zamora described the experience in detail, including the appearance of the "little men" to his fellow officer, Sergeant Chavez; to Police Chief Polo Pineda; and to Mr. and Mrs. James Lorenzen, the two top officers of APRO, who went to the scene at once. Immediately following his interview with the Lorenzens, Zamora was subjected to prolonged and intensive grilling by an Air Force team. One was a Major from Kirtland Air Force

Base at Albuquerque, the other had been rushed to the scene directly from Air Technical Intelligence Headquarters in Dayton, Ohio. This was a major case, and officialdom knew it.

In his original statements, made immediately after the incident and before the military had reached him, Officer Zamora described two aspects of the case which he later refused to discuss: the "humanoids," and the odd insignia which was clearly visible on the side of the craft. Fortunately his original and uncensored statements were made to several credible witnesses and found their way into the public record in spite of hasty efforts to delete or deny them.

The Air Force was in a tough spot here. Since they could not ridicule Zamora—safely for themselves, that is—they had to throw a couple of smoke bombs while they stalled for time.

They flew Dr. J. Allen Hynek, head of the Astronomy Department at Northwestern University, to the scene of Sergeant Zamora's experience. Dr. Hynek has a positive genius for the oblique approach to problems involving UFO's. He was equal to the occasion at Socorro: He told newsmen that he was puzzled as to why the UFO had not been reported on radar "in an area that is infested with radar."

The news wires carried that apparent dismissal of the reported object and it probably had the desired effect—pretending that, since radar did not report it, the thing probably did not exist.

There were two major flaws in the statement.

For one thing, military regulations would have prevented the radar stations from making public statements even if they had picked up the UFO.

189

And as APRO had already determined by a simple check which was also available to the news services, the radar station which covered that area was not even in operation at the time of the incident.

The military censors may have suspected that they might be tripped up on that one and, being very astute operators, they were ready with another. This time it was Dr. Lincoln LaPaz, Director of the Institute of Meteoritics at the University of New Mexico in Albuquerque. His statement to the ALBUQUERQUE JOURNAL was promptly carried by the newswires. The weird craft seen by Sergeant Zamora, said Dr. LaPaz, was nothing more than a "super pogo" device being developed by the military.

Dr. LaPaz and his "super pogo" proved to be a super blooper. He evidently did not know that the military had already announced that they had no device or craft answering the description of the thing Zamora saw . . . and Dr. LaPaz went down waving his explanation when the National Aeronautics and Space Administration revealed that the thing LaPaz was talking about had not yet been built.

At late as January, 1966, in POPULAR SCIENCE magazine, Air Force spokesman Major Hector Quintanilla, Jr., says of the Socorro case: "It has been well investigated and analyzed by experts. But it's still a mystery."

Twenty months after it happened, the case of the egg-shaped craft with the humanoids beside it, in that ravine near Socorro, New Mexico, was still listed on the Air Force public statements as "unsolved." It was too well documented to be ignored; too far-reaching to be admitted.

[Authors note: The appearance of Dr. Hynek on the scene of the Socorro sighting indicated that the Air Force considered it very important and that they dared not ridicule the witnesses.

Dr. Hynek's technique is twofold: First, it delays the issuance of any official statement. Secondly, he refrains from the practice of ridiculing the witnesses.

Dr. Hynek questions some of the key witnesses and then professes interest but need of more information. Then he questions the witnesses again and fires complex scientific questions at them, or makes inquiry of such technical nature that the witnesses can only reply that they don't know. Dr. Hynek is then in a position to say that due to the lack of technical information from the witnesses he is forced to draw his own conclusions, thus putting the whole matter back in the area of doubt.

Another variation is to question the witnesses and then to turn the matter over to an assistant. This stalls the "official statement" and creates an impression in the public mind that the case is so unimportant that Hynek's assistants can handle it.—F.E.]

One of the most bizarre reports dealing with the humanoids who are said to operate the UFO's came from Milan, Italy.

It was 1954, a year when hundreds of landings were reported from many parts of the world, including Europe. The specific date, according to the official records of Milan, was October 28.

A resident of Milan, returning from an outdoor movie on the outskirts of the city, noticed a glowing light inside a seldom-used sports field which was surrounded by a high but rather rickety board fence. Curious about this unusual activity in that field at that hour of night, he got off his bicycle and peered through the cracks in the fence.

He later told authorities that he could see some sizable

191

object, glowing softly like a very dim fluorescent lamp. It was on the ground or hovering a few inches above it—he could not tell since he could see no legs or landing gear. But he could and did see small dark forms moving around between himself and the object. He was frightened. He jumped on his bicycle and pedaled rapidly toward the outskirts of the city.

He had gone only a few hundred yards when he met a group of farmers, on their way home after attending a meeting. They heard his story and hurried back with him. Peering through the fence cracks, they too saw what he claimed to have seen. All of the witnesses, a total of thirty-one, affirmed to police who questioned them after the incident that the creatures moving around the glowing object resembled miniature men, not more than four feet tall, with light-colored pants, some sort of gray jackets, and helmets which appeared to be transparent. All of the creatures, said the witnesses, wore on their backs some bulky equipment connected to the front and bottoms of their helmets, presumably breathing apparatus.

Several passing automobiles, including a truck loaded with rotten fruit, stopped to see what was attracting the crowd around the fence. Presently some of the more venturesome members of the crowd forced the lock on the gate and stepped inside the fence for a better view. As they did so, the dark little figures began scurrying into the object, entering it from beneath. A moment later it began to hum and then to rise; but not before the farmers had thrown scores of rotten oranges at it, scoring some hits, so they told police.

If the details given to the police of Milan are correct, this may well be the only case in the universe where space travelers have been welcomed with a shower of garbage.

"The United States Navy evaluated the Trinidade Island sighting and reported to the Air Force their findings.

The Trinidade Island sighting was determined to be a hoax."

> —LETTER from Major L. A. Tacker, Air Force Public Relations Officer at the Pentagon, to Richard Hall, Assistant Director of NICAP (May, 1960)——

"The Navy has made no evaluation or official statement on the subject of unidentified flying objects in the vicinity of Brazil."

> —LETTER to APRO from the Secretary of the Navy, October 1, 1960, in reference to the Trinidade sighting.

8

The Race Into Space

If we conduct a sequential study of the likelihood of intelligent life elsewhere in the universe, we note that man's early wireless transmissions seem to have been noted and returned. The experiments by Professor David Todd for the U.S. Navy in 1924, previously described, hinted at some sort of intelligence that was capable of putting signals, however bizarre, on our recording device, however crude. The advent of the UFO's which followed our first nuclear explosions, and the flurry of UFO's which seem to manifest interest in our high-altitude rockets and, eventually, our satellites, must also be taken

193

into consideration as an important part of the whole picture of the phenomena.

Prior to the development of the German V-2 rocket in the midst of World War II, man had no effective tool for reaching out into space. The V-2 was a comparatively primitive piece of space hardware but it showed what might be done—given thousands of scientists and billions of dollars.

Some compelling reason induced both the Soviet Union and the United States to embark on fantastically expensive space programs. That these long-range devices would be of great military value was obvious. But both nations quickly showed a remarkable interest in the moon, that non-belligerent lover's lamp which has served Earth so long and so well.

In order to secure Congressional approval to divert so many billions of dollars to such an unusual project, the spokesmen for the Defense Department went to Capitol Hill and solemnly told Congress, and the press, that the moon had great military value. "The conventional slogan of the moon-shooters was that the nation that rules the moon rules the world."

This was pure fiction, of course, but before it could be effectively exposed as such it served to get our "Man to the Moon" program well under way.

For a military base on the moon to have military effect on Earth is sheer fantasy. It takes about a thousand pounds of fuel and rocket gear to get one pound to the moon and back. The same job can be done from one continent to another on Earth—and with far greater accuracy—using only a small fraction of that effort. Attacking our planet from the moon is about like attacking a battleship from a rowboat five hundred miles away.

The Race Into Space

When the "military necessity" theme wore thin and still more billions were needed, the proponents of the drive into outer space pinned their demands on the vital "necessity" for scientific research—and spiced it with hints that we were losing a "space race" to Soviet Russia. Other than a blow to our pride, it was never really explained what great advantages Russia would derive from landing a man on that reportedly bleak, barren, and inhospitable orb 250,000 miles from home.

A few scientists have spoken out concerning the illogical rush to the moon. They urged a more cautious and lengthy program. But their voices were drowned in the clamor of the Do-It-Now-Department of the government. If it made no sense, at least it made jobs. The public had no way to protest, even had they desired to do so. There was no way out for the goofs that lay the golden eggs.

Let us examine the chronological sequence which seems to indicate a relationship between the doings of man and the interest of the UFO's.

It was roughly one year after the first atomic bombs were exploded before these strange craft began to appear in Europe. Since we do not know what maximum speeds they can attain in their various devices, it is idle to speculate on why there was that lapse of time, assuming that they were attracted by the A-bomb flashes or radiation. Perhaps they were surprised by the bombs and it took them some time to organize their expedition. At any rate there was that one-year interval between the event on Earth and the arrival of the UFO's.

Since that time, however, the interval has been much shorter, generally only a matter of two or three days *if there is any interval at all.*

This might be construed to mean that these devices are

based either in some isolated spot on Earth or on some relatively nearby object, natural or artificial.

A logical suspect would be the moon.

The wealth of oddities which have been noted on the lunar surface is nothing short of astounding. In 1879, two years after man first noted that Mars had two very bright satellites, we discovered that our own satellite was pockmarked with lights and lines and geometric figures where none had been seen before. The British Astronomical Society asked its members to report such anomalies as they discovered them, in the hope that scientists might be able to discern some attempt at communication with us. After only two years the Society had to ask to be released from its proposal; more than two thousand reports of oddities on the moon had been recorded in that two-year period. Of this deluge the scientists could only conclude that the moon must be a very strange place, beyond their understanding.

Major Patrick Powers, head of the United States Army Space Development Program wrote in FAMILY CIRCLE magazine that in his opinion "the first men to reach the moon must be prepared to fight for the privilege of landing."

In December of 1962, at the convention of the American Rocket Society in Los Angeles, the speaker was Dr. Carl Sagan, the Advisor on Extra-terrestrial Life to the Armed Services. Dr. Sagan told his audience that mankind must be prepared to face the probability that we have already been visited by intelligent beings from elsewhere in the universe—and that they have—or have had—bases on the averted side of our moon.

By that time we were already involved in a twenty-billion-dollar program to send men to the moon. We had already designed and were building devices to photograph the moon at close range before crashing into it. And we had already arranged for many observatories, including Palomar, to devote as much telescope time as possible to studying the moon—which had long ago been abandoned as a major astronomical project in favor of more distant and more difficult objects.

(One of the problems confronting us in our proposed moon trips was that of communicating with the devices in transit. In 1951, Navy scientists used bulldozers to scoop out a bowl-shaped hole about 250 feet in diameter and about 50 feet deep at the center, near Boulder, Colorado. This hole was then lined with heavy metal foil to increase its reflectivity. A radar transmitter was set up in the center of the depression. Its signals bounced off the moon and returned to the bowl, October 21, 1951. Using radio, recognizable voice returns were obtained by the same process a short time later. Manmade instruments could therefore be sent to the moon under control—literally on the beam. The electronic road was open.)

Major Powers declined to amplify his interesting statement about the possibility of men having to fight for the privilege of landing on the moon—so we must leave it there as interesting but enigmatic.

To date, Russia has sent two photographic devices close enough to the moon to make and return pictures of reasonable quality. Please note that upon both occasions the device photographed the AVERTED side of the moon—they did not take a single picture of the near side of the moon. Russia showed no interest in the side of the moon where she hopes to land a man but devoted all her efforts to filming the averted side, where Dr. Sagan suggested that someone may already have landed.

197

Our own photographic lunar probes had a long record of mystifying failures before we finally scored. Known as the Ranger series, six of them went out and slammed into the moon without returning a single picture. Number Seven finally came through for us by producing, in the summer of 1964, a total of 4,320 pictures of surprising clarity before it banged into the lunar landscape. One of those pictures, which showed two large lumpy white objects in one of the pits or craters, was recalled and briefly "classified"—then re-released with the explanation that the strange objects were only rocks. Since this explanation was only a guess from 250,000 miles away, it carries little conviction.

The pictures by Ranger Seven were featured in newspapers and magazines for weeks; that is, the "selected" pictures which were released were widely published. They were our first close-up look at the moon. They had been frightfully expensive but they were remarkably detailed and interesting.

While Ranger Eight sent back about 7,000 pictures a few months later—pictures that were admittedly far more detailed than those of its predecessor—you will have to dig to find them in any quantity in the public prints. They were so much better, photographically, that they were correspondingly more interesting. But after a small initial release of "selected" frames they dropped out of sight.

Photographically, they were better pictures. They were also pictures of an unusually active area of the moon. But few of them were exhibited—which leads to the suspicion that perhaps they may have shown too much. In the present state of affairs between the government and the public, it seems improbable that we shall ever know just what

the Ranger Eight pictures *did* show. The crater Alphonsus
—true—but what did they tell us about that crater that
was new and different?

Lunar anomalies were by no means restricted to the
late years of the nineteenth century. They continue to this
day.

Equally interesting are the so-called "moon domes"
which are discussed in Harvard Observatory's magazine
SKY AND TELESCOPE for January, 1958. Noting that in
recent years astronomers have been paying increasing attention to "lunar domes, small rounded hills being observed in increasing numbers," the magazine displays a
drawing of one of these objects, made by an astronomer
in France who had studied it through a ten-inch telescope.

The presence of these domes was first noted in the
1930's; by 1960 more than two hundred of these rounded,
white, hemispherical objects had been recorded on the
lunar surface. Whatever they are, they are not *hills;* for
hills do not appear and disappear on an airless orb. The
shadows of these objects show them to be rounded and
they show a marked tendency to appear in areas which
are apparently level.

In order to be seen at all from Earth, these things
would have to be about 600 feet in diameter. They are
admittedly close to the limits of visibility, which may
mean that they are possibly 750 feet in diameter. This
would be tiny for a volcanic cone by our standards, but
it would not be small for an inflatable or portable space
base, such as we ourselves have considered for similar
purposes. Furthermore, these domes are seen first in one
place and then in another. If volcanoes do move on the
moon they differ in that respect from terrestrial volcanoes.
Volcanoes can hardly be expected to pick up their cones

199

and shuffle off to new locations. Space bases would be logically expected to do just that.

The well-documented peripatetic moon domes may be still another hint that the moon is not as lifeless as some scientists profess to believe.

In 1958 and again in 1961, Soviet astronomer Nikolai Kozyrev announced that he had detected what appeared to be volcanic activity near the crater Aristarchus. He had first made the detection of this anomaly by telescope from the observatory at Pulkovo and confirmed it by spectrograms.

The sneers he drew for this report came largely from those western scientists who *knew* that the moon was only a great lifeless orb, alternately frozen and broiled by the sun.

But in late 1963, four prominent American astronomers confirmed Kozyrev's first reports: There was certainly some action "apparently volcanic" in the crater Aristarchus. In the December, 1963, issue of SKY AND TELESCOPE, Lowell Observatory reports that on the night of October 29 it had detected two clusters of bright red lights north of the crater Herodotus; on the night of November 27, the red spots had vanished from their previous location and were clustered in an oval formation along the south rim of the crater Aristarchus!

[Please do not misconstrue these bright red lights moving from place to place on the moon as indicative of life there. They were officially nothing more than that rarest of all phenomena . . . galloping volcanoes.—F.E.]

In June of 1965 an amateur astronomer alerted professional observers in both California and Arizona to a strange brilliant white ray of light that had streamed out of Aristarchus, which was then well over on the dark portion of the lunar disc.

In July, the observatories saw it too—a beam of white light which lasted for about one and a half seconds each time it appeared.

The observatories made arrangements with numerous amateur radio operators to flash the word from one observatory to another when the flash was spotted. Known as "Astronet," by August of 1965 it included "ham" operators of short-wave radio transmitters in Phoenix, Tucson, and Prescott in Arizona; at Mt. Wilson, San Diego, and the Los Angeles area in California; and another in Las Vegas, Nevada.

In July and again in August, the astronomers who were watching this latest moon mystery were able to talk with each other as though they were in the same room, thanks to this hookup of amateur short-wave radio facilities. As each scientist observed the flash he would report it to his colleagues.

Aristarchus is in the south left center of the moon as viewed from Earth and can be seen by a telescope of four inches or more with ease.

And what of the light? The scientists who have logged it in their observatory records do not believe that it is any reflected star light—nor a vagrant sunbeam—for at the time it is seen, Aristarchus is around the curve of the lunar landscape from the sun.

What is it, then, that is flashing that strange light from that unusual crater which has spawned so many enigmas in recent years? The scientists aren't talking. But they and their friends of Astronet are still watching Aristarchus —and are still marveling at what they see there.

Robert E. Curtiss of Alamogordo, New Mexico, is not only a very capable astronomer, he is also a skilled photographer.

On the night of November 26, 1956, Mr. Curtiss was making some test shots with a Mitchell 35 millimeter motion picture camera. It was loaded with highly sensitized film and was coupled to the rangefinder of his 16-inch reflector telescope. With this setup he was able to shoot pictures of the moon at speeds of 24 to 48 frames per second. The telescope was covering that portion of the moon around Fra Mauro, which lies between Parry and Copernicus.

When Mr. Curtiss developed and printed his films he was startled by a peculiarity. Just to the left of the terminator, which is the dividing line between sunlight and shadow on the moon, there was a small white Maltese cross. It was on frame after frame and was unquestionably either on the surface of the moon or very close to it.

SKY AND TELESCOPE ran the picture in June of 1958. They appended a suggestion by Walter Haas, Director of the Association of Lunar and Planetary Observers, who ventured the possibility that the strange white cross with the four arms of equal length might be only a group of ridges or mountain spurs, visible in this particular form only for a fleeting period when the sunlight reaches the lower slopes.

It is an interesting theory. Unfortunately it conflicts with nature. For ridges or mountain spurs to cross each other at right angles is a physical impossibility, according to the U.S. Geodetic Survey, since the forces that created one ridge would automatically destroy the other.

The cross was there. Mr. Curtiss photographed it. Thus far, it seems, no one has been able to explain it.

Something very powerful indeed is the driving force behind our frenzied effort to reach the moon. Dr. Sagan's suggestion, if correct, might explain why the UFO's now appear within such a short time after we do something spectacular. A lunar base would simplify the task of keeping us under surveillance at all times and of conducting intensive surveys on short notice. The conclusion that the moon is, or might be, harboring such a base would serve as an urgent motivation for our drive to reach the moon . . . and would probably explain Russia's singular preoccupation with the averted side of the moon.

To illustrate the frantic haste behind the program we have only to note that twice, in less than a year, the National Aeronautics and Space Administration switched methods on how to land a man on the moon and get him back. The emphasis is on speed; expense has been left at the post; and safety has been a minor consideration.

For at least a million years, man has been able to live on Earth in varying degrees of comfort. Now, as our living standards reach the highest point in human history, we embark on a tremendously expensive and dangerous venture to go to the moon.

When we get there, what do we do if we find that beings from elsewhere in the universe, more advanced than ourselves, are already there?

Conversely, what if we find that the UFO's, which have shown such prolonged interest in us, have shown no interest in the moon? After spending all those billions of dollars to reach the moon on the thrust of a chemical rocket, what have we accomplished if we discover to our chagrin that the thing we are looking for isn't there . . . and doesn't need to be there?

Unless we actually know that our moon *is* being used

as a way station by the UFO's, then our crash drive to get there is not readily understandable. If we DO know that the UFO's are there, or HAVE BEEN THERE, then the urgent nature of the moon program makes some sense.

But as of right now, the space program, like the phenomena on the moon, has a surplus of questions and a shortage of answers.

We have already seen how, on at least one occasion, a Russian space capsule was paced by a controlled UFO. There is one other recorded instance of a similar incident involving a Soviet space capsule.

I made headlines around the world in June of 1962 with the detailed report of five Soviet space casualties. Included in that list was the case of a pair of Soviet cosmonauts, a man and a woman, who were launched into orbit from Baikonour, on the Aral Sea, on February 17, 1961. On that day and for seven days thereafter, tracking stations at Uppsala, Bochum, and Turin, among others, recorded conversations between these hapless cosmonauts and their base stations. Due to some malfunction, they were unable to return from orbit and they presumably died up there. [The Soviet Union refuses to comment on the incident.—F.E.]

As the doomed pair orbited over Europe in the early evening hours of February 24, 1961, tracking stations at Bochum, Meudon, and Turin listened to their reports. The pair described their physical condition as good, but they added that their air supply was about gone and their lights had failed. The man's voice reported that the dials were virtually impossible to read at that time. He added that the incoming radio signals were weak [probably due to the power failure.—F.E.] but that the capsule was maintaining its prescribed orbit.

Then the woman's voice cut in excitedly:

"I'll take it and hold tight with my right hand! Look out the peephole! Look out the peephole! I have it. . . ."

After a few seconds the male voice burst in:

"Here! Here is something! *There is something*—[three seconds garbled.—F.E.] "If we do not get out the world will never know about it! It is difficult—."

At this point there were a few unintelligible fragmentary voice sounds—then their base station [code name: Hole] cut in to announce that it was 8 p.m. Moscow time.

From the study of their expressions and their words, it is clear that the doomed couple in that Soviet capsule had seen something unusual near them in space—something that first startled and then terrified them.

That incident occurred six weeks after a comparable case involving one of our own space shots.

In the files of NICAP is a photocopy of an official log from the tracking facility at Cape Canaveral, Florida, dated January 10, 1961. On that day the principal project was the test firing of a Polaris missile, to be launched from Florida and tracked down range several thousand miles into the South Atlantic.

The official log shows that, while the Polaris was still climbing, it suddenly acquired a traveling companion. The log refers to it as "an unidentifiable object." The object was evidently so much larger than the Polaris and so close to the missile that the automatic radar tracking gear at the base locked on the larger object—the UFO. When the UFO veered away from the Polaris a few minutes later, the automatic gear continued to follow it . . . and it required fourteen minutes, according to the official log, for the technicians to get the radar off the UFO and back on the smaller Polaris.

You will find an account of this incident in TRUE magazine for January, 1965, in an article on UFO's which must have been very annoying to the censorship group in the Pentagon.

Our first orbital launching of a Gemini spacecraft occurred on April 8, 1964. Instead of astronauts, the Gemini carried a load of devices designed to report the performance characteristics of the craft to determine whether it was safe to carry men into space.

The blast-off was excellent and the Gemini went into its predetermined orbit, beeping down its findings.

While the Gemini was still in its first orbit, it was joined by four controlled objects of unknown origin. The astounded technicians and scientists at the tracking stations watched as the four UFO's took up positions near the Gemini; two above it, one behind it, one below it. They maintained these relative positions for one complete orbit; then they swerved away and sped out into space, from whence they had come.

TRUE's disclosure of this incident stirred up a hornet's nest. Among the stung was the Air Force explanation department. Members of Congress who made inquiry were informed by the Air Force that they had been advised by Leo Abernethy, Chief, Mission Support, Apollo Flight Operations, Office of Manned Space Flight, as follows: [Quoted from Air Force letters to Congressmen] "No unidentified objects were observed accompanying or pursuing the GT-I spacecraft launched into orbit on a Titan 2 booster on April 8, 1964. Objects observed, which were detected on radar, have been identified as minor structural pieces which routinely break free from the expendable booster portion in the spacecraft and booster separation process. There is no indication of the presence of any material which was not originally part of the launched vehicle."

The Air Force "explanation" was clearly designed to create the impression that the admittedly observed objects were related to the separation of the capsule and the second stage—or booster—rocket.

The Air Force was caught with its explanations down again, when Howard Nichol, of 65 Somerset Road, Glastonbury, Connecticut, queried the National Aeronautics and Space Administration about the matter. Under date of August 8, 1965, an official NASA letter written by A. P. Alibrando, Public Affairs Officer for Manned Space Flight, NASA, informed Mr. Nichol:

"The answers to your questions on Gemini I are as follows:

"The second stage of the booster and the spacecraft *did not separate* because the flight was a test of only the launch vehicle and guidance system, and the structural integrity and compatibility of the spacecraft and the launch vehicle.

"The first stage of the Titan landed south of Bermuda.

"It is the second stage of the Titan which actually places the Gemini spacecraft into orbit.

"In Gemini I, both the booster and the spacecraft reentered the atmosphere as a *single unit*."

The italics in the above quotation are mine, to underscore the portions which completely refute the alleged "explanation" which had been rushed out to members of Congress and other interested parties.

The report of the UFO's around our Gemini I was based on statements by scientists who were present at the time of the incident. Since the Air Force experts knew that there was no separation of booster and Gemini, it is strange that they should have predicated their answer on

207

such a basis, unless, of course, they felt that it might hold up and they had to take a chance.

When Major Gordon Cooper was making his final orbit of Earth in May of 1963, he radioed down to the tracking station at Muchea, near Perth, Australia, that he was being approached by a greenish object moving east to west—which is contrary to orbits of manmade satellites.

The object was seen on the tracking gear at Perth by more than a hundred persons, most of them technicians and some of them newsmen. The National Broadcasting Company carried the report of this incident immediately after it happened. But when Cooper was fished out of the ocean at the end of his journey, the eager newsmen were bluntly informed that they could not question him about this incident, that any statement on it would have to come from NASA.

Needless to say, no such statement ever came.

Our first two-man team of astronauts Edward White and James McDivitt, were passing eastward over the Hawaiian Islands on June 4, 1965, when McDivitt spotted a "weird object" with some sort of "projections" from it, "like arms." White was asleep at the time. McDivitt took pictures of the thing with a movie camera mounted inside the cabin of the Gemini. A few minutes later, both men saw two more such objects, this time over the Caribbean.

The Department of Instant Explanations was equal to the challenge. The Air Force promptly announced that the men had seen our Pegasus satellite. But the space detection and tracking system showed that Pegasus was actually 1,200 miles from the Gemini capsule at the time of the sighting. This was very embarrassing for the explainers, so the Air Defense Command got into the act and announced that it "might" have been Pegasus after

Front page of a Soviet 'popular science' type magazine, purporting to show a fantastic jet-propelled disc type passenger plane then (1964) being contemplated by Soviet engineers. It never was heard of again. See page 277.

Described as a secret Russian 'anti-gravity' plane this much-retouched picture has been described by U.S. aerodynamics expert as a conventional light plane, with the propellor painted out.

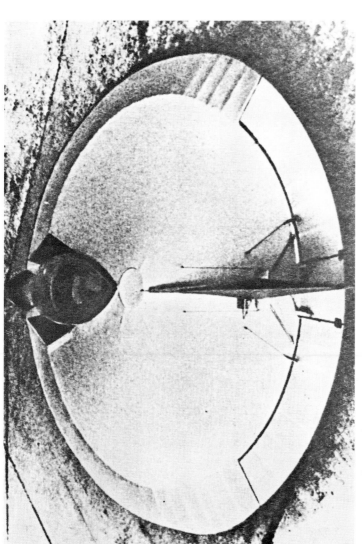

Presumably an overhead view of the same 'anti-gravity' plane on preceding page. This device appears to be a wedding of a metal skin center with fabric and doped rim—a type of construction long outmoded in the United States—and Russia. Story of USSR devices on page 275.

This One Flew: V–173
(Official U. S. Navy Photo)

When UFOs first appeared over the United States in mid-1947, many persons recalled this experimental plane of unusual design, best known as the 'Flying Flapjack.' Underpowered, it was obsolete by the time it was tested. After being flown a few times it was relegated to display in the Smithsonian Air Museum, where it still is.

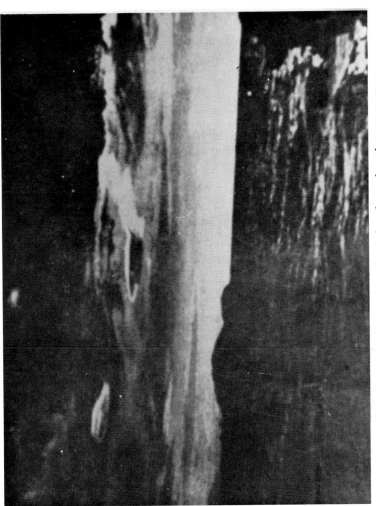

This mushroom shaped UFO, with cabin below dome shaped superstructure, was following a Brazilian Navy officers fishing launch in 1953. The UFO was estimated at about 200 feet in diameter, silent, leaving contrail. It was in view about fifteen minutes. Photo from Brazilian Navy, via APRO, Tucson.

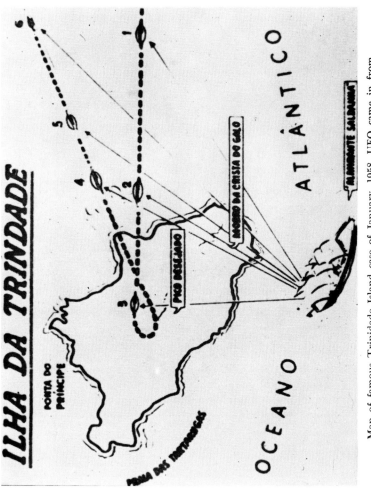

Map of famous Trinidade Island case of January, 1958. UFO came in from right, stopped at numbered positions, finally moved away to east by north after circling radar installations on island.

One of three spots in swamp near Tully, Queensland, Australia, where spinning circular UFO's reportedly landed January 26, 1966. Landings were witnessed and reported by group of high school teachers. Great weight and crushing effect of objects indicated by condition of rushes flattened in thirty foot circles. Photograph copyright 1966 by professional photographer

UFO following B-47 twin jet military plane, near Edwards Air Force Base in September of 1957. Photo made by test pilot from Convair. Enlargement of UFO in upper left of photo (insert). Photo Courtesy NICAP.

UFO with shallow, rounded dome, illuminated from within and blinking in green, red and creamy white. Photographed by a 14 year old boy in Tulsa, Oklahoma. The photo was authenticated and copyright by the Oklahoma City Journal. Story on page 287.

The first of three photographs taken by a Los Angeles County highway employee named Heflin on the morning of August 3, 1965, near Santa Ana, California. Note apparent disturbance on shoulder of road below object. Story on page 300.

Second photograph of same object taken by Heflin from inside Highway Department truck. Rear view mirror in lower left. Photos courtesy Los Angeles NICAP Committee.

Heflin picture number 3. Taken shortly after number two and only a few seconds before object sped away and was lost in smog. Camera was Polaroid, fixed focus, electronic shutter. Film speed ASA 3000.

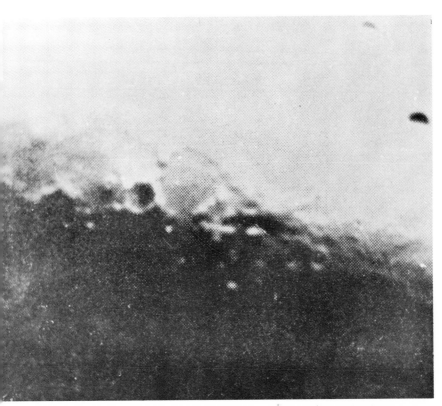

Robert Curtiss, astronomer of Alamogordo, New Mexico, took this picture
with a 35 mm Movie camera through his telescope in 1956. Sky and Telescope, which published the print, expressed the suggestion that the strange
white cross in the edge of darkness was merely two mountain ridges crossing
each other. For details, see story on page 202.

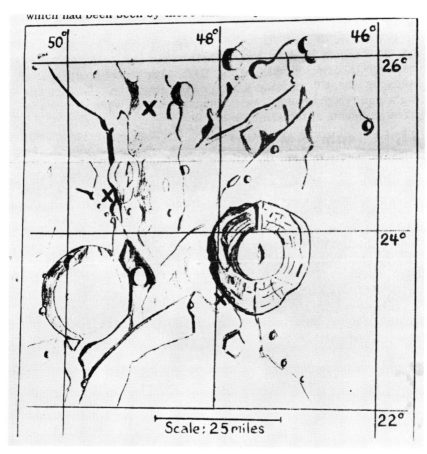

Scene of strange red lights noted on moon by professional astronomers in October-November, 196 . Crater in lower right is Aristarchus, also scene of phenomena in 1965. Courtesy NICAP. Stories on page 200.

Glowing, disc-shaped UFO about thirty feet in diameter according to esti-
mates by witnesses. Time exposure made by Frank Lucci, Beaver Falls, Pennsylvania, August 6, 1965. Courtesy NICAP.

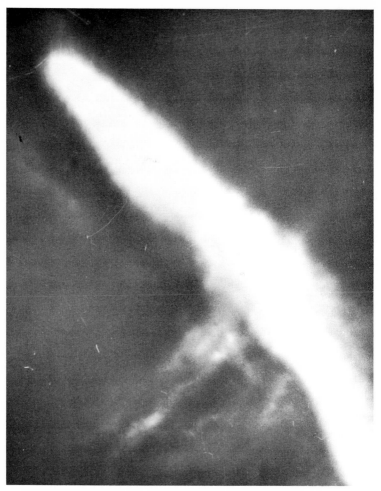

One of two photographs of Portland, Indiana, UFO by Robert Kennedy. Object was in view an estimated four minutes. Shown here streaking from a fixed position. Kennedy, police officer Robert Glentser and other witnesses say object traveled in spurts, stopped abruptly, moved silently. Photo copyright by Robert Kennedy.

all, since a "re-check" of the calculations indicated that Pegasus "might have been" ten or twelve miles from the Gemini as it passed over the United States.

In the first place, the sighting was made over Hawaii—and not over the United States.

In the second place, the Air Defense Command has repeatedly asserted that its functions are so precise that it can *pinpoint the location of any and all Earth-launched satellites at any time.*

But, in this instance, they claim they made an error of 1,200 miles! If that is a pin point . . . what size was the pin?

After the flight of McDivitt and White ended, and their films had been examined, United Press quoted a spokesman for NASA as making this remarkable remark:

"Careful study of the pictures taken by McDivitt of the object seen from the capsule shows nothing that looks like a satellite."

If it didn't look like a satellite—what DID it look like? The spokesman didn't say and presumably nobody inquired.

One of the movie frames taken by McDivitt was released to the press about a week after the incident. It shows an oval- (or disc-) shaped object with a tenuous trail or glow behind it. [See picture section.]

It might be well at this point to take note of the experiences of two famous test pilots who were flying our extreme-high-altitude rocket plane, the famed X-15, at the times of their incidents.

On April 30, 1962, Major Joe Walker was streaking along in excess of 2,000 miles per hour at the fringe of Earth's atmosphere. After the flight, when his rearview movie camera films were developed, it was discovered that for part of his flight Major Walker's plane had been followed by a group of five disc-shaped or cylindrical objects, which were in echelon formation most of the time they were within camera range. Major Walker was permitted to mention the eerie incident on an NBC broadcast from Seattle, and the films were shown at a news conference there. But no prints were available and Walker did not make any further public statements on the case.

The official explanation which followed hot upon the heels of the broadcast was that the objects were in reality only "ice flakes." If so, it was one of those extremely rare incidents where ice flakes flew in echelon formation and followed a plane at 2,000 miles an hour—which you may agree is pretty fast, even for an educated ice flake.

On July 17, 1962, the record breaking X-15 was zooming into the stratosphere again, this time with Major Bob White at the controls. He, too, had an unexpected traveling companion which was also recorded by his camera. It looked to Major White "like a gray-white piece of paper," pacing the ship off the left wing tip for five or six seconds, then it darted above and behind the plane and vanished from the pilot's view.

Both are interesting cases because they seem to indicate the presence of intelligently controlled objects around our high-speed rocket planes, as well as our even faster and higher space capsules.

And the object that flipped over Major White's canopy seems to have had a counterpart in the Gemini 7 flight of astronauts Frank Borman and James Lovell in late 1965. On their second orbit they reported that they were seeing a "bogey"—the airman's term for unidentified aircraft which might be hostile. The ground station suggested to Borman that he was probably seeing the burned-out booster rocket which had sent them into orbit. Borman replied that he was, indeed, seeing the booster rocket and seeing it clearly—" a brilliant body tumbling along in the sunlight"—but the bogey was something else entirely, in a different part of the sky.

The Air Force promptly announced that the thing Borman saw was only the debris of a Titan rocket that had blown up during a faulty launch some weeks before.

That explanation was promptly gunned down by NORAD, the agency charged with the responsibility of knowing WHAT is up there . . . and WHERE it is. Said NORAD: "There is no rocket debris, Titan or otherwise, in that area at this time going in that direction at that altitude." Which seems pretty definite.

From the existing and recorded evidence, you might conclude that our struggle into space has not gone unnoticed. Unless we have advanced by a long series of coincidences, it seems that we have learned much by emulating, to the best of our ability, some of the characteristics of the UFO's. We have yet to duplicate their method of propulsion, whatever it is, but we are making every effort and with a little luck—or another coincidence —we should attain that goal also.

Our expensive scramble to get into space has produced some interesting and unexpected side effects. Among them is the still unsolved case of four of our satellites which suddenly ceased to function—and then returned to service just as suddenly and mysteriously as they had blacked out.

First official admission of this singular matter leaked out in piecemeal fashion in the latter part of August, 1963—not an open and candid description of what had ocurred but a story which newsmen had to assemble by probing and prying and persistent inquiry.

Here it is.

Let us consider the strange cases of the geodetic sphere Anna and of the communications satellite Telstar 2.

Anna went into orbit in October of 1962 and was equipped, as you may recall from contemporary statements, with four brilliant, flashing lights which could be photographed against the stars, to enable our scientists to calculate more accurately the exact size and shape of the earth. Known also as the "Firefly" satellite, it was tracked and photographed for two months. Then, very unexpectedly, Firefly ceased to function. Believing it to be dead and useless, the Air Force abandoned their work with it, and the technicians packed their gear and went on to other duties. But in August of 1963, after a seven-month hiatus, Firefly abruptly came back into action—and the startled but grateful Air Force technicians resumed their work with it.

Then there was the case of Telstar 2—launched May 7, 1963, with great fanfare. It functioned perfectly until July 16, 1963, when it suddenly blacked out. It remained dormant until August 12 and then it suddenly picked up where it had left off.

The bafflement of our scientists would seem to be pardonable. Two satellites which were functioning perfectly stopped cold without any indication of malfunction prior to the stoppage. After they had been dead for weeks or months, the two satellites returned to service within three days of each other, again for reasons unknown.

Richard Kerschmerof of Johns Hopkins University—which built the Firefly—told newsmen: "This sort of thing is hard to believe. We have no explanation for the lights coming back on."

Doren Mitchell, of Bell Laboratories, which built Telstar 2, said: "There is no indication of what caused the failure—but it might have been a meteorite."

The scientists were left with two questions: If the satellites were damaged by meteorites—what repaired the damage?

The other question—which officials declined to discuss —was this: Was something, or somebody, examining the satellites while they were out of service?

In 1964, a total of four of our satellites quit without apparent reason and returned to service without apparent reason.

The question, which remains unanswered, is *why?*

The record shows that quite early in the space race we encountered an enigma which was considered so important that top scientists devoted time and thought to it.

By July of 1960 there were eleven small U.S. satellites in orbit and one large Soviet capsule still following a known and predictable path. But our tracking gear showed a stranger—also in orbit. We had accounted for the products of all the Soviet launchings, on which we kept close records. We knew where our own satellites were and what they were doing. What was this unknown?

NEWSWEEK magazine interviewed scientists at the Nation Space Surveillance Control Center; then NEWSWEEK said: "A growing number of scientists are now convinced that Spacetrack may have overlooked at least one other space vehicle, neither American nor Russian but out of this world, indeed—out of this solar system! This Satellite, they suspect, is a visitor sent by the superior beings of a community of other stars within the Milky Way galaxy—

a kind of United Stellar Organization interested, for archeological and anthropological reasons, in how things are going in this part of the galactic neighborhood."

Dr. Hermann Oberth and others had said virtually the same thing years before—that to them the evidence indicated that somebody from Out There was looking us over.

There had been many hints at such a state of affairs prior to 1960—and there have been a great many more since then.

"There are no such things as flying saucers—nothing to them at all!"

—Dr. Hugh Dryden, Director, National Advisory Committee on Aeronautics, to House Appropriations Committee, February 19, 1957

Gentlemen, I regret that I made that statement . . . about flying saucers. It was just my personal opinion, nothing more.

—Dr. Hugh Dryden, February 24, 1957, to a press conference after being challenged by NICAP

9

Does Science Follow the Saucers?

The vast frozen wastes of the Antarctic had been of comparatively little interest to science prior to 1948—the year in which whaling vessels returning from that area reported numerous sightings of strange disc-shaped objects in the South Polar skies. In late 1949 the Chilean Navy sent Commander Auguste V. Orrego with a portion of the Chilean fleet into the Antarctic. He brought back from that expedition hundreds of feet of motion picture film showing those same objects circling the ships of his command, especially while they were at the Chilean Antarctic base of Arthur Prat. The films were turned over to the Chilean government on February 23, 1950, the day on which Orrego revealed their contents to

231

newsmen. The films have never been publicly screened since that day.

Since the reports of UFO activity at both Poles, from 1947 to 1949, every major nation has taken part in "scientific research programs" in one or both polar regions. Commander Orrego's films seem to have touched off a Cold Rush of monumental proportions. Russia, Sweden, Norway, Canada, the United States, Argentina, Chile, Australia, France, and Great Britain all launched projects into the frigid wastelands of the Antarctic. In a three-year period, 1948-1951, more men, money, and material poured into the Antarctic than had been sent there in the preceding two hundred years.

Was this apparently concerted rush nothing more than coincidence? Whether or not that is the answer, it is but one of a series of such activities which have taken place since the advent of the UFO's. They may be pure happenstance—and then again, they may not.

Let us examine the record.

Earlier, you may recall, I mentioned that the Canadian saucer study, Project Magnet, had detected the electromagnetic disturbance associated with the unidentified flying objects, and the Canadians had designed simple detectors which were capable of alerting the investigators when a UFO entered the field of the detector. Wilbert Smith, who headed the project, said at a news conference in Washington that he and his colleagues had endeavored to construct a disc-shaped device capable of converting the magnetic field into sufficient usable energy to lift itself— but had finally abandoned the project as beyond contemporary scientific knowledge.

In reality, we know little about the nature of gravity. We cannot be sure whether it pulls or pushes and we admittedly do not know why it does either, if it does. Thanks to our space-traveling probes we do know that gravity exists to some degree everywhere in the space between the planets which we have thus far been able to reach. A method which would convert gravity into usable energy should be the ideal power system for traversing the vast reaches of the solar system—or beyond. But first we must learn to use it.

After Dr. Hermann Oberth had studied the UFO problem for West Germany, he said at a press conference that he and his colleagues felt that these objects propelled themselves by distorting the gravitational field and converting it into usable energy. Under the Unified Field Theory of science, which holds that electricity, gravity, and magnetism are different manifestations of the same form of energy, Dr. Oberth may well have been right in his conclusion.

Gravitational research was long the playground of kooks and dreamers. Conventional science held that man was tied to Earth by gravity—he had always been tied to Earth by gravity—therefore it was foolish to suppose that he might learn to break that bond.

By the time Dr. Oberth made his remarkable remark about UFO's and gravitational propulsion, there was so much scientific interest and activity in this field that he did not draw the traditional barrage of criticism that would have been his fate twenty years earlier. Many researchers were already dusting off the old books and reports to see just what HAD been learned by scientific investigation in years gone by. And many of them had found themselves patiently perusing the reports of Dr. Charles F. Bush, M.E., M.S., Dr.Sc., who reported to his fellow scientists in 1926 that he had discovered some strange

233

characteristics in a substance known as Lintz Basalt. For one thing, he found that it generated more heat than did uranium and, later, that it refused to accelerate in free fall as prescribed by the accepted "laws" of gravitation. It did not defy gravitation—neither did it conform. Dr. Bush could not explain it; but he could, and did, report it.

Furthermore, Dr. Bush listed several other substances which showed varying degrees of allergy to falling as they had been expected to fall. The scientist's report was regarded by his contemporaries in 1926 as interesting but not necessarily important. He had pointed a path which he thought worthy of further exploration, but nobody was interested. His works were filed and forgotten—for thirty years.

J. E. Surrat, Jr., Vice President of the Society of Aeronautical Weight Engineers, said in April of 1957, that five major American companies were engaged in anti-gravity research projects which were government-financed. At that same time there was already in existence at Wright Field, Dayton, Ohio (center of the Defense Department UFO investigations, then and now), a multi-million-dollar installation designed and equipped for research and study of counter-gravity and anti-gravity forces.

A tantalizing tidbit indicative of the vast expenditure of time and money going into this field will be found in the magazine ELECTRICAL MANUFACTURING in the issue for October, 1953. The headline over this brief item reads: AIR FORCE SPONSORED MAGNETICS RESEARCH. The article explains that the Indiana Steel Products Company had just received a three-pronged contract for exploring magnetics, possible new magnetic alloys, magnetic characteristics, and the theory of magnetic phenomena—also, please note, applied research, design and application, and *"An advi-*

sory committee will be formed to coordinate the research with existing projects in the same field." [Italics mine.— F.E.] This was the confirmation that this particular gravity-electro-magnetics project was merely part of a much more extensive program. By early 1958 Inland Steel, Sperry-Rand, General Electric, Lear Instruments, Hughes Aircraft, and United States Steel were also participating in the all-out effort to penetrate the secrets of gravity. TRUE magazine for January, 1966, said that *forty-six* military-sponsored gravity research projects are in being now.

All this costly and time-consuming interest in gravity had blossomed *after the arrival of the UFO's* and after their silent, gravity-defying performance had led to the suspicion that they were not really *defying* gravity, but *utilizing* it.

Coincidence again?

The scientific hegira to the Antarctic which followed the acquisition of photographic evidence of intensive UFO activity there also produced an interesting side effect— the suspicion that there might be a good reason for so much activity at the Poles—and so little above our equator. Was there some reason why the UFO's might *prefer* the Poles?

The subject resolved itself into two apparent probabilities: One was the likelihood that the frigid temperatures might be more to their liking. The other suggested that there might be something in space beyond our equator which made entry there undesirable. Since the UFO's used both polar regions at the same time, the temperature theory did not appear to be a transcendent consideration. Since they entered our atmosphere at the Poles and were tracked in Pole-to-Pole movement thereafter, the study of space above the equator was instituted as soon as we were able to contrive rockets capable of reaching extreme altitudes, bearing the necessary instruments. Early in this century a few scientists had cautiously theorized that such study would vindicate their suspicions, if it ever became possible.

On March 2, 1958, it was announced that two of our Explorer satellites had definitely confirmed the existence of a belt of intense radiation girdling Earth at an altitude of about 600 miles above the equator. This zone is now known as the Van Allen Belt, in honor of one of its proponents. There is nothing comparable to it above either of our polar regions and its true nature was a major surprise, even to those who anticipated and predicted its existence; for the NEW YORK TIMES quotes these scientists as saying that the radiation was a thousand times more powerful than they had estimated. It was a deadly ring of radiation through which man may not venture—and which the UFO's seemed to avoid.

When it appeared that these objects preferred to enter our atmosphere only at the Poles, science made haste to examine outer space above our equator—and found a great belt of deadly radiation.

Coincidence again?

Elsewhere in this volume we have discussed at length the multi-nation program of building giant devices for the detection of radio signals from space—and for the tracking of unknown satellites traversing our part of the solar system. Famed astronomer Dr. Clyde Tombaugh revealed in 1952 that he was in charge of a government [Army] program to locate and study two strange satellites which had been detected several times. This was five years before the first manmade satellite was sent into orbit by the Soviets. As we shall see when we turn our attention to our space program, there were several of these strange objects near Earth at various times during the first decade of the UFO phenomena; and their detection was followed by the creation of huge devices capable of locating and tracking them—popularly known as radio telescopes.

Again we note the interesting chronological sequence which has been identified with so many scientific projects paid for by the military in recent years—the appearance of strange satellites around or near Earth—and the development of a project which seems to be directly concerned with the objects.

Coincidence?

Perhaps.

Upon many occasions, some of them dating back to the closing years of the preceding century, officers and crewmen of numerous vessels reported watching disc-shaped craft entering and emerging from the sea. One such incident occurred in 1955 when the crew of a Gulf Oil tanker reported to authorities that a huge circular, double-convex object trailing smoke dived into the Gulf of Mexico only a few hundred yards from their vessel in full daylight. A coastal vessel in the Mediterranean only a few miles off southern Italy, carrying a load of passengers, reported seeing a disc-shaped thing rising from the water in 1953.

As the years went by, and as more and more of these strange spectacles were recorded, an interesting corollary developed: Man began experimenting with disc-shaped undersea craft for the first time. You will find an interesting article on this radically different submarine craft in the NATIONAL GEOGRAPHIC magazine for April, 1960. Its creator is none other than world-famous undersea expert

Jacques Cousteau. And he calls it—"the Diving Saucer."

The same shape that seems to work so admirably in the atmosphere has been found to perform equally well under water. Unknown devices of similar shape have been observed in both elements for years. Now man is trying them himself.

Pure coincidence, no doubt.

To this growing list of such "coincidences" we should by all means add the following cases:

The explosions of the first manmade atomic bombs in 1945 were followed by the appearance of UFO's in numbers in 1946. [The two bombs were exploded over Japan; the 1946 UFO's were over Scandinavia and Russia. If they were looking for the source of those atomic flashes they had the right latitude but the wrong longitude. —F.E.]

The 1947 mass appearance of UFO's over the United States included numerous sightings around our atomic installations at Hanford and Oak Ridge, as well as the great scarred area near Alamogordo, New Mexico, where we had fired our first atomic device. If they were looking for sites and sources of our activity in the field of nuclear fission, they were looking in the right places by 1947.

Our launchings of V-2 rockets from White Sands in 1948 were also marked by visits from UFO's. [I have a sound film interview with Charles Swartz, who was in charge of radar at White Sands during one of these UFO incidents. The UFO, a disc, climbed alongside the V-2 at about 1,000 miles per hour, circling the rocket. It was observed visually through binoculars, telescopes, and theodolites—as well as on radar. It climbed straight up past the rocket at an estimated 5,500 miles per hour and went

238

out into space.—F.E.] On April 24, 1949, White Sands scientists tracked still another UFO there. The case is reported in detail by Captain R. B. McLaughlin, USN, in TRUE magazine for March, 1950.

Between the disc-shaped objects which followed our rockets in 1949 and the launching of the first manmade satellite in late 1957, the pattern of UFO reports indicated that they were involved in pacing our ships, planes, trains, and automobiles, as well as making systematic surveillance of important military, industrial, and communications centers all over the world. [French mathematician Aimé Michel's books cover this program in detail and are highly recommended. See Appendix.—F.E.]

Close on the heels of their first dramatic satellite launching, the scientists in the Soviet Union made headlines again on November 2, 1957, when they launched into orbit a device they called Sputnik 2—which carried a living passenger—a dog named Laika.

This memorable event was followed a few hours later by a UFO demonstration which jarred the Pentagon. There was the landing on the highway near Levelland, Texas, of a huge red-glowing object which knocked out ignition systems and headlights of approaching vehicles. A few hours later another strange, brilliantly glowing thing was seen to settle down briefly on an isolated part of the White Sands Proving Ground. It was reported by three different military patrols which observed it from three separate points on the range.

The Ever-Ready Explainers at the Pentagon dismissed the huge, dirigible-shaped object on the highway at Levelland as nothing more than "ball lightning" (which never attains a size greater than eighteen inches). And the brilliant object which landed on the White Sands military range? Why pish! tush! and twaddle! children—that was only the planet Venus!

It was, you see, one of those unforgettable nights in the annals of astronomy when Venus came down and rested briefly on the gypsum sands of New Mexico. At least, that was the official "explanation."

Man had just launched a living creature into orbit—and Unidentified Flying Objects began to appear in numbers—and to make their presence known by creating interference with man's electrical gear.

And what of the orbiting dog, Laika? Were the UFO's interested in that hapless creature, too?

Very definitely—and it was the beginning of an interesting and important phase of the space program, as we shall see.

The Soviet scientists who had launched Laika into orbit were anxious to know how her heart and blood pressure and other bodily functions would react to the foreign element of orbital weightlessness. Her body had been wired to transmitters which reported regularly on the space traveler's performance. Scientists in many parts of the world tracked the capsule as best they could—and among this group was Dr. Luis Corrales, of Caracas, Venezuela.

In the early evening hours of December 18, sixteen days after Laika had been sent into orbit, Dr. Corrales made a time exposure on a photographic film to record, if possible, the passage of Sputnik 2. He got not only the luminous trail of the Soviet space capsule—but alongside it a second trail which indicated that the capsule had company—intelligently controlled.

Scientists who studied the photograph released a statement to the press. EL UNIVERSAL, for December 19, 1957, quotes their conclusions:

"It cannot be a double exposure, for the stars would also have registered double images on the film, and they did not. It cannot be an internal reflection [lens flare? —F.E.] for the path is not the same as the one left by the Sputnik. It is not a scratch on the film, for examination under magnification reveals that it is a precipitation of the emulsion on the photographic material, which is accomplished by light alone. The camera photographed something which we cannot identify. . . . If the luminous trail running parallel to the satellite's trail is the path produced by another body and if it became luminous during a short period of time, we would be making a hypothesis hard to prove."

The photograph shows clearly the long straight path of the Sputnik bearing the dog. Another trail is clearly visible beside that of the Sputnik but traversing only about one-seventh of the Sputnik path. The clue to the real nature of this second object lies in one clearly visible change of direction—it veered away from the Sputnik and then returned to pace it again.

Something—or somebody—was taking a close-up look at man's first orbiting satellite with a living creature aboard—although by that time the dog was dead.

Man's drive into space had begun—and it was already under scrutiny by something—or somebody—from somewhere.

It was a pattern that would be repeated in the days to come.

"The surprising thing is the level of intelligence of the observers and reporters of UFOs—certainly above average, and in some cases decidedly above average. The typical [UFO] witness is honest and reliable."

> —Dr. ALLEN HYNEK, top Air Force scientist on UFO's, quoted in Yale Scientific Magazine, April, 1963

"Instead of investigating the reports of UFOs it might be better if we investigated the people who report these things."

> —Dr. ALLEN HYNEK, top Air Force scientist, Associated Press, November 8, 1965

10

Muzzles for Americans?

The existence of an extensive program of censorship relative to the UFO problem is neither debatable nor surprising. The ground rules for everyone on the government payroll are spelled out in JANAP 146, and the regulation by which the Air Force carries out its part of JANAP 146 is Air Force Regulation 200-2.

The JANAP order promulgates the rules under which Unidentified Flying Objects shall be "explained" only as conventional objects or conditions, and it names the Air Force to do the explaining.

AFR 200-2 specifies how the Air Force shall conduct its investigations and specifies how and by whom the public statements shall be made.

Heavy penalties are provided for anyone under these regulations who fails to abide by them.

The application of those restrictions is evident in the innumerable and conflicting statements which have been offered to the public, and even to members of Congress, in response to questions about UFO's.

But why the censorship in the first place?

Why should the government of this nation embark on a program of this scope—and of this nature—unless the need was urgent or imperative?

One clue to the generation of this tortuous policy on UFO's may be found in the fact that, when they first appeared in numbers over northwestern Europe in 1946, the major powers were less than a year away from the end of the most catastrophic war in human history. Suspicion on an international scale was in full bloom; the common-law marriage of Communism and the Western Powers to bring about the fall of Hitlerism had run its course. The old, old struggle to outmaneuver the opposition was underway with little pause.

It is more than likely that the appearance of these strange craft in the skies in '46 and '47 led both Russia and, later the United States—to suspect each other of trying out some new weapon of remarkable performance characteristics. Until that supposition could be confirmed or refuted, both nations seem to have pursued a policy of saying as little as possible.

Also, in 1947, the near-panic which resulted from the Orson Welles 1938 radio program, War of the Worlds, was still fresh in the minds of many persons in authority. That unfortunate radio broadcast showed how mass hysteria could be triggered by fear of the unknown. I have never felt that official statements playing down the "flying

244

saucers" were unwise at the time of the first mass appearances of the "saucers."

In later years, after the UFO's had been around for a while and the public had begun to suspect that not all those who reported such things were as looney as the official statements might lead one to believe, still another factor may have entered the picture to make UFO censorship desirable from the official point of view.

By 1952, when the UFO's swarmed over the capital of the United States on at least three memorable occasions, the military budget was by far the largest single item in the entire national budget. The military had the obligation and the responsibility for controlling the airspace over the nation as well as everything that sought to use that airspace. They could not control the UFO's. The question that had to be decided was whether to admit that there was something up there that they could not control, even with all those billions of dollars to do the job, or whether they should deny the existence of the problem while they studied it and sought means of coping with it.

That alternative was the one they chose. It was at least an extension of their previous policy, intensified by the need to carry out the responsibility they used to justify their fantastic income.

Somewhere in this complex of circumstances lies the reason (or reasons) for the censorship. Precisely where— we can only surmise.

Governmental truth-twisting is by no means confined to Unidentified Flying Objects. It was brought sharply into focus by Arthur Sylvester, Assistant Secretary of Defense, who told newsmen on October 29, 1962, that the government took the position that falsification was all right if the results were good.

[It was simply another way of repeating the old Nazi line that it's all right to lie to the public if it is for their own good. Whether it was justified would be decided by those who did the lying, of course.—F.E.]

The Air Force, as a separate entity, was only seven days old when Captain Mantell met his death chasing an Un-identified Flying Object over Kentucky. The official state-ments of explanation, three in number, were indicative of confusion. This seems to me to be pardonable under the circumstances, for the brand new military agency was dealing with a brand new problem.

It was, to my knowledge, the first application of the multiple-explanation technique which has proved so suc-cessful in more recent years.

A classic of this type is the famous Killian case. Captain Peter Killian and his flight officer, John Dee, were flying an American Airlines cargo plane from Newark to Detroit on the night of February 24, 1959. They were over Penn-sylvania when they discovered that they were being paced by three brightly lighted objects which changed their relative positions in flight. Other airline crews in the area saw the same objects, from different angles.

Captain Killian was a veteran pilot with a fine record. When he and his co-pilot reported their experience they were given the multiple-explanation treatment. The Air Force first explained the lights as those of a military tanker refueling some jets. When this was rejected by the pilots concerned, a second "explanation" was offered from still another Air Force source—Captain Killian and the other pilots had been watching three stars in the constellation Orion. This also had certain defects, including the fact that the lights changed formation. Then came the third offering. An otherwise "unidentified" Air Force spokesman told New York newsmen that Killian had probably been drinking too much.

When Killian rightfully threatened action over this latest accusation, which could have cost him his job, the smear was retracted. Net result: No acceptable explanation—but a confused public. Results, from the censor's standpoint—at least acceptable.

When the Socorro, New Mexico policeman, Sergeant Lonnie Zamora, reported coming upon an egg-shaped object in a ravine on the outskirts of the town on the afternoon of April 24, 1964, he described to his fellow officers and to his superior two small manlike creatures he had seen beside the object, and the strange insignia on the side of it.

Later, Zamora refused to discuss either the insignia or the alleged humanoids, on the ground that he had been asked to keep quiet about "some things" that he had seen.

In return, perhaps, Sergeant Zamora was not ridiculed or embarrassed by the official investigators.

He did get the triple-explanation treatment, however. First, from an astronomer who was hurriedly flown to the scene, who hinted that lack of radar detection of the object was puzzling. (The radar wasn't working.)

Then came another eminent astronomer who "identified" Zamora's UFO as a secret U.S. spacecraft (which had not even been built). And finally, there came the admission that the Air Force was still interested, but mystified.

Nothing had really been admitted and the case finally dropped out of the news, spread-eagled in three directions.

Sergeant Zamora's remarkable experience was of especial interest to me because of a strange coincidence in which I was a participant.

In April of 1964 I was in Hollywood to be a guest on Art Linkletter's television program "House Party"—on which I had appeared several times before. On the day of this particular program one of the officials of the company which produces the show called me at my hotel and asked me to be certain that I did not mention "flying saucers" during my interview with Art that day. I agreed to avoid the subject, which was really no problem for me, since we were going to discuss mysterious occurrences cited in my book *Strange World*, and there were many types of phenomena other than UFO's from which to choose. I assumed that he wanted to avoid further mention of UFO's because Art and I had discussed them on the occasion of my last appearance on his show, a few months prior to that of the April visit.

Much to my surprise, when I got there I found that the writer who was going to interview me prior to the program, paving the way for the on-the-air discussion with Art, wanted to discuss UFO's. I explained to him that I was willing, if that was what he wanted—but I warned him that I had been asked NOT to discuss that subject on that show. The writer seemed a bit puzzled by this request, so he went to check with the man who could give him the answer, Mr. Linkletter.

Art told him he wanted to talk with me about UFO's and about the so-called "Little Men" who were sometimes reportedly associated with them.

That was precisely what we talked about.

The program was broadcast on April 24, 1964—*just a few hours before Sergeant Zamora found the two humanoids beside that strange egg-shaped craft in the ravine near Socorro, New Mexico.*

The timing was so close that I sometimes wonder if Somebody Out There was listening to CBS that afternoon?

I first contradicted the Pentagon censors in late 1949 when I broke the story, over the full Mutual Network, that TRUE magazine was going to say, in its January 1950, issue, that "The Flying Saucers Are Real."

The American Federation of Labor became my sponsor in January of 1950, which meant, among other things, that the members of the Airline Pilots Association were among my sponsors. The pilots furnished me with countless sightings reports, ofttimes before they reported them to the airlines. I built a tremendous audience, and my consistent broadcasting of UFO reports from credible witnesses was a factor in the success of the program. In 1953, the trade paper RADIO DAILY held its annual nationwide poll of radio-TV editors. Edward R. Murrow, Lowell Thomas, and Frank Edwards were named the three top news broadcasters in the nation. The Mutual Network estimated, on the basis of audience-rating figures, that I had an audience of about thirteen million people every night. As the magazine NATION'S BUSINESS said of my work: LABOR'S RADIO PROGRAM PAYS OFF.

Through the Washington grapevine, various friends in the news business had told me that the Pentagon was very unhappy because I continued to broadcast reports of UFO sightings. By late 1953 the news services had virtually ceased to carry such reports; if they were carried at all it was on a strictly local or regional basis. The major leak—and just about the *only* major leak in the censorship of UFO's—was my radio program.

Matters evidently came to a head in 1954 when the Air Force put out one of its semi-annual press releases which explained everything as being nothing. The release said that UFO's were virtually a thing of the past and, to back up that statement, they added that in the first four months of 1954 they had received a total of only eighty-seven sightings reports.

I made arrangements to check with Air Technical Intelligence Center (ATIC) at Dayton, the clearing house for all UFO sightings reports; and I got a statement from Lieutenant Colonel John O'Mara, the officer in charge of such matters. I ran the two statements in sequence on the same broadcast:

The Air Force in the Pentagon said only 87 cases had been reported in four months.

Lieutenant Colonel John O'Mara of ATIC at Dayton said: "This is the biggest year yet! We are receiving 700 sightings reports per week."

I was fired in August of 1954.

On the night of August 10, I had ten million sponsors and thirteen million listeners.

Twenty-four hours later I had neither.

When George Meany, President of the American Federation of Labor, was asked by newsmen what had brought about my abrupt dismissal from such a popular program, he told them:

"Because he talked too much about flying saucers!"

At the time I concluded that he had chosen that remark to make it appear that my work had been unsatisfactory. This seems to be contradicted by a laudatory article about me in the AFL's own house organ at the same time that I was fired. I felt that there must have been some other reason, beyond Mr. Meany's personal dislike of me. It was several years before I was finally told what may well have been the principal reason why the AFL would scuttle a multimillion dollar investment in public relations which was, by their own admission, succeeding beyond expectations.

My informants were two members of the AFL high command who had been close friends of mine. They were so situated that they would have had to know what took place. They told me this:

My frequent mention of Unidentified Flying Objects was irritating to the Defense Department. When I continued to make these reports, the Defense Department complained to the Network, which declined to censor me, and then to the sponsors, who finally instituted censorship in the form of a so-called editor. This editor was a henpecked misfit who had been eased out of the AFL publications ranks and was moved over to ride herd on me.

The final straw was my broadcast which contrasted Lieutenant Colonel O'Mara's statement with that of the Air Force. From that point forward the fat defense contracts showed up with increasing frequency in the hands of non-union contractors. This was hitting the sponsor where it hurt—right in the pocketbook. Something had to be done—and it was.

So when George Meany told newsmen that I "talked too much about flying saucers" there was probably more truth to what he said than I realized. I do not believe that was the major reason for my being ousted—but it certainly provided a convenient peg on which to hang my scalp.

The individuals in the AFL who were jealous of my growing popularity with the members of that organization—and the censorship group in government—had found the excuse to silence me which they had been seeking for some time.

They could only win, and they did.

But it was a rather transient victory for the Pentagon censors. They had silenced me only for the time being and only on one broadcast per day.

Today I am heard on hundreds of stations many times per day—and many of those broadcasts deal with UFO's.

Today my newspaper column is carried in great numbers of newspapers, in this country and around the world. In those newspaper columns I frequently include new and important developments in the UFO field.

My books have sold millions of copies in both hard cover and paperback—and in many lands and many languages.

This international multiplicity of outlets not only gives me a far greater audience than I had at the time of my tumble in 1954, but it also provides me with many more sources of information. I have become a sort of clearing house for phenomena, including that of the UFO.

Censorship has changed, too, during these past eleven years. It has become, if anything, more brazen and more direct. I say this because the experience of a friend of mine is typical of so many instances which have come to my attention recently.

This man is a minor official in a large industrial plant. He has an excellent record of long standing with that particular corporation.

One morning in early December, 1965, he was on his way to work, about 4:30 a.m. As he drove along a new superhighway that gave him a bypass around the large city where he lived, he was startled by a great orange-yellow ball which came from behind his car and passed overhead. It was in sight about thirty seconds. He stopped and reported the case to the State Police, who in turn gave the story to newsmen. He told the State Trooper: "That thing was as big as a house and was so bright that I could easily have driven with my lights off! It was frightening!"

Shortly before noon he was called into the main office of the plant where he is employed and the Plant Superintendent introduced him to two military officers, who in turn told him they were there to question him about what he had seen.

These men grilled him for two hours and then they closed their brief cases and turned off the recorder.

One of the officers said: "We can't tell you what to do, but we can offer a suggestion: Don't talk about this matter to anyone. May we rely on you?"

When my friend said that he would like to think about it, the other officer took over.

"This plant handles government contracts and we would hate to feel that you had caused them any difficulties, of course. But, if necessary, we would take the appropriate action if you decline to cooperate."

He cooperated.

Repeated Air Force press statements, generally issued after each series of important sightings, had, by early 1954, evidently led many publications to believe that the statements were veridical and that the UFO's were nonexistent. As of January, 1954, there were but two major sources of UFO information: airline pilots and my radio program on the Mutual Network.

The systematic elimination of those factors was evidently undertaken immediately; for on February 17, 1954, officers of the Military Transport Intelligence met with officials of the Airline Pilots Association at the Roosevelt Hotel in Hollywood. Purpose of the meeting was to urge the commercial pilots to "cooperate" in what was described as a serious matter for the government. Commercial pilots were urged to radio the nearest airport *immediately* upon sighting a UFO—*and to make no public statements on such incidents.* This was subsequently amplified by the airlines themselves notifying the pilots that their "cooperation" in this matter was requested—and "suggested." By mid-1954 most, if not all, commercial airlines in the United States had established procedures for handling UFO reports.

The Killian case is an example of what can be expected by the pilot who deviates from the rules set by the censors in the Pentagon.

But continued sightings by tens of thousands of credible witnesses have gradually warped the lid of censorship. The great flap of 1957; the sightings by astronauts; the even greater flap of 1965, followed by an "explanation" so preposterous that the newspapers were suddenly brought face to face with the brazen falsehoods which had been meted out to them by the military—all these things have created a new outlook in many minds in the opening weeks of 1966.

The military department was created to be Uncle Sam's bodyguard. It has no authority, real or implied, to deceive him as to the nature or extent of anything with which it deals on his behalf.

Truth is not repellent except to those who abuse it.

"No reports of unidentified flying objects have been withheld. As Director of NICAP, Major Donald E. Keyhoe has received all the information in the hands of the U.S. Air Force."

—LETTER from Major General Joe Kelly, USAF, to Representative Peter Freylinghuysen, September 12, 1957.

"I assure you that the Air Force never intended to turn over "For Official Use Only" files (on UFOs) to your organization."

—LETTER from Major General Joe Kelly, USAF, to NICAP, November 15, 1957.

11

In the Dark

Few things are more disturbing than to be plunged into pitch darkness without warning. It is alarming for individuals; it is dangerous for masses of people. It paralyzes cities, blocks highways, stops trains, leaves elevators suspended between floors. In general, it simply plays hell with the modern way of life.

At great expense the utilities have installed complicated and ingenious equipment to make mass power failure unlikely. They have also spent large sums of money assuring the public that mass power failures such as the one that struck New York and New England in late 1965 are impossible.

This is not to imply that the utilities have deceived the

public on this matter, even though the utilities may be wrong about their claims, as the events indicate.

The utilities have spent tens of millions of dollars designing and installing complicated equipment capable of preventing the conditions that generally result in power failures. It was this realization that left the utilities authorities mumbling to newsmen that they simply couldn't understand it—it couldn't happen, but it had!

As FDR used to say—"Let's look at the record."

It has been known since 1947 that some sort of field associated with the Unidentified Flying Objects causes observable disturbances in electromagnetic instruments. It was first noted in connection with compasses. Later, pilots found that with a UFO in their vicinity the ignition systems of their internal combustion engines were adversely affected. Ships, automobiles, and tractors reported malfunction of their engines in the presence of UFO's. Motorists and airline pilots made many reports of radio interference which prevented transmitting or receiving signals when the UFO's came near.

Were the UFO's also able to disrupt the transmission or generation of electrical power at the utility level?

The first indication that these things might interfere with commercial electric distribution systems in my records does not have enough substance to definitely link it with UFO activity, largely, if not entirely, because of the extremely brief duration of the incident.

It occurred in November, 1953, in New Haven, Connecticut. A glowing orange-red object which witnesses said appeared to be about the size of a football suddenly swooped down over the tops of some trees near an intersection in the residential area. The object came down to within ten feet of the ground, traveling at high speed, leveled off, smashed through a metal billboard from the rear, and rose swiftly above the treetops and vanished. In sight only a few seconds. Apparently unimpeded by the collision with the light metal of the commercial signboard.

The matter is of interest because, as the thing passed over the neighborhood, house lights dimmed or went out for about two or three seconds at the precise time of the object's passage.

If this was a controlled UFO (it left copper fragments around the hole it blasted in the billboard) then we have here an early (1953) case of interference with commercial electricity distribution. But the disturbance, like the duration of the sighting, was very brief. That does not rule it out as a UFO interference case, but it enables scoffers to dismiss the short blackout as pure coincidence—and we have no way to prove that it wasn't.

A strange glowing object swooped down over a part of New Haven, Connecticut, on that November evening in 1953. Intentionally or otherwise, it blasted through a billboard. Accidentally or otherwise, the lights in the homes nearest the billboard went out for a few seconds as the object passed; homes a bit more distant from that corner noted their lights going dim. Since this variation in the lights existed on both sides of the object's path, it would seem reasonable to assume that the disturbance was related to the subject and that distance from the object diminished the effect. This is only my conclusion, based on the known facts in the case. But as we shall see, it fits into the pattern of subsequent cases where there can be no doubt of the relationship.

NICAP's study of UFO association with power failures includes the case at Mogi Mirim, Brazil, in 1957. Three glowing disc-shaped UFO's passed slowly over the town and, as they did so, the power simply ceased to flow and the lights of the town went out. Again, there was an area of total blackness directly beneath the path of the UFO's and a dimming in varying degrees as the distance from the UFO's increased.

Also in 1957, says NICAP Investigator (Volume 3, No. 5), at Tamaroa, Illinois, there was a power failure which lasted until a huge hovering UFO moved away from the town.

On August 3, 1958, a large section of Rome, Italy, was blacked out when a luminous and very large UFO maneuvered overhead. Again, when the UFO left—the lights came on. (NICAP reports that this was a duplication of an incident a short time before—on July 22—in Salta, Argentina.)

A particularly well-documented case occurred in Minais Gerais, Brazil, on the night of August 17, 1959. The instruments began indicating some sort of power-flow interruption, temporary in nature. Presently the officials at the various stations along the distribution system began phoning each other: Their circuit breakers were opening automatically as Unidentified Flying Objects moved slowly along at low altitude above and along the power lines.

At Uberlandia, one of the key stations on the system, the staff had been alerted several minutes prior to the arrival of the UFO. When the circuit breakers started opening, the technicians were standing by and they promptly closed the switches. But their efforts were futile; for the presence of the single oval-shaped UFO nullified the normal procedures which would have kept the current flowing through the lines. It did not flow until the UFO had sailed serenely away into the night.

In the Dark

The record year for major power failures in the United States was also the record year for UFO activity—1965. Again this may be mere coincidence—or it may not.

The 1965 blackout season got under way in Cuernavaca, Mexico, on the night of September 23. The press reports from the scene listed among the witnesses General Rafael Vega, a commander of a military zone; the Mayor of Cuernavaca, Valentin L. Gonzalez, and Governor Emilie Riva Palacie. They, along with a great many other persons, observed a glowing, disc-shaped UFO hovering over the city at low altitude. The lights and all electric power failed when the UFO arrived. The power failure lasted ONLY while the UFO was there. It ended automatically when the UFO suddenly zoomed up and out of sight.

The granddaddy of all blackouts to date was the stygian blanket that fell over thirty million people in the northeastern corner of the United States during the early evening rush hour period on November 9, 1965. Pilots who observed this phenomenon from the air described it as awe inspiring: One moment there were the lighted cities with their scores of millions of inhabitants. The next moment there was only a great black carpet, apparently devoid of life.

Said one pilot to me: "I felt like I had just seen the end of the world!"

From New York City to Maine, most of the area was literally power-less.

How could this be? What of the great power grid with its several generating sources? What of the devices which were designed to automatically shift the load in case of failure in one area—so the malfunction would be bypassed and power restored?

The military quickly announced that there was no

military emergency—they were in communication with their bases in the blacked-out area, as usual.

Later, it developed that they were hard hit by the power failure—for many military communication points and circuits were predicated on the use of public power. When the power failed, military equipment based on it also failed. However, the military assurance that all was well probably had merit to the extent that it had a tranquilizing effect on those who were inclined to be jittery. And the shock of finding military circuits knocked out by a public power failure not only exposed the incredible stupidity of such an arrangement but, more importantly, forced it to be corrected.

The developing story of the great blackout of November 9, 1965, received superb coverage from every angle in the nation's news media and we need not recount it here. It was all over by the morning of November 10—all over but explaining to the public why the impossible had happened.

There was no general agreement among the great power supply concerns which were contributors to this multi-state grid. But the official explanation was that a small device in a Canadian hydroelectric generating plant had malfunctioned and that other instruments had subsequently mis-functioned—and that steps would be taken to try to prevent its recurrence. Strangely missing from the explanation was any further explanation of why the millions of dollars worth of electronic gear had failed to detect the disturbance and shift the load.

Since I am certainly not an authority on such complex and intricate systems I took the explanation to utilities engineers who are experts. They said that to them it seemed a little vague, like the blind men's description of the elephant.

The INDIANAPOLIS STAR promptly carried an editorial suggesting that the government not only investigate the cause of the blackout . . . but that the possibility of a UFO being involved should not be overlooked.

In this connection, the INDIANAPOLIS STAR could have—and *may* have—known of the experience which befell two well-known Indianapolis people on the early evening of that big blackout. Here is their story:

Renato Pacini is the Assistant Conductor of the Indianapolis Symphony Orchestra. He and his wife had flown to Syracuse for a visit with Pacini's two brothers, Humbert, an electronics engineer, and Ramon, a construction engineer. The brothers and their wives had met the Indianapolis couple at the Syracuse Airport, and the six of them got into the car to drive to their destination in Rochester.

There was still considerable light in the western sky at 5:22 p.m. as they turned onto the expressway. Renato noticed a peculiarly brilliant light in the sky . . . clearly noticeable in spite of the skylight. He called it to the attention of the others in the party. All agreed that it was most unusual.

As they drove along the highway, the light sank rapidly and moved toward Syracuse. They watched it for several minutes until it was so low that it was lost to sight in the clutter of hills and houses and darkness. Just then came the announcement over the car radio that the big blackout had struck.

(This was just about one hour after two commercial fliers, Jerry Whitaker and George Croninger, in Whitaker's plane over Tidioute, Pennsylvania, had radioed that they were watching two shiny disc-shaped objects being chased by two jets. The UFO's put on a burst of speed and ran away from the jets, the fliers reported.)

UFO's being chased across Pennsylvania at 4:30.

A strange, brilliantly glowing light coming down near Syracuse at 5:30.

Presto! The blackout was on.

Had anyone else seen such a spectacle as the six Pacinis witnessed?

Very definitely they had.

The SYRACUSE HERALD-JOURNAL reported that Robert C. Walsh, Deputy City Aviation Commissioner for Syracuse, had been flying at about 1,500 feet above down town Syracuse when the blackout struck. Said Walsh:

"It was an eerie feeling. I thought my eyesight was going and for a minute I didn't know what to do. Then I saw cars moving in the streets and I knew that at least I could see. I thought of sabotage. I thought of a lot of things. I even looked off into the distance to see if I could see any flashes of any kind."

Walsh then contacted the tower at the Airport, which was on emergency power, and they told him that they had no idea what had happened. After a moment of looking over the black void which should have been studded with millions of lights, Walsh decided to head for the Airport. He lined himself up with the radio tower of WFBL, a familiar landmark to him, and made an uneventful landing. A few minutes later, Walsh was standing on the runway with some friends discussing the blackout when he and his companions saw a great ball of fiery light go rolling up into the air. Said Walsh: "It appeared to be about one hundred feet in the air and fifty feet in diameter."

The fireball rose swiftly—then suddenly blacked out. At the time of the incident Walsh said he had no explanation for what he had seen. (Subsequently, there was speculation that he might have seen a ball of gas from the De-Witt town dump. Oops! The DeWitt Town Supervisor squelched that guess—no fire at the Dewitt dump. Well, then, the Manlias dump—surely— Sorry! No fire there either! The explainers had to dump the dumps.)

There had been two "fireballs," visible from the Airport and reported by several credible witnesses there. The "fireballs" were not denied. Neither were they explained, although the usual "reliable sources" hinted at the possibility that the witnesses may have been seeing after-burners on jets, etc. This supposition matches everything except the known facts in the case.

At the time Walsh and his companions at the Airport were watching that giant fireball rising into the pitch-black sky, it was also being watched from overhead. Veteran Flight Instructor Weldon Ross and his student, James Brooking, were cruising around over the blacked-out city on a training flight when they saw a glowing ball-shaped body, like a red hot globe, over the power lines leading to the generating plant at Niagara Falls. Their signed report of this interesting angle of the case is in the files of the National Investigations Committee on Aerial Phenomena in Washington.

On the evening of November 16, the HERALD-JOURNAL carried a front-page story on the seven-day-old case: FLYING FIREBALL PHOTOGRAPHED. The story was illustrated by two two-column pictures, taken by William Stilwell, sexton of St. Paul's Episcopal Church.

Stilwell told authorities that he had seen several of these glowing objects in the sky. He watched one of them

263

through his 117-power telescope and said: "The center was rotating, around and around and around." He also told the newsmen that he had observed these objects suddenly stop, hover for as long as two hours, and then go streaking away. He, too, saw a glowing object in the sky the night of the big power failure.

"It came from the direction of Dewitt," Mr. Stilwell told newsmen, "and it shot off at an angle and then went back the way it came."

Altogether, says the SYRACUSE HERALD-JOURNAL, it has received more than a hundred reports of strange glowing objects in and around Syracuse since the night of the blackout.

NICAP has many members in the Syracuse-Rochester area and several of them were assigned to check out the UFO reports, which the paper calls "fireballs." Weeks of patient work by these investigators has confirmed what the earlier reports indicated—the strong possibility that one or more UFO's were over Syracuse at the time of the power failure—but there are no clear-cut indications which would justify connecting them with the power failure itself. Officially, the failure was due to a relay break at the Sir Adam Beck Plant No. 2, four miles north of Niagara Falls. This break is said to have overloaded the American lines, and the overload detectors and trippers failed to function properly.

Unexplained, however, if it is known, is why the relay failed—and why the overload trippers failed.

One other aspect of the Big Blackout remains to be dealt with here: A picture of New York City in the blackout, published by TIME magazine. Up in the corner is a little spindle-shaped object apparently suspended in the sky. Asks TIME: "Could this be a UFO?"

If they were being facetious, a lot of folks missed the little joke. The spindle-shaped thing could have been a UFO—but it certainly wasn't. It was nothing more than an optical ghost, the result of reflections between the elements of an air-spaced lens. Cute—but not interplanetary.

Time gets "E" for effort but they must take second place; for the best line comes from Professor Robert L. Brown, Astronomer at South Connecticut State College, who said that the glowing thing seen over Syracuse might have been the after effects of the Russian moon probe which had plunged into the moon a few days before the blackout.

How could that have caused a fireball over Syracuse?

The professor was equal to the occasion. He explained that the moon is covered with dust. The Russian probe, smashing into the moon, had sent out a cloud of moon dust.

I tip my wig to Professor Brown!

He never sent out any lunar probe—but he got the same results.

According to the ST. PAUL PIONEER PRESS and other papers in the area, power failures of a local nature occurred in and around St. Paul on the night of November 26, 1965—and they occurred as one or more UFO's were moving about the area. Shortly after 8 p.m., witnesses watched an object with blinking blue lights which sent down occasional flashes of bright blue light like that from a welding torch. As it passed over two of the witnesses, Nick DeVara and Mark Wilcox, a brightly lighted service station suddenly blacked out—only to light up again seconds later after the UFO had passed.

The community of Totem Town, on Highway 61 near

St. Paul, got a sharp taste of the apparent effect of a pair of objects giving off blue and orange flashes which crossed the community at low altitude. Many persons—including several police officers—were among the witnesses who reported to Northern States Power Company that simultaneously with the presence of the UFO's all electric power was off. The utility said that the blackout was of short duration and that they could find nothing which could have caused it.

The tremendously vital part that electricity plays in our national existence was re-emphasized by the rash of blackouts which occurred in late 1965. As we have seen, both civilian and military functions were hampered or prevented during the blackouts. And it was something less than reassuring to be told by authorities in charge of the generation and distribution of this all-important electricity that it could happen again.

And it did happen again . . . and again . . . and again.

The great New York-New England blackout occurred on November 9.

On December 2, about 700,000 persons in Texas, New Mexico, and Mexico were struck by a power failure which originated in El Paso. Cause? Failure of a regulator which dumped an overload into the circuits and the overload equipment failed to cope with it. Sounds like old times, doesn't it?

Please don't leave your seats — there's more of the same.

Three nights later—December 5—another massive power failure in the Southwest—this time in East Texas where 40,000 homes suddenly found themselves plunged into darkness. Cause? Another of those doggoned overloaded parts and more of those non-tripping trippers.

266

That El Paso blackout on December 2 hit not only the civilians in that area, but it also blacked out such important military installations as Holloman Air Force Base, White Sands Missile Grounds, Fort Bliss, and numerous airports. *None of these vital installations had been equipped with emergency power.* Through the magic of politics they all bought their electricity from the same source that supplied the washing machines in El Paso.

But there is another aspect to the blackout of December 2—one that brought about some changes.

On that night, President Lyndon Johnson was in his ranch home in Texas. He was on the phone, talking to an assistant in the White House in Washington. Suddenly, right in the middle of the conversation, the line went dead.

Naturally, the President wanted to know what had happened. The explanation he received from the Federal Power Commission Chairman was this:

His phone calls were being fed into the transcontinental cable system at Fairview, Kansas. LBJ, I Love Lucy, Ben Casey, and the Jimmy Dean show all went the same way at the same time . . . through that cable. When the regulator blew up at El Paso, a surge of power hit the cable at Socorro, New Mexico. That was supposed to cut in reserve power from storage batteries but, once again, the equipment failed to perform. Phone calls, including that of President Johnson, were interrupted until the power supply evened itself out.

Mr. Johnson was assured that his calls between wherever he is . . . and the White House . . . will henceforth be carried on lines which can be instantly switched in case of emergency. Sounds good, but one thing bothers me. If the line goes dead, how is he going to get the operator? Will his line be equipped with a tripless tripper?

We have discussed several instances where, in this and other countries, UFO's have interfered with the transmission of commercial electricity. UFO activity in our major blackouts up to the end of 1965 was highly debatable and in my opinion, unproved.

But there is one case, confirmed by the proper military spokesman at the time it happened, where a UFO knocked out a sub-station by its presence until it was driven away by jet fighter planes.

The best-documented UFO case is also one which involves a power blackout due to the proximity of the UFO. You will find it in full detail only in the newspapers in the immediate vicinity, such as the LAS VEGAS SUN for the day following the incident.

A few minutes past 7:30 on the night of April 18, 1962, there was a blinding flash in the sky over the desolate Mesquite Range in southwestern Nevada, about seventy miles south of Reno. The glare was so intense that witnesses said the streets of Reno were lighted as though by a gigantic photographic flash bulb. The glare was reported from five states. And scientists in the area told newsmen that the flash was, in their opinion, some form of atomic explosion.

The Atomic Energy Commission quickly assured the news media that they were not conducting any nuclear explosions or tests which could have been involved in this incident.

Whatever it was, its presence over the United States that night had the military in such a tizzy that they sometimes talked out of school.

Could the thing have been a meteorite, reporters inquired of the authorities at Nellis Air Force Base?

Not a meteorite, certainly, was the official reply. This thing was being tracked on radar and followed by armed jet interceptors at the time it exploded. Radar can only pick up ionized meteor trails, not the meteors themselves. And jet interceptors are not used to chase meteors.

Other reporters reached the officer in charge at the nerve center for aerial protection of the United States—Lieutenant Colonel Herbert Rolph of the North American Air Defense Command Center at Colorado Springs, Colorado. He told newsmen that a Ground Observers Corps center at Oneida, New York, had reported a red, glowing object moving westward at great altitude. Radar tracking had determined that it was neither plane, missile, nor meteor. Since it was moving east to west it could not have been a satellite. It was therefore listed as a UFO and tracked as far west as Gridley, Kansas. It turned northwest and descended until it was lost from the radar screens.

A few minutes later an Unidentified Flying Object landed near an electrical power substation at Eureka, Utah. *The Air Force spokesman at Stead Air Force Base admitted that the object had landed and that the power substation had not been in operation during the forty-two minutes the object was on the ground near it. He also told newsmen that the presence of this object had not been admitted to newsmen until the power station was in operation again—after the object had left.*

Jet interceptors (armed with air-to-air missiles) had admittedly been summoned from the base at Phoenix and also from Stead Field, at Reno. They were pursuing the object at the time it exploded over the Mesquite Range in Nevada.

Here was a case where flustered officials confirmed that

269

an object beyond their control had crossed most of the United States, had landed beside a power station which remained useless until the object took off, pursued by armed interceptors. While under this pursuit, the object had admittedly exploded with a brilliance visible over five states.

Quite a story. A story that was easy to confirm, as the LAS VEGAS SUN learned when it contacted the official sources directly concerned with this problem.

But most people never heard of it, for the simple reason that the news services did not carry the report. One of them ran a four-line item calling the object a meteor (which the Air Force had already denied) and that was all.

Yet the full story was readily available, although it received no national coverage until I reported it through FATE magazine in August, 1962, and later in my book, *Strange World.*

I recount the story here because of its obvious importance, both from the standpoint of what happened and because of the subsequent disappearance of the story on a national basis. The incident is classic in both respects.

"... the 'flying saucers' to which you refer do not have any relation to true reality since these things have never been observed by us."

> —Letter, dated June 11, 1957 from
> A. G. Karpenko, Scientific Secretary,
> Commission for Interplanetary Communications, Moscow, USSR

"Citizens of the Soviet Union who report watching these bludza [flying saucers] are either feeble-minded or delicate liars."

> —Pravda, January 9, 1961

12

Meanwhile, Back in the Soviet Union

The relative silence from Russia on the matter of UFO's has been broken from time to time, but the references have been as sharply contradictory as those of the American Pentagon. But 1965 was for the Soviets the year of change. Something has brought into the open some evidence that the Soviet Union is definitely concerned about these objects and that it is belatedly following the deception policy of our own government.

My source of information on the Soviet activities is the distinguished researcher, lecturer, and writer on Soviet matters, Mr. Paul Voronaeff. He is an avid reader of innumerable Soviet publications and is a frequent witness before Congressional Committees as an expert on Soviet Russia.

271

From the newspaper KAZAKSTAN PRAVDA for September 10, 1965, comes the article headlined FLYING SAUCERS which is based on a report made to the Soviet government by a Soviet scientist, Dr. Mitrovan Zverev, who was on special assignment to the Chilean Observatory, Serro Galan.

Says the report:

Santiago, Chile,—Recently a group of hunters, while hunting in the valley of San Kintin, suddenly were confronted by a fleet of "flying saucers" twelve in number.

At midnight four of the hunters witnessed over their heads a large (glowing) saucer. The hunters wisely did not lose their presence of mind. They directed their electric spotlights from their automobiles toward the object in the sky. Soon eleven arrivals joined the first saucer and all of them began to circle well above the heads of the hunters. One of the hunters started blinking his light on and off. The saucers turned their lights on and off, evidently blinking in response. All of the witnesses confirmed this.

The reports of flying saucers have become the subject of serious research in Chile. Recently three scientists in Santiago signed a public statement about the strange objects which for some time now have been seen in the skies. They said: "We have scientific proof that the mysterious objects are visiting our planet." This statement was signed by Chilean scientist Dr. Gabrial Alvial and his two colleagues.

The Soviet scientist Dr. Mitrovan Zverev, now on a special assignment and working at the Chilean Observatory Serro Galan, has stated that some unknown objects which we do not understand are moving freely around the earth.

The Director of the Observatory, Professor Klaudio Angita, insists that we are not alone in this world. His statement was published in the Chilean newspaper LA TERCERA DE LA HORA—which has also published hundreds of reports from credible witnesses who have observed these flying objects in the Southern skies.

Why should an article of this type appear in a daily newspaper thousands of miles from Moscow, in remote Kazakstan?

Mr. Voronaeff pointed out that the item had to be approved by both scientific and political censors in Moscow before it could even be considered for publication. That it was published at all, he says, indicates that the Soviets were hard pressed in this area.

He says:

"This [Kazakstan] is an area which has been buzzing with rumors and reports of flying saucers, objects from space, and tales of an impending invasion from outer space. The reports never appeared in print but they were spread by word of mouth and distorted to such an extent that widespread alarm and near-panic had been reached.

"Recently the Soviet government sent a veritable army into the villages and settlements in that area to try to 'explain.' These flying saucers had resulted in widespread religious revival and a return to God . . . the last thing the Communists wanted. The flying saucer phenomenon was being interpreted by the natives of that region as some sort of warnings by supernatural beings of an impending catastrophe—the end of the world.

'The Soviet press in that area is filled with reports on astronomy, weather, cosmology and space, all written in layman's language. Some of the best brains of the Communist world—including Brezhnev himself—have been sent there. He went to Alma-Ata, the capital of Kazakstan, where he spoke before their Supreme Soviet and also made a secret speech before the Communist party leaders there on the breakdown of Communist morale, and the unexpected developments in Kazakstan resulting from the flying saucer sightings and interest in them."

Why did the Moscow regime permit any mention of this phenomenon which was already causing trouble for them?

Mr. Voronaeff reasons:

"The prolonged silence on the subject of flying saucers by the government of Russia and its controlled press has led to the belief that they, and their scientists, were helpless—and could not explain the flying saucers. This was held by the government to be responsible for the resurgence of religion—fear of the unknown was driving the peasants back into the churches.

"Early this year [1965], when many reports began coming out of South America on the UFO activity there, the Soviet government dispatched several Soviet scientists to study and report on the phenomena. Zverev was one of those on the study missions and probably the first to report back to Moscow. As of September 22, all those Soviet scientists are still in various South American countries trying to learn all they can about this subject with the aid of the local scientists who have had ample opportunity to be informed."

Two interesting features of the report carried in the Kazakstan paper were those portions which identified Dr. Zverev as being on special assignment at the Chilean Observatory near which this UFO activity centered. By publishing the report as they did, the Soviet leaders probably hoped to crystalize the BLUDZA (saucer) rumors with just enough information to indicate that they were aware of them and were making a study.

274

Meanwhile, Back in the Soviet Union

One of the early features of the U.S. censorship and propaganda programs in the UFO field was the hinting that they were "probably" some secret device with which the U.S. was experimenting. The oft-mentioned "secret saucer" project at the AVRO plant in Canada was such a maneuver. It worked rather well for several years until it occurred to newsmen that this was probably the most widely advertised "secret" of the century. Each year the Air Force would drag out its "artist's conception" of this alleged secret and send it out to be published and discussed.

It is not surprising that Russia has tried the same stunt; but what is surprising is that they waited so long and did it so badly.

Our own mythical 1955 "secret saucer" fizzled in 1959 and upon exposure turned out to be nothing more than a huge ducted fan, of high cost and low performance.

Russia was two years late getting on the "secret saucer" bandwagon. They published in the newspaper SOVIETSKAYA ROSSIYA, October 5, 1957, a story and an "artist's conception" of the alleged saucer they were building. It was nothing more than a circular object with four ducted fans. It would have been subject to the same limitations which beset our own craft in that category. There is no evidence that it ever flew—but the fact that the story appeared in print in Russia in late 1957, only a few days prior to their forthcoming satellite launching, may indicate that they had timed this story as a piece of propaganda to cope with the anticipated UFO sightings which followed their space rocket shots.

By 1952, when the UFO phenomenon was already in its sixth year over Russia, Professor Boris Kukarin, a top

Soviet astronomer, said: "Flying saucers are an optical illusion growing out of sheer war psychosis . . . encouraged by those interested in war."

In other words, for a Russian to report seeing UFO's was to stamp him as unpatriotic and pro-war!

On December 7, 1953, Radio Moscow offered this gem: "Flying saucers are figments of the imaginations of Western War Mongers designed to make taxpayers swallow heavier military budgets."

But by 1957 they were on a new kick: "Flying saucers do exist and Russia has them!" So sayeth Professor S. Zonshtein, a U.S.S.R. scientist. He was one of those identified with the four-motored ducted fan device announced four days after he made this statement.

On January 9, 1961, PRAVDA got into the act by denouncing all Russians who dared to report UFO's as either weak-minded or deliberate liars. Pravda asserted that most of the UFO reports in Russia were merely parroting things previously described by Americans. Which was another instance where they were denouncing those who reported UFO's as unpatriotic by implying that they were listening to the Voice of America broadcasts and repeating what they had heard. Anyone who talked about UFO's, by PRAVDA's definition, was either weak-minded, a liar, or a traitor who listened to foreign radio broadcasts. Not much of a choice for those who sighted these things in the skies over the Soviet Union.

As NICAP pointed out in a study of the Russian policies on UFO's—after this PRAVDA blast of January, 1961, the Soviet official statements on UFO's constituted virtual reprints of the hokum that poured out of the Pentagon on the same subject. Which of those three unsavory categories designated by PRAVDA did the Muscovite explainers then select for themselves?

In the magazine TECHNOLOGY AND YOUTH, Volume 2, 1964, the entire front cover is taken up by a beautifully drawn disc-shaped device apparently hurtling through the skies above a city. It is a giant disc, driven by jets, with a strangely anachronistic conventional fuselage protruding front and back. It gives the impression of a giant jet passenger plane being gobbled in the middle by a flying saucer. It is the feature of the magazine, no mistake about that.

TECHNOLOGY AND YOUTH is a popular science publication put out by the Central Committee of the Communist Youth Organization, the "Komsomol."

The cover illustration carries the banner:

A FLYING SAUCER? YES!

What promised to be such a dramatic disclosure turned up on pages 16 and 17 as an article by M. Suchanov, identified as a candidate for science and technological advances. His article is titled: "Man Overcomes Gravity."

Reading Mr. Voronaeff's translation of "Man Ovecomes Gravity" gave me a feeling of wading through cobwebs. The article purports to divulge to its awestruck readers the secrets of a great scientific discovery. But upon careful examination the discovery turns out to be nothing more than a rehash of stale science fiction mixed with thick slices of experimental programs long since abandoned. For example, the photographs which supposedly illustrate this anti-gravity type of discoid plane are unmistakably the progenitors of such hapless aircraft as our own Chance-Vought flying flapjack which is now in a museum in Washington, D.C. The devices in the photographs with

277

the article are clearly designed to obtain their lift from the passage of conventional airfoils through the atmosphere. Any device capable of conquering gravity would not need any of the guiding surfaces shown on these craft . . . but any craft lifted by conventional passage through the air would need every one of the controls shown. The allegedly remarkable craft differed only in the circular or disc-shaped wings . . . the type which we tested and abandoned in 1942 for the simple reason that new type engines—jets and turboprops—made the circular wing planes obsolete before they ever got into production.

The article hints that newer types are not shown but leaves you to assume that the nonpublication of information on the new machines is presumably to prevent their great secret from being divulged.

There is, however, one portion of the article which indicates quite clearly that whoever wrote it was familiar with some of the flight characteristics of UFO's. This includes the mention of an air cushion being attracted to the craft by its own gravitational field—and how this air cushion would react under certain speeds and conditions. The air cushion report is a bit on the vague side and does not go beyond the 1953-1954 theories of Dr. Smith of the Canadian UFO study nor those of Dr. Oberth and others of that same period.

As a topper for this montage of the tripe and the trite, TECHNOLOGY AND YOUTH brings the subject to a close by reprinting an item from an American publication, AVIATION WEEK, for August 15, 1960. It lists the various gravity research programs being conducted in this country at that time—programs which had grown both in size and numbers in the ensuing four years.

Meanwhile, Back in the Soviet Union

There was nothing to indicate that the title had any basis in fact; nothing to indicate that it was based on any scientific breakthrough having to do with the control of gravity—but much to indicate that it was not.

As with ourselves and many other nations, by 1964 the Soviet Union was having its problems with UFO's plus its own special problems. Damning those who reported such things had not worked very well—or very long. By publishing this latest assertion of a nebulous craft of secret construction, the Soviet Union was providing a source for quotation by other publications to further bolster the official story that the things being seen in the skies over the Soviet Union were their own experimental devices . . . the ones that TECHNOLOGY AND YOUTH mentioned in 1964. Remember, Ivan?

It is my personal opinion that the publication of this article is a further indication that the Soviet Union's troubles with the UFO's are similar to our own. And it is undeniably a further indication that they have again, by this article, followed the policies of our own propaganda departments in the Pentagon by hinting at possible experimental devices which in reality are either already outmoded or which exist only in the imaginations of the harried authorities.

I had not realized, until I began assembling the material for this chapter, how closely the Soviet policy on UFO's has paralleled our own.

There was the initial flurry, in which theirs preceded ours by one year. In both countries the first rash of sightings was met with the flat official denial that anything unusual was going on—that the alleged objects were anything more than hallucinations.

When that failed, both countries began planting stories

of "secret devices" allegedly being tested. Russia denounced those who reported such things as loonies, liars, or traitors. We categorized them as victims of hallucinations, publicity seekers, or drunks.

After that approach had worn thin, both countries went back to the "secret device"; in our case it was the AVRO ground effects machine; Russia has used both the ground effects machine and the bogus anti-gravity planes such as those in TECHNOLOGY AND YOUTH which I have just mentioned.

And in both countries, while the propagandists were throwing sand in the public eye, the government itself was engaged in an all-out program of investigation and counter-measures of the UFO problem, and both are still similarly engaged to this day. In summary, we can say that Russia and the United States have used similar procedures and techniques to cope with the same problem.

"Project Bluebook people in Washington, D.C., say that only two percent of the UFO cases of the past five years have not been solved. . . ."

—NEWPORT NEWS, Virginia, Times Herald, January 25, 1965

"Based upon unreliable and unscientific surmises as data, the Air Force develops elaborate statistical findings which seem impressive to the uninitiated public, unschooled in the fallacies of the statistical method. One must conclude that the highly publicized periodic Air Force pronouncements based upon unsound statistics serve merely to misrepresent the true character of UFO phenomena."

—YALE SCIENTIFIC MAGAZINE, Yale University. Volume XXXVII, No. 7, April, 1963

13

1965—The Dam Breaks

July, at the South Pole, is midwinter. It is a time when the scientific bases there are virtually isolated from the rest of the world.

Isolated, yes. But they were not alone in July of 1965. Radio amateurs in South America picked up the startling story first while listening to official broadcasts to and from the scientific base maintained by the Argentine Navy on Deception Island, on the western side of the Antarctic land mass. From the amateurs the story quickly spread and on July 7, 1965, the Secretary of the Navy of Argentina made a public statement to put the subject in focus. He said:

"The Navy garrison in the Argentine Antarctica, Deception Island, observed on July 3, at 19:40 hours local time, a giant, lens-shaped flying object, solid in appearance, mostly red and green in color, changing occasionally with yellow, blue, white, and orange shades. The object was moving on a zigzag trajectory toward the east but several times it changed course to the west and north with varied speeds and without sound. It passed at an elevation of forty-five degrees over the horizon at a distance estimated to be about ten to fifteen kilometers from the base.

"During the maneuvers performed by the object, the witnesses were able to register its tremendous speeds and also the fact that it hovered motionless for about fifteen minutes at an altitude of about three miles. The meteorological conditions for the area of the sighting can be considered as very good for this time of the year: clear sky, some stratocumulus, moon in the last quarter and perfect visibility.

"The object was witnessed by the meteorologist together with thirteen members of the garrison and three Chilean sub-officers visiting the base. The observation lasted for twenty minutes and photographs of the object were taken.

"On the afternoon of the same day the same object was sighted from the Argentine base on the South Orkney Islands, moving away toward the northwest, about thirty degrees above the horizon, estimated distance ten to fifteen kilometers [six to nine miles—F.E.]. The Chilean base also observed the same object on the afternoon of that same day."

Two days later came the second official statement concerning an Unidentified Flying Object over the scientific bases in the Antarctic. This time the Secretary of the Navy of Argentina reported direct contact (by radio) with the commanding officer on Deception Island, Lieutenant Daniel Perisse. That officer confirmed the details of the previous day's announcement and that the object was extremely brilliant; that it changed course and speed far beyond the capabilities of any kind of manmade device; and, the officer at the Base added, that the efforts to photograph the thing may have been hampered by the relatively insensitive film that was used and the distance of the UFO from the cameras.

Then came this interesting disclosure:

"From the Base at the South Orkney Islands comes a message of extreme importance; during the passage of the strange object over that Base, two variometers working in perfect condition registered sudden and strong disturbances in the magnetic field, which were recorded on their tapes."

Two official statements from the government of Argentina confirming that a large lens-shaped UFO had maneuvered over two scientific bases of that nation in the Antarctic on the same day. Scientists had tried to photograph the object in color and they had recorded its powerful electromagnetic influence on their various instruments.

On the day of the first Argentine report (July 7) the government of Chile had given to the press the contents of reports it had received by radio from the Pedro Aquirre Cerda Base, which actually antedated those of the Argentines, but had been kept under cover until after the Argentine report.

The text of the Chilean messages indicated that they had been received in Santiago on June 19, 1965. They reported that an object similar to that which the Argentine scientists had described appeared over the Chilean Base for about twenty minutes on the afternoon of the preceding day. It changed colors, speeds, and direction in fantastic fashion while being observed by officers and men at the Base. It was a huge, double-convex object and it made no sound.

Appended to this message was still another which the Chilean government made public on the same day, July 7.

It noted that the English Base (Hallet) had also reported watching a similar or the same object for eight to ten minutes on the afternoon of July 2.

Continuing, the report said:

"Communication with the Argentine Base on Deception Island disclosed that on July 3, sixteen persons, including three Chilean sub-officers, had observed an aerial object over the northern end of that island . . . leaving a contrail at thirty degrees elevation. Round shaped, it disappeared into cirrus clouds. Was tracked by theodolite and high-powered binoculars. Corporal Duran, from this garrison [Aguirre Cerda—F.E.] took ten color photographs *through the theodolite*. [Italics mine.—F.E. Theodolite pictures should have produced excellent close-ups, if the exposure was good.]

In a subsequent broadcast, Commander Mario Barrera spoke directly from the bases he commanded in the Antarctic to the Chilean Air Force radio center in Santiago. He described how this brilliant object had changed colors from time to time, yellow to green to bright orange. How it had stopped suddenly while moving at high speed and hovered at that point for twenty minutes.

Then, said Commander Barrera:

"While we watched it through high-powered binoculars, it suddenly ceased hovering and shot away at tremendous speed.

284

"I do not believe this could be an aircraft of terrestrial manufacture. As an officer of the Chilean Air Force my knowledge of manmade machines gives me absolute certainty that nothing similar exists on Earth in shape, velocity, or mobility in space. We have taken ten color photographs which will be developed in Santiago.

"As soon as we sighted the object we tried to contact by radio the Argentine and English bases. But we found such contact impossible because there was a strong interference on the radio on all channels. With our radio useless and with strong emotions, we continued to observe this thing in space—"

One of the most important portions of the story, the Chilean scientist's assertion that this was positively NOT any kind of manmade object, *did not appear in the news stories which reached the news media of the United States.* Where, or why, the deletion was made I do not know, but in order to get the full story it was necessary to secure translation of the official press releases carried by South American papers and by Reuters News Service, an international agency which does not seem to suffer from the same censorship restrictions which afflict the newswires of the United States.

Condensed and denatured as they were, those reports made headlines in this country and constituted a topic of conversation that was still going strong when the next wave struck . . . just one month to the day—or the night —after the incident which stirred the scientists at Deception Island.

Before the events of August 2-3, however, dramatic activities similar to those of the UFO's which visited the scientific bases in the Antarctic occurred on July 11. This time the strange objects were sighted over Portugal: One in the province of Motoshinos, near the city of Oporto, where witnesses described it as resembling "some sort of giant balloon that was flattened out. When it rolled from side to side we could see that it was more like two huge plates stuck together."

One witness, Manuel Fernandes, an employee of the Fishermens Union there, watched the spectacle with his wife and he told authorities:

"The thing was very luminous and had orange coloring and was nearly red at times—and at other times bright rays of green light shot out of it. It stopped for three minutes near the coast and then, with incredible velocity it rushed away toward the North."

In the Azores, at Villa Do Porto, the government weather station had a strange visitor that same day. A luminous white thing, sometimes cylindrical and sometimes more nearly lens-shaped, circled the Base slowly at an altitude of between twenty and thirty thousand feet. It then moved away toward the northeast, said the meteorologist, who also told newsmen that the electromagnetic clocks of the weather station were stopped by the field of the object, and as it passed overhead the compasses gyrated wildly.

Vessels of the International Geophysical Year fleet were in the Azores at the time of this incident. Their officers declined to comment to newsmen on whether their instruments had also been adversely affected by the presence of the UFO reported by the weather station.

The Antarctic, South Africa, France, Australia, Portugal, Argentina, the South Atlantic—the tempo was rising steadily.

North America was next.

On the night of August 2-3, 1965, tens of thousands of American citizens, taxpayers one and all, stood along highways beside their automobiles, in the streets before their homes, in parks and on bridges and other vantage points to watch a fascinating and eerie spectacle.

From South Dakota to the Mexican border and beyond, legions of witnesses watched formations of brightly colored lights zipping back and forth across the heavens. Some witnesses reported that the things were in diamond-shaped formations and that they made sharp right-angled turns. Sometimes the lights were single and they hovered from time to time. Some were at high altitude and they occasionally came plunging down to a much lower level. Some were at low altitude and, as the awed witnesses watched, the things would streak straight upward.

Occasionally one of the glowing objects would come to a halt, generally for only a few seconds; and that is what enabled a fourteen-year-old boy in Tulsa, Oklahoma, to secure a remarkable picture with a cheap little snapshot camera.

For hours, citizens of Tulsa had been watching this strange spectacle as it developed in the skies on this warm, clear night. Among those who watched was Alan Smith, the fourteen-year-old son of A. L. Smith, a turbine engine specialist with American Airlines.

About 1:30 o'clock on the morning of August 3, Alan, his father, and three other persons were watching the unusual movements of a multicolored object that seemed to be approaching them in a shallow glide. When it was still several hundred yards away, it paused momentarily. Alan pointed his camera and snapped the shutter. Afraid to try another shot lest he double expose on the one he had just tried to take, Alan took his camera back into the house and ran back outside just in time to see the object moving swiftly into the distance.

He had aimed the camera entirely by guess, for in the tiny viewfinder of his $6.95 plastic box he could see nothing of the object so small and so far away. Had he actually had it in the field of view when he snapped the shutter? And was the thing bright enough to photograph on the relatively slow color film (ASA 64) which he was using?

The film was developed along with a jillion other films in an automatic color processing machine. When the transparencies and prints came back there was not a sign of the one which might have contained the UFO. No print, that is, but the reason was understandable. The negative of that particular snap showed only a tiny object in the lower right quadrant of the film. The processor had assumed that the snap had been a failure . . . and had not printed it.

But when that tiny portion of the film was highly magnified the results were startling. There was the UFO, clearly divided by two opaque bands into three segments. It was disc-shaped, apparently flat-bottomed, and the sections were blue-green, orange yellow, and creamy white, just as witnesses had said.

The picture was examined by the OKLAHOMA CITY JOURNAL, which also had the negative examined by photo experts who, after lengthy investigation and careful study of the negative, pronounced it genuine and produced as described by the boy who took it.

The OKLAHOMA CITY JOURNAL ran the enlargement made from the original negative on the front page of that paper on October 5, and it created something of a local sensation. [Unfortunately, in their enthusiasm at securing

288

such an exceptional picture, they headlined it the FIRST UFO COLOR SHOT—which it was not.—F.E.]

The INDIANAPOLIS TRIBUNE, a newspaper which had printed just one edition when it heard of the picture we are discussing, made arrangements with the OKLAHOMA CITY JOURNAL to print the picture on the front page of the second edition of their infant paper. It appeared there on November 13, 1965, and the entire edition of more than a hundred thousand copies was a sellout. Some people even drove miles to the printing plant in another city to be sure they got a copy of the picture and the explanatory material which I had written for it.

During that same memorable night, August 2-3, 1965, a glowing UFO hovered near Sherman, Texas. Broadcasting stations, police, and other agencies had been flooded with reports for hours. Television cameraman Robert Campbell was out with Patrolman Peter McCollum, interviewing witnesses and watching the objects for themselves. Campbell took a still picture of the hovering UFO —a two-minute time exposure while he and the police officer watched the thing. The picture was overexposed, possibly due to the brilliance of the UFO, but it showed conclusively that there was something there in the sky, just as the witnesses said.

The Air Force lumped this object with all the others when they tried to dismiss them as nothing more than stars—their first "explanation" of the events of this memorable night.

Of this matter [the Sherman, Texas, picture] the CHRISTIAN SCIENCE MONITOR said:

"Flying saucers" sighted earlier this month over Texas may give scientists something to think about for a long time.

"They were among many reported sightings around the world lately. But they give the clearest evidence of all that something strange was actually in the sky."

Many Texans definitely saw something that even experienced investigators now admit defies explanation. Police officer Lewis Sikes noticed a strange lighted thing in the sky about 1:30 on the morning of July 31. He was attracted by its regular emission of alternate red, blue, and white light. After watching it for forty-five minutes as it hovered, Officer Sikes radioed to the Oklahoma Highway Patrol to report. The State Highway Patrol queried Tinker Air Force Base, and Tinker advised them that the object was there all right at about 8,000 feet—and that no aircraft were in the area. A few minutes later, Carswell Air Force Base in Fort Worth also located the object on radar; the two stations tracked the thing to a spot about fifteen miles west of Tinker, where it vanished from the scope.

After the Air Force officially "explained" the objects that swarmed over the Great Plains states in early August as nothing more than stars and in the same breath told newsmen that the radar stations at Tinker and Carswell had positively not picked up any such UFO blips as reported by State Police in both Oklahoma and Texas, the FORT WORTH STAR-TELEGRAM had had enough. It said, editorially:

"They can stop kidding us now about there being no such things as 'flying saucers'.

"Too many people of obviously sound mind saw and reported them independently from too many separate localities. Their descriptions of what they saw were too similar to one another, and too unlike any familiar object.

"And it's going to take more than a statistical report

on how many reported 'saucers' have turned out to be weather balloons to convince us otherwise."

When the great August 2-3 UFO inundation hit the headlines, the Air Force promptly—or hurriedly, perhaps —reached out and gave the crank on its Explanation Machine one full turn: Presto! Next morning's headlines quoted the Air Force as saying that all those strange things that people had been watching were nothing unusual at all . . . just four stars in the constellation Orion; Betelgeuse, Rigel, Aldebaran, and Cappella. By this time it appears that some newsmen were beginning to be skeptical of the glib explanations: Somebody asked professional astronomers if those four stars could have been the answer.

Never to my knowledge has the Air Force been knocked down with more celerity. The same wire stories which carried the Air Force "explanation" carried the withering blast of rebuttal from such incontrovertible authorities as Walter Webb, Chief Lecturer at the Hayden Planetarium in Boston, and Dr. Robert Risser of the Oklahoma Science and Art Planetarium.

Said Dr. Risser: "The Air Force assertion that these lights were nothing more than stars in the constellation Orion is about as far from the truth as you can get."

Said Professor Webb: "At the time of these sightings the constellation Orion *was visible only from the other side of the world!*"

The Air Force "explanation" was a miss—by 12,000 miles. Cynics will conclude that even then it was better than usual for them.

This fantastic faux pas by the government censors attracted widespread editorial attention as more and more newsmen became aware of the falsity in these Air Force pronouncements on the UFO.

To keep things in proper chronological sequence, let us put into the record here this United Press International report headlined in the Duluth, Minnesota, paper as: THOUSANDS SEE FLYING OBJECTS—JETS CHASE UFO's OVER DULUTH AREA.

"Houghton, Michigan, August 7—Personnel at the U.S. Air Force Radar Base in the Keweenaw Peninsula today reported solid radar contact with up to ten unidentified flying objects moving in a "V" formation over Lake Superior yesterday.

"The objects were moving out of the southwest and were heading north-northeast at about 9,000 miles per hour" the radar men said. They were from 5,200 to 17,000 feet high.

"Elsewhere seven other objects were spotted over Duluth and jet interceptors gave chase but they could not maintain the speed of the UFO's and were easily outdistanced."

After comparing the facts against the official "explanation," the ALAMEDA (California) TIMES-STAR said on August 10, 1965:

HOW MANY HAVE ANOMIA IN U.S.?

According to Air Force spokesmen a powerful assortment of police officials, sheriff's deputies and other individuals, including even some members of the Air Force itself, were suffering a mild form of anomia—the loss of ability to name an object correctly, as evidenced by their failure to recognize such obviously common objects as weather balloons, planets, comets, etc., when they spotted them in the skies over an area of some eight states. They saw the objects plainly enough of course, but their error lay in terming them unidentified flying objects, more commonly called flying saucers.

Just how the Air Force spokesmen were able to tell that hundreds of reports of UFO's from an area the size of Free Europe were faulty—and especially how they were able to do it within 24 hours of the time the reports came in—ought to rank as one of the most remarkable examples of lightning-like mass diagnosis of all time.

That is, it ought to if the Air Force spokesmen were actually correct.

However it now appears that—as countless thousands of well-informed persons have suspected for years—the Air Force spokesmen were wrong again. According to a UPI story from Houghton, Michigan, this past weekend, personnel at the Air Force Radar Base on the Keweenaw Peninsula reported "solid radar contact" with 7 to 10 Unidentified Flying Objects moving in a "V" formation over Lake Superior. The objects were moving out of the Southwest and were heading North-Northeast at about 9,000 miles an hour, at elevations ranging from 5,200 to 17,000 feet.

What distinguishes that story from many others involving Air Force personnel during the past several years is that it was not accompanied by a paragraph "explaining" that the objects had finally been identified as a flight of ducks, comets, balloons or something else equally commonplace.

Why wasn't it?

The most likely reason is that the Air Force spokesmen, whose duty is to explain away the seemingly improbable in terms of the commonplace, have been getting such a workout lately that either they are starting to break down or their superiors are coming to the conclusion that they are making the Air Force appear ridiculous.

Of the two, the latter seems more likely. The business of attempting to protect the public from panic—as the

293

obvious reason for the Air Force's traditional policy of identifying flying objects as weather balloons, etc.,—is something that cannot be indefinitely sustained, particularly when the source of the presumed potential panic is a mass of peculiar things that persist in flying around where large numbers of persons can see them. To do that is no more possible than it is for the panic to be sustained by individuals for more than a few hours at most. It's too exhausting. One can flee a horde of little green men from outer space only so long. Presently one gets tired and decides to do something else, even if it is no more than sitting down.

But whatever the reason may be why the Air Force spokesmen are becoming less vocal, the time is long overdue for the Government to disclose to the public all that it knows about UFO's.

It is now generally admitted in the scientific fraternity that Earth is not the only heavenly body to have intelligent life, and since we ourselves are now invading outer space, it would be nonsensical to suppose that inhabitants of other worlds have not already done so.

In other words, it should surprise no one today to learn that the UFO's are spacecraft from elsewhere in the solar system—or beyond. In fact, it would be even more surprising to learn that they were not. Hence, the only way in which the public interest may be served in this matter is for the Government to disclose what it knows about these phenomena.

As remarkable as were the sightings themselves during the July and August epidemic, equally as remarkable and fully as important was the sudden and dramatic awakening of many segments of the American press to what was going on . . . and to the realization that they had been systematically misled for years, by bogus pronouncements, as a matter of government policy. This was the long-awaited break for which we at NICAP had been working and hoping. Under persistent pressure of this sort from this source the government must eventually open its classified files and secret cases to public scrutiny.

The Air Force, which is to say the Defense Department in this context, came out of the July and August events bedraggled and bedamned. They had lost their grip on the American press and news services. That segment of the population which had *not* been deceived by the meaningless "explanations"—and which had been demanding more facts and less fiction from the Air Force—had gained some powerful new adherents. August added up to a major setback for the censorship policy.

And there was more to come.

Place: A highway near Damon, in Brazoria County, Texas.

Time: Approximately 1 a.m.—September 3, 1965.

The Principals: Chief Deputy B. E. McCoy and Patrol Deputy Robert Goode, both from the Sheriff's Office in Angleton and both police school graduates.

The official report:

The two men spotted a huge flying object as they drove along in their patrol car. In the bright moonlight they could see it clearly. They estimated it to be about two hundred feet long. Forty to fifty feet thick at the center, tapering at both front and back ends. The front end carried a brilliant purple light, the rear end a fainter winking blue light. It was the lights which had first attracted their attention.

Goode drove back toward Damon for about three quarters of a mile and pulled off the road so they could observe this strange spectacle. They took turns leaning out of the car windows and examining the thing through binoculars.

Without changing speed, it suddenly nosed down and started toward the car in a shallow dive. When it was only about a hundred feet above the earth, the officers could clearly see its shadow racing over the ground in the bright moonlight, coming straight for their lighted automobile. Officer Goode, leaning out the driver's side, distinctly felt heat from the blazing purple light which fronted the approaching UFO. When he got the car into gear the object was not more than fifty yards behind them.

Driving at speeds which at times reached one hundred and ten miles an hour, on a highway which was not designed for such performance, the officers soon reached Damon. They later admitted to the Air Force officer who questioned them that they had been badly shaken by their experience.

After a few minutes in Damon, both Deputies regained their composure and decided to return to the scene of this singular experience. McCoy told newsmen: "We were still jittery but we wanted to find out what that thing was —so we went back."

When they reached the area, McCoy and Goode discovered that they were not alone. They told authorities that they soon made out the lights of the enormous craft, and the lights were changing in intensity just as they had previously seconds before the thing dived toward them. The Deputies had had enough. They again "hastened" back to Damon—at the same speed as before.

(They made written reports to the Sheriff and next day were interrogated by an Air Force investigator from Ellington Air Force Base, Major Laurence R. Leach, Jr.

The account given here is from their signed report, a copy of which is in the files of NICAP in Washington.)

On that same night, and two thousand miles away, other officers were having their problems—this time in Exeter, New Hampshire.

Shortly before the Texas deputies had their unnerving experience, two veteran police officers of Exeter had been sent to investigate a car which was parked near the city limits. It was not entirely off the highway and so constituted a hazard. The call came in at 12:30 a.m.

The officers found two women in the car, evidently in a state of shock induced by fright. The driver of the car told Officer Bertrand that they had been closely followed for twelve miles by some sort of huge aerial object which gave off a brilliant red glow. The police calmed the ladies, looked around and saw no such object, and got the women started on their way.

An 18-year-old Exeter youth, Norman Muscarello, came stumbling into the Exeter police station at 1:45 a.m., exhausted from running and—so the desk officer later told newsmen—"He was white with fear and shaking so bad that he could hardly talk."

When Muscarello had calmed down and recovered his breath, he told Desk Officer Reginald Toland and Patrolman Bertrand a fantastic story.

He had been on his way home along Route 150, said the young man, when the area ahead of him was suddenly lighted with a red glow—and a strange craft of some sort rose above a grove of trees. As it came closer, he said that he could see four or five extremely brilliant red lights in a line from front to rear in the bottom of the craft—and the lights were blinking in sequence: 1-2-3-4-5-4-3-2-1.

297

Badly frightened, Muscarello said that he dived behind a low stone wall and crouched there as the thing passed slowly overhead, silently and not more than a hundred feet above the spot where he was hiding. He told officers that the object hovered just above a nearby house owned by Clyde Russell and as it did so, the youth said that he could see that it was longer than the house. He estimated that it was possibly ninety feet in length. A moment later it moved back in the direction it had come from and vanished behind the trees where Muscarello had first seen it.

Muscarello ran to the Russell home and began pounding on the door, yelling at them to get up and let him in. Russell, presuming that it was some passing drunk, ignored the clamor. When the youth realized he was not going to be admitted, he began running toward the police station.

After the two officers had heard the young man's story— the second time that night that they had had a report of this weird thing with the red lights in that area—Toland sent Officer Bertrand back to the scene to look around . . . and to quiet down any commotion which the boy's door-pounding might have created.

Bertrand parked the police car along the road beside the field which bordered the grove of trees behind which the object had reportedly vanished. Both Bertrand and Muscarello got out of the car. The youth pointed out the approximate location where he had last seen the thing. They could detect nothing unusual. Bertrand got out a powerful flashlight and sent its beam into the field.

Just then, so he later reported to authorities, they both "saw a large dark object displaying a row of bright red lights underneath" gliding toward the field above the treetops. It had just turned on the lights and swung around

298

in the direction of the two men behind that flashlight. Height . . . not more than seventy feet.

Bertrand jerked out his heavy service pistol . . . then decided against using it. Muscarello dived into the police car, as did the officer. Both said later that the red light was so blinding they feared they might be burned or blinded by it. The lights blinked in sequence from front to back and return: 1-2-3-4-5-4-3-2-1. Both men agreed that the extreme brilliance seemed to create a halo around the craft.

Officer Bertrand radioed for help. Muscarello said later that while Bertrand was using the microphone, his own attention was attracted by a commotion in a nearby barn where the horses were whinnying and kicking their stalls and where dogs were barking furiously. This aspect, confirmed by Bertrand, is ofttimes reported where UFO's are present at low altitude. Animals seem to hear or sense the UFO's presence before men do.

Officer Bertrand and Muscarello are quoted in the Exeter police record as being unable to determine the *exact* size or shape of the UFO because of the brightness of its lights, but both witnesses said that in the glare from those same lights they could see that the body of the craft was a solid object. It was, said the two men, egg-shaped and metallic looking. They could detect no wings or tail or fins of any kind on it.

In response to Bertrand's radio appeal, Officer David Hunt came on the double quick. He arrived in time to confirm the sighting; in fact, Hunt watched the UFO for about six minutes. It was then moving slowly away, its bright red underlights blinking steadily in their strange sequence.

In accordance with a previous agreement, the Exeter Police Department notified Pease Air Force Base at once of what had transpired and on the following day two officers from the Base interrogated the three witnesses.

The same police officers were also interviewed by an investigator for NICAP, after the Air Force man had gone. Raymond Fowler, who conducted the interview for NICAP, was told that the Air Force men had shown especial interest in the size and shape of the UFO. And they assured the policemen that there had been no planes or balloons in the area at the time—and that Pease had been getting other UFO reports nightly for about a week prior to the Exeter case. Perhaps most interesting of all, the Air Force investigators urged the policemen to keep the story away from the newspapers. Fortunately, it was too late for that kind of "cooperation"; the report on the Police Department blotter was already public knowledge.

The Texas case and the Exeter case which I have just reported are unusual in that they constitute two instances on the same night of civil police officers being alarmed by close-range sighting of UFO's. The objects were similar but not identical—and the same may be said of the police reaction to them.

As previously reported, the most extensive and prolonged mass-sighting in the history of the UFO's occurred on the night of August 2-3, 1965—it lasted for hours and it extended from the Canadian border to the southern part of New Mexico.

On the morning of August 3, three of the best UFO photographs in civilian hands were made near Santa Ana, California. They are published in the picture section of this book from duplicates of the original prints.

Rex Heflin is a Highway Accident Investigator for the Los Angeles County Highway Commission. As an important part of his job he photographed the scenes of traffic accidents—and for this purpose he carried a Polaroid camera. As was customary with him, on the morning of August 3, the camera was loaded and ready for use. It contained film rated at 3,000 ASA. The camera itself is equipped with an electronic exposure device which automatically adjusts for the proper exposure setting; the operator is obliged only to aim the camera and trip the shutter.

Heflin reported that as he drove along on Myford Road, near Santa Ana, in his County-owned truck, he spotted an unusual object approaching the road. He stopped the truck, grabbed the camera off the seat beside him, and made three pictures as rapidly as possible from inside the truck—in two of the pictures the rear-view mirror outside the truck is clearly seen. As the object moved away, Heflin says that he scrambled out of the truck and took his fourth and final picture.

When Heflin tried to contact his office by radio, while the UFO was near the car, the radio refused to operate [confirmed by Heflin's superior—F.E.]. But as soon as the UFO had gone, the radio functioned perfectly.

Several weeks later the United Press International news service in Los Angeles heard about the pictures and induced Heflin to permit them to examine the photos. UPI turned the pictures over to their own photographic specialists. After considerable study of the pictures themselves, and after experimenting with the same equipment that Heflin had used, at the same spot, the UPI photo experts concluded that the pictures had been made as Heflin said they had; that, whatever the object might be, the pictures were genuine.

United Press distributed the pictures to newspapers and magazines and television stations across the country.

Meanwhile, a man purporting to be from NORAD, induced Heflin to let him have the original prints for "official study"—which Heflin unwisely did. Later, both NORAD and the Air Force denied having the originals.

That the Air Force should denounce the pictures as "a photographic hoax" was to be expected. Indeed, under the censorship regulations, they could "identify" the object as nothing else. To have accepted the pictures as bona fide photos of an unknown object would have negated the official contention that UFO's are nonexistent. The Air Force, whatever their findings really were, had no choice but to dismiss the Heflin pictures as they had dismissed all the others before it—as phonies.

The "hoax" assertion was quickly knocked down by Ralph Rankow, photographic analyst for NICAP, in New York; and by a group of investigators working with Mrs. Idabel Epperson of NICAP in Los Angeles. Mrs. Epperson identifies the Los Angeles probers as Ed Evers, engineer; John Gray, an engineer at North American, working on the Apollo program; an unidentified photogrammetrist with another major space industry in Los Angeles; and Zan Overall, technical advisor on the probe.

After a patient and thorough study of the photos and the photographer, these probers came to the conclusion already reached by Rankow and by Clay T. Miller, the Chief Photographer for the SANTA ANA REGISTER: That there was no hoax involved in the Heflin photographs.

The Air Force claim fizzled on several points.

First: That it was not possible to take three Polaroid pictures as rapidly as Heflin had stated.

Tests showed that it could be done—by doing it.

The Air Force claim that the background was fuzzy due to being out of focus was also insupportable. The NICAP investigators—and others who examined the evidence in a search for the facts—found that the alleged fuzziness was actually camera movement; in other words, Mr. Heflin's hands were not absolutely rock-steady at the time he took the pictures. This would seem to indicate that he was operating under strain—can't say that I blame him, either.

What may well be the most important feature of the pictures is one that the Air Force failed to mention—perhaps for that very reason.

In picture Number 1, Heflin's nearest approach to the object, you will note that directly beneath the object there is a circular patch, lighter in color than the surrounding area. It is sharply defined and clearly visible—under the object and nowhere else.

Under magnification it appears to be a mixture of dust and sand and light debris, rising to a height of a foot or more—agitated *only* directly under the object.

Whatever it is, this effect has been associated with UFO's many times before. Over snow, where witnesses report that the snow swirled upward toward the UFO. At Diamantina, Brazil, August 20, 1962, witnesses told authorities that a phenomenon of this type removed every speck of dust from the surface of the hard soil where the UFO hovered only a few feet above the ground. In still another case which I have in sworn affidavits from the General Manager and Chief Engineer of a St. Louis broadcasting station, they state that they were starting out to fish one morning in 1953 on the famed Lake of the Ozarks. Out some three or four hundred yards from shore, their outboard motor died. They were sitting there in the fog, listening for a passing boat which might help them, when they heard a heavy humming sound. They could see nothing until the fog parted briefly; then about a hundred feet from them, and not more than five feet above the still waters of the lake, they saw a shiny disc-shaped thing. It was oscillating slowly, and both men noticed that directly beneath it the water was dancing in thousands of tiny sharp pointed waves. A moment later the fog closed in and my friends waited no longer for help, they began paddling back toward the dock, using their hats for paddles.

The same effect they mentioned, the agitated dancing wavelets under the UFO, were also noted by Clint Walker, best known for his work in the television serial "Cheyenne." He told me in 1962 of an experience that he and another fisherman had on a river when their boat drifted under an overhanging tree limb. As they sat there taking a break and smoking, a disc-shaped UFO came slowly and silently down the river, about six feet above the water. As it silently crossed the pool where Walker and his companion had been fishing, they noticed that the water beneath the UFO was dancing madly—a circular patch of tiny waves that moved along with the UFO and was unquestionably caused by it.

As with my other friends on the Lake of the Ozarks, Walker and his fishing buddy felt that they had had all the fishing they wanted that day.

So I was not particularly surprised to see those tell-tale circles on the ground in Mr. Heflin's pictures. In fact I rather imagine that the Air Force had seen them too but somehow they neglected to mention them in their "analysis" of the pictures.

Well, at least they tried.

By the end of 1965, after a year studded with landings and electromagnetic interference by UFO's; after numerous occasions on which the UFO's were reportedly witnessed by great numbers of people simultaneously, scores of the nation's newspapers and magazines had demanded an end to the censorship and secrecy policy which the government had inflicted on the American public for so many years. By the end of 1965 all these publications which I have just listed, and many, many more, were in reality proposing the same things which NICAP had been advocating since 1956.

These publications felt, as NICAP has long felt, that the citizens of America who pay the bills for the Defense Department are sufficiently intelligent to receive the courtesy of being told the truth about this military probe of the UFO's; and that the average American is sufficiently level-headed to handle the information, however bizarre, which was gathered at public expense for public benefit.

In the closing days of 1965 (with the possible exception of the numerous electric power failures) UFO activity in the United States was at low ebb and the Pentagon propagandists got a respite. But there were indications that it was nothing more than a brief hiatus—for the January, 1966, issue of TRUE magazine opened the year 1966 with an article by Major Donald E. Keyhoe, Director of NICAP, with access to all NICAP's files and sources. Entitled "U.S. Air Force Censorship of UFO Sightings" it included reports of UFO accompaniment of some of our space capsules and missiles, as well as authorized quotations by Vice-Admiral R. N. Hillenkoetter, former Director of both the Central Intelligence Agency and, later, of NICAP; Rear Admiral Delmar Fahrney USNR, former head of the Navy guided missile program; Colonel Dewey Fournet, Jr., former Air Force headquarters Intelligence monitor on the UFO project, all of whom went on record as agreeing with the statement made by Albert M. Chop, Deputy

Public Affairs Director for the National Aeronautics and Space Administration (NASA) who said: "I have been convinced for a long time that the 'saucers' are interplanetary. We are being watched by beings from outer space."

The report from the Antarctic scientific bases that they had been visited by a huge double-convex UFO which knocked out their electromagnetic gear received widespread publicity early in July. When the spectacular events of August 2-3 made headlines and the Pentagon sought to brush it off as nothing more than four stars in Orion (which were not even visible to the United States at the time of the sightings) outraged editors all over the nation lowered their sights on the perpetrators of Operation Hoodwink.

A headline in the FORT LAUDERDALE NEWS said: UNIDENTIFIED FLYING OBJECTS CAN HAVE BASIS IN FACT DESPITE DOUBTING EXPERTS—LIGHTS IN THE SKY STARS, AF INSISTS.

From the RICHMOND (Virginia) NEWS-LEADER:

"Attempts to dismiss the reported sightings under the rationale as exhibited by Project Bluebook [the current UFO investigation—F.E.] won't solve the mystery, however, and serves only to heighten the suspicion that there's something out there the Air Force doesn't want us to know about. If Project Bluebook officials want the UFO's to go away they'd be well advised to wish on another star."

From the CHRISTIAN SCIENCE MONITOR:

"Many persons saw something that even experienced investigators now admit defies explanation.

"It was photographed (over Texas)—

"There was no temperature inversion—

"It was not a scientific balloon.

306

"It makes the clearest case yet for a thorough look at the saucer mystery."

The WALL STREET JOURNAL also carried a lengthy and well-written article on the riddle of the UFO's in the days following the August events. Its appearance in that publication and at that time indicated that the nation's largest financial publication also had its doubts about the official "explanations."

MERIDEN (Connecticut) JOURNAL:

"There are many reports in Air Force files made by qualified pilots, who, in flight, have encountered UFO's with fantastic flight patterns. These officers are not quacks, nor are many of the intelligent people who have spotted phenomenal objects in the sky."

And the DALLAS MORNING NEWS:

"The Air Force says all sightings can be explained in terms of known phenomena and then adds that it can't explain 633 of the reports it has had. Which reminds us of the English Astronomer Royal, who spoke up in 1957 just before the Soviet Union startled the world with its first Sputnik launching. He said: 'Space travel is utter bilge!'"

WICHITA EAGLE:

"The subject of UFO's remains not only an area of sustained interest but one which legitimately demands investigation."

SEATTLE TIMES:

"Do you ever get the feeling that when it comes to flying saucers the Air Force makes its denials six months in advance?"

Coos Bay (Oregon) World:

"We think the time has come when the Air Force's knowledge of these objects and the results of the investigations which have been carried out should be made public."

Probably the two greatest developments in the field of Unidentified Flying Objects in the year of 1965 were these:

The repeated appearances of these objects within view of groups of witnesses.

The remarkable and encouraging change in editorial opinion, as expressed in their editorial columns and treatment of UFO information.

On January 24 through January 27, 1965, newspapers in Washington, D.C., and Staunton, Norfolk, and Winchester in Virginia, reported numerous UFO cases within a hundred miles of this nation's capital. The reports frequently came from groups of witnesses who told of watching beehive-shaped craft, glowing brightly, ofttimes on the ground. Witnesses included staff and students at two schools. And on October 16, a four-foot disc touched down briefly within a hundred feet of students at the Elementary School in Spring Grove, Pennsylvania. Classic of the group sightings was the fantastic night of August 2-3rd, when tens of thousands of witnesses, including many police and fliers, reported the things which flitted through the clear skies over the Great Plains states.

True magazine, no advocate of Pentagon censorship, carried to its millions of readers an article on the vast governmental effort to unravel the secrets of gravity in the hope of duplicating the flight and power characteristics of the Unidentified Flying Objects. And the January, 1966, issue of Popular Science magazine carried an article by famed writer MacKinlay Kantor, winner of a Pulitzer Prize for

308

his book *Andersonville.* In the POPULAR SCIENCE article, Mr. Kantor describes his own sighting of a UFO. In the article, Kantor reports a conversation he had with General Curtis LeMay while he was writing his book *Mission with LeMay* in late 1964. LeMay said:

"Many of the mysteries might be explained away as weather balloons, stars, reflected lights, all sorts of odds and ends. I don't mean to say that, in the unclosed and unexplained or unexplainable cases, those were actual flying objects. *All I can say is that no natural phenomena could be found to account for them. . . .*"

"Repeat again: There were some cases we could not explain. Never could."

Please note that under the censorship regulations handed down by the Defense Department, the Air Force was not permitted to issue any public statements about these cases which it admittedly could not explain.

In print, the UFO's began the year 1966 auspiciously with the TRUE and POPULAR SCIENCE magazine articles.

It was indeed only the beginning. At least one UFO played a personal appearance two consecutive nights, January 11 and 12, 1966, over and around a vast frozen reservoir within fifty miles of New York City—and in the presence of hundreds of witnesses.

The NEWARK NEWS covered the story in its issue of January 12, under the headline: UFO SIGHTED AT WANAQUE— FLYING SAUCER CASTS SPOTLIGHT ON RAMAPO AREA.

"By Cecelia King, Staff Correspondent—

"Wanaque—An Unidentified Flying Object—'very white, very bright and much bigger than a star'—hovered silently over the astounded Ramapo (N.J.) countryside last night for hours.

"Hundreds of eyewitnesses in a 20-mile periphery testified to seeing a flying saucer, first in Oakland, later over the Wanaque Reservoir where it hovered longest and then above Lakeland Regional High School and finally over the Houdaille sandpit in Haskell. From there it appeared to move southeast toward Pines Lake in Wayne and suddenly disappear."

Mayor Harry Wolfe of Wanaque was notified by police that a UFO was circling over the Raymond Dam which impounds the waters of Wanaque Reservoir. The mayor and his 14-year-old son, Billy, drove at once to the Reservoir, taking with them two Wanaque City Councilmen, Arthur Barton and Warren Hagstrom. They spotted the object as soon as they got out of the car—a glowing thing that was flying slowly and very low over the frozen Reservoir. The city officials and the police who were also present estimated that the thing was somewhere between three and nine feet in diameter. They all agreed that it did not twinkle or flicker like a star, but that it was a continuously bright thing that changed color from white to red to green and back to white.

The NEWARK NEWS reported that the New Jersey police post in Pompton Lakes was deluged with calls from many persons in that area, reporting a strange light in the sky. The officer at the post radioed to the Wanaque city police and told Officer Joe Cisco that many persons were reporting a flying saucer moving down over the Wanaque Reservoir.

"Cisco quickly flashed the message to Reservoir Patrolman George Dykman and, even as he was giving Dykman the message, a group of teenagers ran up to Dykman's car and yelled at him to get out and watch the thing that was coming across the lake.

"Dykman gaped along with Michael Sloat, 16, and Peter

Melegrae, 15, and a few seconds later they were joined by Civil Defense Director Bentley Spencer and his assistant Richard Vrooman. 'What the heck is it?' exclaimed Dykman. 'Never saw anything like it in my life.'"

Spencer hurried to the top of 1,500-foot-long Raymond Dam with Reservoir employee Fred Steines. From that vantage point he reported later that he could see "bolts of light shoot down as if attracted to the water." He said it looked like "beams emitted from a porthole."

While this group on the dam was observing the weird antics of this strange object, Reservoir Police Lieutenant George Destito was at the entrance gates to the area, turning away swarms of pedestrians and scores of automobiles which were converging on the area to witness the spectacle.

"The saucer hovered over the dam for about two hours before it soared out of sight," says the NEWARK NEWS. "It reappeared over Lakeland Regional High School in the Midvale section of the borough. A bevy of photographers converged on the spot but before any pictures could be taken the mystery object vanished. The last good view of it was had in Highland Avenue, where volunteer firemen were burning Christmas trees in the Houdaille sandpit."

Shortly before 2 o'clock the following morning Wanaque City Police Officers Joseph Cisco and David Cisco radioed that the thing was back and darting around over the Reservoir again, and that they were watching the antics through binoculars.

This was not only the first major sighting of 1966 but it had two other noteworthy aspects: Subsequent newspaper reports said that when Reservoir police went on the frozen surface in the area where the UFO had reportedly sent down those bolts of light, they found, according to local newspaper reports, unexplained holes and pools of water

311

atop the ice. [NICAP reports that the holes and watery pools angle was a misunderstanding of a statement that some of the witnesses saw the lights reflected from water on the ice, which was not necessarily a result of the UFO presence.—F.E.] However, if the water had resulted from the UFO it would not have been surprising, since there have been hundreds of reports where the pronounced heat effects from the UFO's have been well documented.

Another interesting facet of the Wanaque case is this:

Officers Jack Wardlaw and Charles Theodora, described the UFO as "definitely disc-shaped and at certain angles, egg-shaped."

A psokesman for Stewart Air Force Base at Newburgh, New York, told the officers and officials who had reported the case that they had been watching nothing but "a helicopter with a bright light on it."

At long last the Air Force was explaining an egg-shaped object with an egg-shaped answer.

Next day, however, the Air Force admitted that there had been no such helicopter in that area at that time. Major Donald Sherman, at Stewart AFB, admitted to newsmen that the helicopter "explanation" of the night before had been without foundation. The Major could tell them what the UFO was NOT. He declined to speculate on what it might have been.

A week later the Pentagon "explained" that the objects seen over Wanaque were only the planets Venus and Jupiter! If so, this is probably the only time those two planets have ever come within twenty feet of any New Jersey reservoir.

After more than nineteen years, the UFO's are with us in greater numbers than ever.

1965—The Dam Breaks

At long last the American press and the American public are demanding to know what the Defense Department knows about these strange craft and their strange operators.

The Defense Department is clinging doggedly to its policy of pretending to ignore a problem which it really considers very serious.

The day of the denouement cannot be far away.

The time may be shorter than we realize.

Credible observers have reported these objects in the air, in and on the water, and on the ground. We have seen the objects go through various changes in shape, evidently design changes. They have visited all of man's important military, communications, power, and transportation bases. They have demonstrated flight characteristics beyond any vehicles presently used by man. And they have shown the ability—and sometimes the apparent inclination—to interfere or to prevent the functioning of our electrical and electronic systems.

The Unidentified Flying Objects have developed a program of newsworthy appearances immediately following each of our major endeavors in space. This began with the Soviet space launchings of late 1957 and continues to this day. The evidence shows that both Soviet and U.S. space capsules have been approached and upon occasion, followed. Somebody out there is interested.

A careful study of the mass of evidence indicates that there is a definite purpose in the reported landings of UFO's in isolated areas such as swamps and deserts: There is a strong likelihood that they are making inspections or adjustments to the craft or its mechanism. By landing in areas unfrequented by man such work could be carried out with little or no hindrance. We propose to operate in this same fashion should we find ourselves confronted with the same set of circumstances, when we visit other planets.

If the conclusions of the scientists in NICAP are correct, then we are probably witnessing the sixth phase of a seven-phase program of the UFO's—the appearance to the greatest number of people to demonstrate both the presence and the lack of hostility of the UFO's. And if last summer's mass sightings were that sixth phase—or a major part of it—then the seventh phase—known to the military as the "Overt Landing" or deliberate contact, cannot be far away. If we have, indeed, gone through six phases in nineteen years—then the final phase would seem to be due in the next two or three years—although it could come tomorrow.

What these things are, where they come from, and why they come here at all are questions which I doubt that anyone can answer.

It is my personal belief that the day is not far distant when these questions will be answered for us.

I see no reason to fear the revelation, whatever it may be. I feel, as General Douglas MacArthur expressed it, that contact with intelligent beings from elsewhere in the Universe will be the greatest experience of the human race.

We shall see.

* * * * * * * *

"UFO's SERIOUS BUSINESS"

Unidentified Flying Objects—sometimes treated lightly by the press and referred to as 'flying saucers'—must be rapidly and accurately identified as serious Air Force business in the ZI [Interior Zone]. As AFR 200-2 points out, the Air Force concern with these sightings is threefold: . . ."

—OPERATIONS AND TRAINING ORDER from the Inspector General of the Air Force to Base Commanders, December 24, 1959

AND

"I'm convinced that saucers have an out-of-world basis."

> Dr. Walter Reidel, noted German rocket expert. LIFE 4-7-1952.

"Flying saucers come from distant worlds."

> Dr. Herman Oberth, American Weekly magazine, Oct. 24, 1954.

"The Air Force maintains a continuous surveillance of the atmosphere near Earth for Unidentified Flying Objects."

> Secretary of Air Force to Base Commanders, August 15, 1960.

"If the intelligence of these creatures were sufficiently superior to ours, they might choose to have little, if any, contact with us."

> Brookings Institution report on extraterrestrial life. Quoted in New York Times, December 15, 1960.

"Of course the flying saucers are real—and they are interplanetary."

> Air Chief Marshall Lord Dowding (head of Royal Air Force in World War Two) quoted by Reuters, August, 1954.

"I've been convinced for a long time that the flying saucers are interplanetary. We are being watched by beings from outer space."

> Albert M. Chop, deputy public relations director, National Aeronautics and Space Administration, True magazine, Jan. 1965.

"I feel that the Air Force has not been giving out all the available information on these Unidentified Flying Objects. You cannot disregard so many unimpeachable sources."

> Honorable John McCormack, Speaker of the House, January, 1965, True Magazine.

"Unidentified flying objects are entering our atmosphere at very high speeds and obviously under intelligent control. We must solve this riddle without delay."

Rear Admiral Delmar Fahrney, USNR, letter to NICAP, 1956.

"The case of UFO interference with our naval transport, the Punta Mendota, was but one of fifteen such cases which the Argentine Navy has reported since 1963."

Lt. Commander O. R. Pagini, special assistant to Sec. of Argentine Navy, letter to NICAP, September, 1965.

"Something unknown to our understanding is visiting this earth."

Dr. Mitrovan Zverev (USSR), Santiago, Chile:

"We are not alone in the Universe!" and

Prof. Claudio Anguila, director of Cerro Calan Observatory.

"There is scientific evidence that strange objects are circling our planet. It is lamentable that governments have drawn a veil of secrecy around this matter."

Professor Gabriel Alvial, Cerro Calan Observatory. Zverev, Anguila and Alvial quoted on August 26, 1965, by Reuters.

Appendix

Recommended books on UFO activities:

1. The UFO Evidence, compiled by NICAP, $4.95
   Probably the best of all UFO reference books
2. The Truth About Flying Saucers and Flying Saucers and the Straight Line Mystery. Aimé Michel. $4.50
3. Flying Saucers Top Secret. Major Donald Keyhoe, $3.95
4. The Flying Saucer Hoax. Coral Lorenzen-Apro, $4.45
5. Challenge of UFOs; Dr. Chas. Maney-Richard Hall, $3.50
6. Anatomy of a Phenomenon, Jacques Vallee. $4.95
7. Captain Edw. Ruppelt. Report on Unidentified Flying Objects. $2.95.

Out of print. Available only at libraries: Flying Saucers Are Real and Flying Saucer Conspiracy by Major D. E. Keyhoe.

UFO Investigating organizations:
—National Investigations Committee on Aerial Phenomena 1536 Connecticut Avenue NW—, Washington, D.C. $5 per year. Eight-page bulletin to members every six weeks.
—APRO—Aerial Phenomena Research Organization, 3910 Kleindale Road, Tucson, Arizona. Write for information.